# THE FIRST BOOK OF enoch

## THE OLDEST BOOK IN HISTORY

### WITH THE RESTORED NAME OF YAHUAH

Adapted From The 1912
# R.H. CHARLES
Original Translation From The Ethiopic Text

Compiled, Edited, Commentary, Maps, Charts, and Research By Timothy Schwab, Anna Zamoranos and The God Culture Team

---

# CONTENTS

But thou, O Daniel, shut up the words, and seal the book, even to the time of the end: many shall run to and fro, and...

knowledge shall be increased.

DANIEL 12:4 KJV

THIS TIME HAS COME THAT ANCIENT KNOWLEDGE IS BEING RESTORED. Not esoteric occult but His Torah which included Jubilees.

# FOREWARD

By Timothy Schwab
*Author, Publisher, Researcher, Speaker, Singer/Songwriter,*
*Founder of The God Culture, Non-Pharisee and proudly so...*

Of all the editions for the modern church to censor and attempt to discard, imagine the first book written among men by the first great prophet and we are supposed to ignore it. As we have proven in The Book of Jubilees: The Torah Calendar, that text vets as Torah even according to the Temple Priests who label it and use it as Torah also. Read that work for our position as we prove it. No Pharisee wrote that but Moses firmly did. Jubilees as Torah records the Prophet Enoch most certainly was the first scribe among men in all of history to write. You will not find another writing, rock carving, or anything written by human hands that will precede this First Book of Enoch. That includes history, science or any category. He was the first. Your professor was not.

> **Jubilees 4:16-19**
>
> *And in the eleventh jubilee Jared took to himself a wife, and her name was Bâraka, the daughter of Râsûyâl, a daughter of his father's brother, in the fourth week of this jubilee, and she bare him a son in the fifth week, in the fourth year of the jubilee, and he called his name* **Enoch.** *And he was the* **first among men that are born on earth who learnt writing and knowledge and wisdom** *(Section 2: The Book of Parables)* **and who wrote down the signs of heaven according to the order of their months in a book** *(Section 3: The Astronomical Book), that men might know the seasons of the years according to the order of their separate months. And he was the* **first to write a testimony, and he testified to the sons of men among the generations of the earth, and recounted the weeks of the jubilees** *(Section 1: The Book of The Watchers)*, **and made known to them the days of the years, and set in order the months and recounted the Sabbaths of the years** *as we made (them) known to him. And* **what was and what will be he saw in a vision of his sleep** *(Section 4: The Book of Dream Visions)*, **as it will happen to the children of men throughout their generations until the day of judgment** *(Section 5: The Epistle of Enoch);* **he saw and understood everything, and wrote his testimony, and placed the testimony on earth for all the children of men and for their generations.**

Jubilees not only affirms Enoch wrote a scroll in ancient times before the Flood as the first among men to write, Moses details in this full description, the content of First Enoch. The First Book of Enoch is segregated into five sections. In Section 1: The Book of the Watchers, Enoch records the history of the world from Creation to the days of Jared when the Watcher Fallen Angels took an oath to set the Earth on a course of destruction requiring Yahuah to step in and rescue mankind, plants and animals with the Flood. The beginning words of Section 2: The Book of Parables express that it is Enoch's *"visions of wisdom"* and *"beginning of the words of wisdom"* in exact language identified here in Jubilees. Multiple mentions of times and seasons are made by Moses referring to Section 3: The Astronomical Book. Direct reference is made to the visions Enoch saw in his sleep in Section 4: The Book of Dream Visions which includes the history of mankind through the days of Israel to the time of Messiah. Finally, Moses points out this includes prophesies of the time of the end found throughout but specifically in Section 5: The Epistle of Enoch. Moses recognized all five sections of Enoch in this endorsement of a volume he is defining as inspired scripture *"for all the children of men and for their generations."* Is Moses not an authority far greater and better qualified than any modern scoffer calling themselves scholar? Yet, today, there are many scholars who censure and marginalize this book Moses defines as one of the foundations of the whole of scripture. This publishing will dismantle every one of their illiterate assertions.

We are handed the end of the debate that the occult Sumerian Tablets or the Nephilim Epic of Gilgamesh among others could possibly predate this book or the Bible. They cannot and even if they did, they are lies. An older lie is still a lie. Gilgamesh was a Nephilim and is actually recorded in the fragments of another writing of Enoch also found in Qumran known as the Book of Giants which we will publish in a separate book. Thus, Enoch even wrote about Gilgamesh before the stone dated in fraud. Also, the writers of the Sumerian Tablets were Nephilim and Fallen Angels. Talk about Bizarro World. However, instead, illiterate scholars try to bury the point which obliterates such a position because they can't read and comprehend. They have failed us once again.

### 1 Enoch 1:2
*Enoch a righteous man, whose eyes were opened by Elohim, saw the vision of the Holy One*
*in the heavens, which the angels showed me, and from them I heard everything, and from them*
*I understood as I saw, but not for this generation, but for a remote one which is for to come,*

Prior to Enoch, the very first accounts including history and geography, were written and kept by the Angel of the Presence in Heaven. By all means, please produce a modern historian or scholar who parallels his intellect. Enoch was the first man but not the first. The Angel of the Presence wrote these down as events unfolded since Creation. These are the very accounts in which Moses was given access and copied in the writings he received on Mt. Sinai. After being called up to Mt. Sinai where Jubilees begins essentially at the end of the story and then flashes back, Moses is instructed to receive the writings and accounts of the Angel of the Presence and dictate them.

### Jubilees 1:27, 29
*27 And He said to the Angel of the Presence: "Write for Moses from the beginning of creation*
*till My sanctuary has been built among them for all eternity.*

*29 And the Angel of the Presence who went before the camp of Israel took the tables of the divisions of the years -- from the time of the creation -- of the law and of the testimony of the weeks, of the jubilees, according to the individual years, according to all the number of the jubilees [according to the individual years], from the day of the [new] creation †when† the heavens and the earth shall be renewed and all their creation according to the powers of the heaven, and according to all the creation of the earth, until the sanctuary of Yahuah shall be made in Jerusalem on Mount Zion, and all the luminaries be renewed for healing and for peace and for blessing for all the elect of Israel, and that thus it may be from that day and unto all the days of the earth.*

Moses was not around for Creation nor was Enoch and many inept scholars, attempt to undermine Moses and Enoch as a result of their ignorance. Moreover, most scholars use this claim that an angel assisted Moses as if that is somehow unthinkable. How inept a scholar would have to be to think in such a ridiculous manner of scoffing. However, most of them are scoffers not Bible scholars. They sit in the seat of the scornful offering the most illiterate of paradigms they call "textual criticism." They will, then, redefine that as constructive. No, it is not. It is destructive and no way to read the Word. Certainly, we are to prove all things but they don't even research and clearly most do not even know or understand the Bible. For instance, is it new that Moses in Jubilees would claim to receive assistance from the Angel of the Presence? Such scoffing is uneducated and unbiblical as Luke and Paul agree Torah came to Moses with the assistance of an Angel.

### Acts 7:53 KJV
*Who have* **received the law by the disposition of angels**, *and have not kept it.*

### Galatians 3:19 KJV
*Wherefore then serveth the law? It was added because of transgressions, till the seed should come to whom the promise was made; and it was* **ordained by angels in the hand of a mediator**. *(Cf. 4Q180, p. 553 [22])*

Why would very plain Bible doctrine be ridiculed by so-called scholars? Very clearly, they do not know or represent the Bible position and though they claim to be New Testament scholars, they do not even know how to read Luke and Paul evidently.

The occultists would then claim Moses plagiarized these occult frauds. The claim is ridiculous but because modern scholars have proven so incapable of understanding and illiterate of what is scripture and who was ordained to keep it, they contribute to these occult lies. This is why Paul admonished us all to prove all things and hold fast that which is good *(1 Th. 5:21)*. We will test and prove the historicity of this magnum opus of Enoch with a full Torah Test in this Introduction including our research on the Qumran community and what they represent. For any scholar to attempt to marginalize these exiled Temple Priests and insert Essenes, we will prove they are not scholars, not honest and not logical. No Essenes lived in Qumran which is utterly stupid.

In this Introduction, we will address the incredibly illiterate view of willing ignorance which claims First Enoch to be written as late as the 2nd Century or so B.C. None of those scholars have an ounce of such proof nor do they appear to be able to read and comprehend. There is no factual, logical basis for such an uneducated assumption yet many accept this ignorance as fact. It is not and we will prove it. Unfortunately, we find these kinds of nonsensical narratives surrounding the Dead Sea Scrolls in propaganda. These are not honest men seeking the truth, they are liars and not Bible scholars. They are Pharisees and modern church Pharisees who are covering their tracks as those two groups changed the Bible and will not be able to escape their curse. They are complicit.

As you see, we use firm language in our publishings. We do not placate stupid scholarship of the illiterate. It is called rebuke and without such, one does not show love. If one finds this offensive, you are welcome.

**James 3:2 KJV**
*For in many things we offend all. If any man offend not in word, the same is a perfect man, and able also to bridle the whole body.*
**Romans 3:23 KJV**
*For all have sinned, and come short of the glory of God;*

Enoch composed this masterwork before the Flood to an audience he says is the End Times remnant. That is us today. He wrote this so in the Last Days especially, we would have this knowledge restored in the midst of a strong delusion in which we were warned and it has been in place for centuries. We are bombarded with a culture who hates Yahuah and will march against Yahusha in the end including many in the church. They will unite for that singular purpose, not in Him, and this has been growing for thousands of years. This is why we are called the Remnant and there are not over one billion believers on the Earth today but very few in number proportionately as predicted by Messiah and the Prophets including Enoch. The way of Yahuah is foreign to this world including scholarship and the church. They generally do not know the Elohim of the Bible, His Son nor His Word. This book will expose this many times.

**1 Enoch 1:1-2**
*The words of the blessing of Enoch, wherewith he blessed the elect and righteous, who will be living in the day of tribulation, when all the wicked and godless are to be removed, And he took up his parable and said—Enoch a righteous man, whose eyes were opened by Elohim, saw the vision of the Holy One in the heavens, which the angels showed me, and from them I heard everything, and from them I understood as I saw, but not for this generation, but for a remote one which is for to come.*

Enoch will clarify he speaks of the Day of Final Judgment with fire and not the Flood here. He certainly shared these texts with his family and especially Noah who carried these scrolls from Enoch on the ark surviving the Flood. This masterpiece has remained in circulation throughout time since the Flood. It is relevant not just to history of all ages, but to us today in the End Times. Without First Enoch, we are missing part of Yahuah's word we need now. You will know this by the culmination of this Introduction.

In this book, we will cover only the First Book of Enoch including its five sections. We will reserve the Book of Giants also by Enoch for a separate publishing as fragments were found in Qumran. We will assess these fragments in a coming book where we will address occult frauds purporting to originate in these fragments. In that book, we will also test the Books of 2 Enoch, 3 Enoch, 4 Enoch and 5 Enoch which were not found in Qumran thus classifying them as suspect. Finally, we will also tackle testing the Book of Modern Jasher in that publishing as well including if Modern Jasher is not the Biblical Yashar, what book qualifies for the book quoted in Joshua and Samuel? Coming soon.

In this Introduction, we again offer our research on the Qumran community identifying who lived there, why they kept so much scripture and why it qualifies as the only Bible Canon in history up until the first century. We offer several supporting charts. We, then, apply a comprehensive Torah Test to First Enoch proving out its historicity, use as scripture and Bible Canon, and a plethora of citations including direct quotations with attribution in the modern Bible Canon – far more than a verse or two in Jude. Finally, this Introduction includes an assessment of the "Lord of Spirits" and "Head of Days" terms used by Enoch for the Father as well as "Son of Man" referring to Messiah in Heaven before the Flood whom Enoch met. Yahusha uses that term often as well.

We will address the supposed "missing" Second Section: The Book of Parables in which fragments were not found in Qumran. Yet, we will prove it was in use as scripture near that time, quoted and named within 1 Enoch by other portions of that book by name and content, and affirmed in other sources. If only scholars could read... We will also cover the former Dead Sea Scrolls Chief Editor's claim that he saw a complete Aramaic First Book of Enoch from Cave 11 both in print and microfilm.

As we move into the full publishing of the R.H. Charles translation of First Enoch from the Ethiopic, we have curated massive margin notes, produced charts, maps and graphics as well as history for enhanced understanding. No one needs to agree with every chart we create but we encourage you to read this book with an open mind as it has been greatly misunderstood. Follow our test and prove it out for yourself.

It is time to understand Enoch's 7 Weeks *(not 10)* with Daniel's 2,300 Days which we fully chart over 4 pages. We will answer the question with abundant evidence – Where Did Enoch Go? As Enoch well describes it, we will identify the type of tree representing the Tree of the Knowledge of Good and Evil. In Israel, many place names are an emulation of the Ancient Mt. Zion, Heavenly Jerusalem and we will locate even the true Armageddon where the final battle will amass, which is not Israel.

In this major work, we will not ignore Enoch's very obvious cosmology of the Earth including in most maps used, but we will embrace the ancient perspective in the shape of the Earth. Those who reject that will never understand this ancient text nor the Bible. The Lord of Spirits identified by Enoch many times is not a title but in fact, includes His name as Enoch specifies many times. We will substantiate that and restore this and the name of YHWH in this entire publishing. The ramifications of Messiah in Enoch are so incredibly profound which is why Pharisees want that section removed. He met Yahusha in Heaven in spirit before the Flood and renders the very first prophesies of Messiah coming in the flesh and His role in the End Times for eternity.

First Enoch includes extensive maps such as Enoch's Complete Journey Around the World on the surface where he was taken by angels to the most extreme ends of the Earth in all directions. Along the way, Enoch defines markers such as the four holy places of Yahuah on Earth including Mt. Zion in the North Pole *(not Israel)*, Great Deserts he visited including Mt. Sinai and the Garden of Eden and Mount of East. His extensive understanding of the Inner Earth brings the whole of scripture into context and full clarity for all to see supported by a large catalogue of Bible passages.

As we plot Enoch's journey, we find exact directions to the Garden of Eden in the modern Philippines after the Indian Ocean*(Erythraean Sea)* in the Easterly direction exiting to the Northeast as he defines. That can only be the Philippines*(see map)*. This concurs with Jubilees, Genesis and all of our research on the topic and has never been lost. Enoch further defines 7 Mountains of Eden *(the Garden)* from within the Earth and from the surface which match the 7 great islands of Visayas even in orientation just above the Garden which before the Flood, would be mountains. We include another fragment from Qumran written by or in the perspective of the Archangel Michael. Within, this proves to render another confirmation of the story of the migration of Ophir and the sons of Joktan *(Gen. 10:26-30)* from the area of Shinar *(Mesha, Mashhad, Iran)* during the time of the Tower of Babel fully affirming Genesis 10. This righteous lot returns to the ancient land of the Garden of Eden *(Sephar = Tree of Life, Mount of the East = Holy Mountain, both in the Garden)* formerly Havilah where the Archangel Gabriel, the Angel of the East resides*(see chart)*. We also compare Enoch's 7 Antediluvian Rivers with the Rivers From Eden from Genesis 2 which appear to agree.

Not being scientists, we were able to generally comprehend and chart the course of the sun by month over twelve mappings. It is uncanny how these seem to match the seasons appropriately as Enoch understood. He definitively agrees with Jubilees that the sun is the measure for the days, weeks, months, and years – NOT the moon!

This First Book of Enoch, much like Daniel, has remained in circulation but its understanding has been hidden or shut up until the days of increasing knowledge as Daniel predicted. We believe this is now. It is time we all understand and restore the full Word of Yahuah. Review this research and this will change your life. May this bless all who read. Yah Bless.

# INTRODUCTION Who Lived in Qumran?

In 1947, the voice in the wilderness cried out yet again. Did you hear it? The entire modern Old Testament canon was found in Qumran with the exception of the Book of Esther in what is inappropriately labeled and expanded in scope as the Dead Sea Scrolls as the find was specific to the Qumran area and truly remains so. This included other books as well. For many of these books, these are the oldest copies found and some were complete such as the 24-foot long Isaiah Scroll. After over 70 years, we still know little about this community yet the archaeology, writings of the community and the large compound found there confirm these were the Aaronic Levite Priests, the sons of Zadok, who had been exiled to the Wilderness of Yahudea by the Hasmoneans and Pharisees. They were the Temple High Priests replaced by a new unbiblical order.

However, today, the world allows the Pharisees who defiled the Temple to teach us about this community. No wonder we know so little about them or at least we are taught so. This was the base of operations for John the Baptist and his disciples where he baptized Jesus *(Yahusha)* and was visited by Him later privately. It is among the most well-documented New Testament communities on record and the church does not even know because it is too busy defending a control narrative that the other books found with the Old Testament are somehow cursed when Yahusha and John set this library as a time capsule to preserve His Word.

*Note: This "Who Lived In Qumran?" section of this Introduction only is the same as The Book of Jubilees: The Torah Calendar. The rest of the book is new.*

*Photo: Stone Sundial from Qumran site. The Qumran community were the keepers of the Biblical calendar based on the sun and the canon of scripture according to the decrees from Yacob and Moses.*

Several other books were found among these scrolls which must be considered and tested. The First Book of Enoch was ranked #3 in most scroll fragments found there. There were no fragments from the latter Enoch additions which become questionable especially with their occult leaning content. We will cover this too. Clearly important among that community of Levite priests, this tells us much as the Temple Levites were the keepers of scripture. Yacob entrusted Levi with this role in Jubilees 45:16 and Moses authorized these same Aaronic Levites in Deuteronomy 31:24-26 to do the same. If one truly wanted to know what books were and were not included in the Bible canon at the time of Messiah, they need not look far as this preserved the Old Testament canon of scripture up until His time. There were no books yet, just scroll libraries like the one found in Qumran.

Some attempt to force the books in the Septuagint that can be a useful publishing indeed in comparison but never as a standalone text as inerrant scripture. In fact, it too was a scroll library created in Egypt and the Aaronic Levites were not in Egypt at that time. They were in the Temple where they should be soon to be driven out into the Wilderness of Yahudea. They would take their Bible, scroll library in that time, with them. This was rediscovered in 1947 and immediately the Catholic Church and Pharisees moved to redefine the Bible that was found to protect the fraud they perpetrated in those days and since. The sect that created the Septuagint Greek translation in Egypt were not Aaronic Levite priests. These were Essenes in their attempt to hijack scripture which they would later write what they would call scripture in the Gnostic Gospels also found in Egypt. Not one Gnostic Gospel was found in Qumran nor do they coalesce with the New nor Old Testaments.

Essene is a name not found in the Bible even in the Greek Septuagint version demonstrating that cult has nothing to do with the Bible. The Qumran community never uses it nor anything similar. It is derived from the writings of Pliny, Josephus and others as ESSENOI, or ESSAIOI. As this is not a Bible word, we must go to an occult source to learn this originates in Egypt. In 2007, the Rosicrucian Digest weighs in on this.

*Origins of the Word "Essene"*

*The word truly comes from the Egyptian word kashai, which means "secret." And there is a Jewish word of similar sound, chsahi, meaning "secret" or "silent"; and this word would naturally be translated into essaios or "Essene," denoting "secret" or "mystic." Even Josephus found that the Egyptian symbols of light and truth are represented by the word choshen, which transliterates into the Greek as essen. Historical references have been found also wherein the priests of the ancient temples of Ephesus bore the name of Essene. A branch of the organization established by the Greeks translated the word Essene as being derived from the Syrian word asaya, meaning "physician," into the Greek word therapeutes, having the same meaning. [9]*

Again, this is an occult source and they take credit for the Essenes as a secret cult of sorcerers. To them, that is a good thing where those of us believers know better. However, what they do not connect is the "chsahi" *(kashaph:* ‏כָּשַׁף‎*: H3784)* were the sorcerers and magicians in which Moses and Aaron faced in Egypt*(Ex. 7:11)*. Some of them exited Egypt in the Exodus and settled in Ein Gedi in ancient times and not Qumran. Pliny notes they are a very ancient cult. This same sorcery and witchcraft is recorded in Canaan*(Dt. 18:10)*, in Israel*(2 Chr. 33:6)* and even in Babylon*(Dan. 2:2)*. It is the enemy of the Bible.

Some even further connect this Aramaic word "asaya" as the origin of the word Hasmonean. These are the conquerors of the Temple in 165 B.C. who exiled the Levite Temple priest system who are rebuked by their Qumran community as the "sons of darkness." What a world in which we live. This word is the origin of the Hasidim or Hasidic Jews of today. They are Essenes. The breakdown of the factions still exists as Rabbinic Judaism generally are Pharisees essentially with a sect of Hasidim, Essenes. Sure, they call themselves pious but they do not even remotely know the relationship of Torah. This is why we find them referring to their god as Hashem. This name is a variant of Ashima, the god of the Samaritans from whom they originate. Who would replace the name of Yahuah 6,800+ times with Lord or Ba'al in Hebrew? These Samaritans would. Any attempt to associate them with Messiah and John the Baptist is ridiculous. We were warned in the end times evil would be called good and good, evil.

One of the main reasons employed by many is this assumption that Essenes lived in Qumran which they never did. Attempts are even exercised claiming Jesus*(Yahusha)* and John believed in resurrection and somehow that is supposed to be equated to the reincarnation doctrine of the Essenes which is among the most illiterate of positions. The two doctrines are opposites as are the Essenes from the Qumran community. In fact, human spirits cannot reincarnate. The only spirits who do are demons or spirits of Nephilim when they die. They wander the dry places and when invited, they can enter a human and possess it or even an animal as Messiah cast demons into swine. Reincarnation is literally a doctrine of demons as only they reincarnate possessing the body of another.

Essenes originated from Egypt, though perhaps truly Mesopotamian origins ultimately thus the Aramaic, where they were known as physicians or alchemists of sort. There, they were called the Therapeutae in Greek. In Biblical terms they were sorcerers such as the false prophet identified as from Yahudea, Barjesus, an Essene*(Acts 13:6)*, the "child of the devil" according to Paul, Elymus*(Acts 13:8)* and the bewitching Simon the sorcerer*(Acts 8:9)*. In Greek, Paul calls this pharmakeía*(φαρμακεία: G5331)* meaning medication *("pharmacy")*, i.e. *(by extension)* magic *(literally or figuratively):*—sorcery, witchcraft."

Revelation tells us this is the end times deception in fact playing out as "by thy sorceries were all nations deceived"*(Rv. 18:23)*. This same sorcery is exactly what has happened with this entire narrative. Only a fool would claim Essenes lived in Qumran with no evidence, writings identifying themselves as Levites and incredibly significant Essene finds 25 miles South in Ein Gedi matching Pliny's directions to their headquarters. No scholar could logically draw such conclusion yet the mantra is vast. This false story permeates Judaism(Pharisaism according to the Jewish Encyclopedia) and those who manage the Rockefeller-funded museum doling out the idiotic control line. The church has bought this especially in seminaries. It is a lie.

The other list of Bible canon immediately thrown out there is that of Josephus who propagated a closed canon according to him of course. Josephus was an admitted Pharisee, Hasmonean and he was Essene trained by Banus in the wilderness*(Ein Gedi)* [11: *The Life of Flavius Josephus]*. Realize his "closed canon" which some Christians actually cite would mean the entire New Testament is not scripture and was already rebuked as ignoring part of the law or Torah according to Messiah*(Jn. 5:46-47)* and what they did use, they turned against scripture according to Him*(Mark 7:9)*. That is an oxymoron many do not even think through. His listing of what the Pharisees considered scripture educate us all on the paradigm at the time of Messiah and shortly after when the New Testament was just written as it already censored Jubilees especially. That is no canon.

However, whom did Yacob and Moses entrust with the keeping of scripture, Torah and what we would call Bible? The Temple Levite Priests of Aaron and Josephus was not nor were the Rabbis/Pharisees or Hasidim/Essenes. We have now found this scroll library which is the only which qualifies as the Bible canon for the entire history up until the time the Temple was destroyed. The question is, whom was ever given authority to overrule these Levites? Who was given their responsibility to keep scripture? Who was given authority to overturn Messiah's endorsement of this canon as well? Certainly not Pharisees who already threw out the Book of Jubilees in the days of Messiah. Most certainly not the cowardly general, Josephus, who ordered all of his troops to commit suicide while he failed to do so himself. Josephus is useful for history and geography to a point. However, he was no authority on scripture and his list is a spouting of Pharisee doctrine rebuked by Messiah many times. Only the Levite library records canon. Any Catholic council changing that was usurping Biblical authority it never had.

This community left history and scripture behind so that we would all know just what was and was not considered canon. They even include commentaries on different books, additional prophecy especially of the war of the "sons of darkness" versus the "sons of light," hymns, calendars, etc. The Hasmoneans*(Essenes)* and their priests *(Pharisees and Sadducees)* who exiled the true Aaronic Priests from the Temple are called the "sons of darkness" as they conquered the Temple and Yahudea in 165 B.C. This battle will last until the very end times in their writings. The Temple was the center of worship in Yerusalem. Though the Second Temple no longer housed the ark of the covenant with Yahuah's presence, it still received His blessing until that time. Priestly courses continued such as that of Zacharias, father of John the Baptist, in the course of Abiyah *(Abia)* but the leadership in the Temple, in all of Yahudea and essentially the world in a spiritual sense had been usurped by these "sons of darkness." This was a fulfillment of the Psalm 83 war in which David predicted the Temple, not even built at the time of his prophecy, would be defiled by neighboring enemies in this exact sense.

For the Hasmoneans did not attack just the Greeks nor did they originate in Yahudea. They inhabited an area called Modi'in which is across the border into Dan controlled by Samaria and the Philistines. They were not Hebrews nor Israelites. They were Samaritans who were the replacements of the Northern Tribes of Israel when they were taken captive into Assyria since around 700 B.C. This is why even in Messiah's parable of the Good Samaritan *(Lk. 10:25-37),* what was unthinkable in

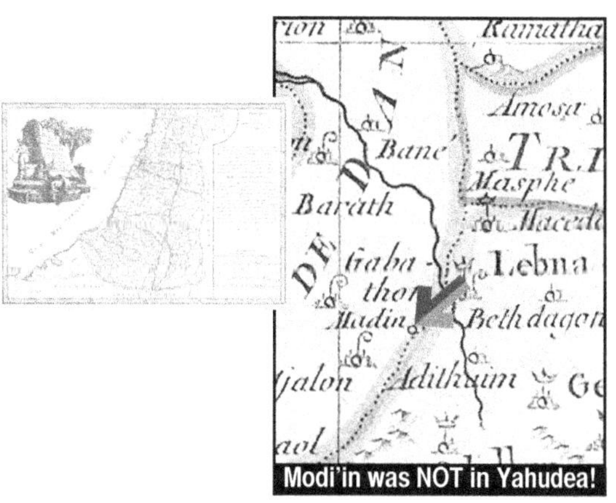

1770, Bonne Map of Israel. Rigobert Bonne 1727 – 1794. [12]

the paradigm of that day, was that a Samaritan could be good. These replacements were brought into the Northern Kingdom of Samaria and kept the name. They then attempted to infuse the worship of Yahuah into pagan religions of their gods Ashima *(Hashem),* Adrammelech *(Melech/Molech/Ba'al)* and others. However, this was never a sincere gesture. It was a response to the land that had been rejecting them as they were being attacked by wolves. They brought in a Levite Priest to teach them the rituals of the Bible. Yahuah rejected this infusion *(2 Ki. 17).*

The Pharisees and Sadducees did not exist in Yerusalem until the so-called Hasmonean Revolt in 165 B.C. You will find the Books of Maccabees as well as Esther were not found among the Qumran scrolls because neither are scripture. Both are the stories of what would become Zionism today. This was predicted not only by David but identified in Revelation as Messiah discusses the Synagogue of Satan who say they are Jews and are not but do lie *(Rev. 2:9, 3:9).* Even the term Jew is fraud and it never should be used in scripture as it is not of Ancient Hebrew,

Aramaic, Greek, Latin, Old French, Old German nor Old English origin. The name of Yahuah's people includes His own and such tribes would never remove His name from theirs. His people in the Old and New Testament are the Yahudim in Hebrew and Greek really. The shortened form of this word is Yah's never Jews as there is no "J" in any of the languages in which the Bible has been interpreted through. The first two letters are YH*(יה)* and that is Yah not Jew or Yah's not Jews. This fraud wraps into the rest of this false narrative coming from the modern Pharisees and the Catholic Church who changed scripture and attempt to cover it up.

Many do not realize that Qumran is identified in the Bible. However, Qumran is it's Muslim name oddly continued by Pharisees and modern Israel. Why would they do so when the Bible identifies this area by the name as Bethabara*(Greek)* or Betharabah*(Hebrew)*. Joshua*(Yahushua)* identifies the Western coastline of the Dead Sea geographically when he outlines a list in North to South progression of the cities of the Dead Sea wilderness.

*Joshua 15:61-62 KJV: In the wilderness, **Betharabah**, Middin, and Secacah, And Nibshan, and the city of Salt, and Engedi; six cities with their villages.*

He begins in the North with Betharabah on the Northwestern tip. That is called Qumran today. Joshua continues as he heads South to Middin which is due South of Qumran, then further South all the way to Ein Gedi. He defined a 25-mile distance from North to South. Notice there are several cities between Betharabah*(Qumran)* and Ein Gedi so even if somehow Pliny meant just North instead of just above in the mountains, which is obvious, he still would not be identifying Qumran as the headquarters of the Essenes. Of course, Ein Gedi has the archaeology called "The Essene Find."

The Madaba Mosaic Map*(left)*, c. 6th century A.D., contains the oldest surviving original map of especially the Dead Sea and right on the intersection where the Jordon meets the Dead Sea, is labeled in Greek as Βηθαβαρά or Bethabara. This is right where Joshua placed it and it is modern Qumran.

The reason this is important as well is John the Baptist baptized Messiah at Bethabara. This was not some random journey into the wilderness but a visit to the very compound

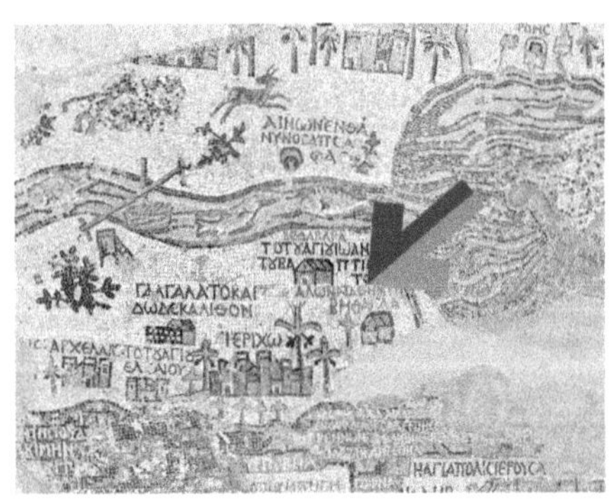

*Above: Jordan. Madaba (biblical Medeba) - St. George's Church. Fragment of the oldest floor mosaic map of the Holy Land - the Jordan River and the Dead Sea. [13]*

and library designed similar to the Temple where scripture was now kept outside of the Temple. Messiah Himself visited it more than once. Jesus *(Yahusha)* grew up and initially operated in Galilee *(Mt. 2:22)*. He came from there, headed South to beyond Jordan. The Jordan is not simply the Jordan River in scripture but the entire Jordan Plain or Jordan Valley *(Gn. 13:10)*. This does not indicate crossing the river but into the Wilderness of Yahudea at Qumran right on the border.

*Luke 3:2-4 KJV: ...the word of God came unto John the son of Zacharias in the wilderness. And he came into all the country about Jordan, preaching the baptism of repentance for the remission of sins; As it is written in the book of the words of Esaias the prophet, saying, The voice of one crying in the wilderness, Prepare ye the way of the Lord, make his paths straight.*

*Matthew 3 KJV 1: In those days came John the Baptist, preaching in the wilderness of Judaea...*
*5-6: Then went out to him Jerusalem, and all Judaea, and all the region round about Jordan, And were baptized of him in Jordan, confessing their sins.*

The Wilderness of Yahudea *(Chambers Map, right)* is very specifically the area along the West coast of the Dead Sea. It is not nor ever has referred to the Jordan Plain or Valley nor River other than before

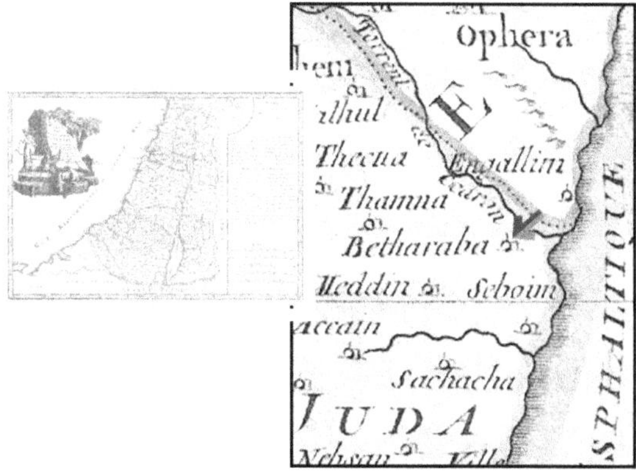

1770, Bonne Map of Israel. Rigobert Bonne 1727 – 1794 [12].

1836, Tanner Map of Palestine, Israel, Holy Land. [14]

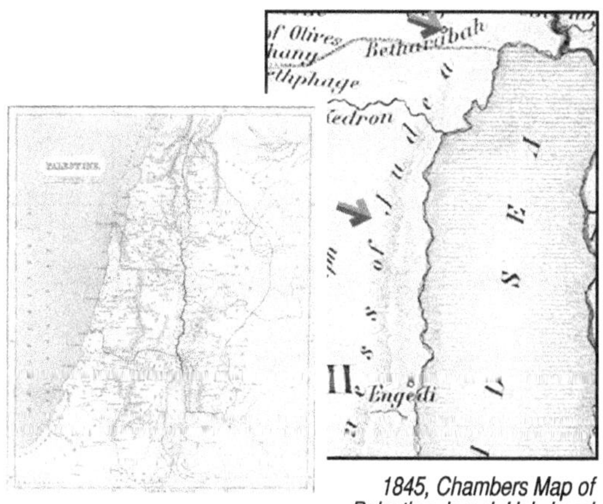

1845, Chambers Map of Palestine, Israel, Holy Land. [16]

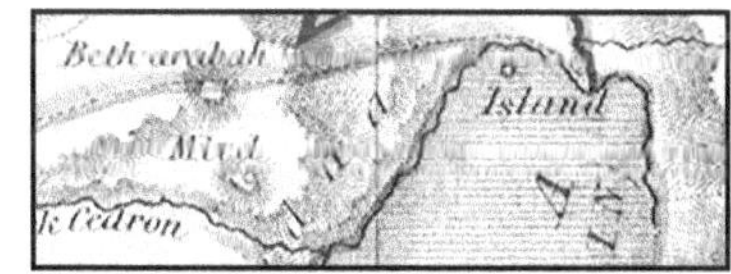

Inset of 1852, Philip Map of Palestine, Israel, Holy Land. [17]

there was a Dead Sea perhaps which was likely created by the destruction of Sodom. This has been known all along even on many maps until the 20th century *[previous page]*.

> **Matthew 3:13 KJV:** *Then cometh Jesus from Galilee to Jordan unto John, to be baptized of him.*

Where did Jesus *(Yahusha)* come from? Galilee. He travels South to Jordan. Where in Jordan? This verse is not specific.

> **John 1:28 KJV:** *These things were done in Bethabara beyond Jordan, where John was baptizing.*

Now, we have details rather than a general area. Jesus *(Yahusha)* came from Galilee heading South. He enters the Jordan Valley region and he travels "beyond" the Jordan Valley to a place called Bethabara. Where is this? The Jordan ends to the South at the Dead Sea and on the Northwest corner of the Dead Sea is Bethabara where John operated and baptized Messiah. It does not say he crossed the Jordan changing directions to go to the East. It says he travels South beyond Jordan to Bethabara. This is very clear and maps agree. This is Qumran.

The word beyond in Greek here is peran *(πέραν)* meaning "other side, beyond, over, farther side." This is where many scholars go wrong by forgetting the orientation of the region from Galilee South which does not enter the East side of the Jordan which is still the Jordan Valley. It progresses beyond the Jordan Valley to the Wilderness of Yahudea where John is said to be based. There is a reason.

John was an Aaronic bloodline Levite Priest qualified to be of High Priestly caste. He was not some hermit living under a tree eating locusts and honey. He was a righteous Aaronic Levite Priest operating in the place where his people had been exiled in the Wilderness of Yahudea in Bethabara which today is called Qumran. This forerunner to Messiah, the Elijah come again, wore camel's hair clothing *(Mt. 3:4, Mk. 1:6)* akin to sackcloth as in mourning. John ate locusts and honey which are both in the Biblical, covenant diet. He was essentially living the oath of a Rechabite but he was not poor and he did not live under a tree. He also is in no way the same as Banaah from the Talmud though attempts are made as Banaah lived 2-3 centuries later. John the Baptist was no Essene nor Pharisee nor was anyone in the Qumran community. John baptized mostly in fresh springs in clean water not the muddy waters of the Jordan River that few would desire to participate. Bethabara *(Qumran)* had fresh water. There is no disputing Qumran is Bethabara where Messiah was baptized and John and the Levites operated. This is the new location of the Temple practice where scripture was kept thus Bible.

## THE ESSENES OF EIN GEDI

*"On the west side of the Dead Sea, but out of range of the noxious exhalations of the coast, is the solitary tribe of the Essenes..."*
*"Lying below the Essenes was formerly the town of Engedi..." "Next comes Masada..." [10]*
*– Pliny the Elder, Natural History (Book V)*

Pliny, a geographer, indisputably located the Essenes in the mountains overlooking Ein Gedi, 25 miles South of Qumran. He even anchors it to Masada just to the South and that is the Southern tip not near Qumran.

This is affirmed in mass scale archaeology called "The Essene Find" in Ein Gedi. This included a very ancient temple identified as a Chalcolithic Temple, c. 4th millennium B.C., which was not built by the Essenes but likely part of their compound in the mountains.

Also, archaeologists discovered a synagogue with many symbols identifying these Essenes as the secret cult throughout history fitting to everything we know about the Essenes who never lived in Qumran.

They were obsessed with peacocks as they worship the Peacock Angel*(Persian)* identified by many as the Nephilim deity known as Asmodeus. They etched swastika on the wall, very prominently display an 8-pointed star of Ishtar on the floor in tile, etc. They even offer what appears a very freemasonic warning on the wall.

There is no actual coherent data placing Essenes in Qumran.

Remnants of a Chalcolithic Temple (4th millennium BCE). [18]

Essene synagogue in Ein Gedi. [18]

Tile mosaic on synagogue floor in Ein Gedi. [18]

Peacock symbols in Ein Gedi synagogue. [18]

## SONS OF ZADOK = 20 times

From the days of King Solomon, these are the Temple Priests. They are Levites and sons of Aaron both. However, they were given charge of the Temple worship and are the only Biblical keepers of scripture. They never call themselves Essenes but they identify themselves over 100 times and any scholar confusing the two is no scholar. They remained holy according to Ezekiel:

*Ezekiel 48:11 KJV*
*It shall be for the priests that are sanctified of the sons of Zadok; which have kept my charge, which went not astray when the children of Israel went astray, as the Levites went astray.*

They remained faithful when exiled from the Temple to Qumran and they will stand again in the End Times.

*"The sons of Zadok are the elect of Israel, the men called by name who shall stand at the end of days."*
*–The Damascus Document, p. 132 [22]*

Scripture was found in their library meaning this was Bible canon kept by the Sons of Zadok as was Biblical tradition. Essenes are never mentioned in scripture and never a Biblical tribe nor found in or near Qumran. That is blatant fraud!

*Moses in Deuteronomy 31:25-26 KJV (Cf. Jubilees 45:16)*
*That Moses commanded the Levites, which bare the ark of the covenant of the LORD, saying, Take this book of the law, and put it in the side of the ark of the covenant of the LORD your God, that it may be there for a witness against thee.*

SONS OF AARON = 16 times
LEVITES = 71 times
SONS OF LEVI = 5 times
SONS OF LIGHT = 27 times
TEACHER OF RIGHTEOUSNESS = 53 times

"...this concerns the Wicked Priest who pursued the Teacher of Righteousness to the house of his exile..."
–COMMENTARY ON HABAKKUK, p. 515 [22]

"the city is Jerusalem where the Wicked Priest committed abominable deeds and defiled the Temple of Elohim. The violence done to the land..."
–COMMENTARY ON HABAKKUK, p. 515 [22]

"Words of blessing. The M[aster shall bless] the sons of Zadok the Priests, whom Elohim has chosen to confirm His Covenant for [ever]"
– The Blessing of the High Priest, p.388 [22]

"When Elohim engenders (the Priest-) Messiah, he shall come with them [at] the head of the whole congregation of Israel with all [his brethren, the sons] of Aaron the Priests" – The Messianic Rule, p.161 [22]

*From a search of "The Complete Dead Sea Scrolls in English" by Geza Vermes [22]. Some are his mentions in commentary but that further affirms he knew who these were and still ignorantly concluded in fraud that these were Essenes with 0 mentions, 0 archaeology and Pliny indisputably placing them in Ein Gedi confirmed in archaeology.

# ESSENES = 0 times

When groups of scholars make themselves so stupid as to say this group were Essenes, you know they are only offering propaganda.

# WHO DEFILED THE SECOND TEMPLE?

The Books of Maccabees, not found in the Dead Sea Scrolls make the claim Greece defiled the Temple. That is a lie!

## Greece Did NOT Defile the Temple

From the account of the Temple Priests which appears within their commentaries of prophetic interpretation of events that had already occurred in their time, they record that Greece did not defile the Temple nor even attack Yahudea with their military. This is consistent with Greek history that does not mention this Maccabees account which is not history nor Bible. This is a major problem for modern Judaism which has only this claim to link it to their being Hebrews. They are not.

"Whither the lion goes, there is the lion's cub, [with none to disturb it] (ii, 11b).
[Interpreted, this concerns Deme]trius king of Greece who sought, on the counsel of those who seek smooth things, to enter Jerusalem. [But Elohim did not permit the city to be delivered] into the hands of the kings of Greece, from the time of Antiochus until the coming of the rulers of the Kittim. But then she shall be trampled under their feet..." –COMMENTARY ON NAHUM, p. 505 [22]

Thus, from the time of Demetrius to the time of Antiochus I including the time of Antiochus Epiphanes and until the time of the Kittim takeover which is the Roman Empire, Yahudea is not subdued with Greece's military. Even Alexander the Great was welcomed in a peaceful takeover not military conquest especially in the Temple where he even burnt the sacrifice of the Temple. Greece wanted the tax revenues and Israel agreed to that in all accounts even Josephus, Tacitus, Origen and others agree on that. However, who trampled Yahudea? Who defiled the Temple? This community did not keep that a secret...

"[For the violence done to Lebanon shall overwhelm you, and the destruction of the beasts] X II shall terrify you, because of the blood of men and the violence done to the land, the city, and all its inhabitants (ii, 17). Interpreted, this saying concerns the Wicked Priest, inasmuch as he shall be paid the reward which he himself tendered to the Poor. For Lebanon is the Council of the Community; and the beasts are the simple of Judah who keep the Law. As he himself plotted the destruction of the Poor, so will Elohim condemn him to destruction. And as for that which He said, Because of the blood of the city and the violence done to the land: interpreted, the city is Jerusalem where the Wicked Priest committed abominable deeds and **defiled the Temple of Elohim**. The violence done to the land: these are the cities of Judah where he robbed the Poor of their possessions."
–COMMENTARY ON HABAKKUK, p. 515 [22]

The Wicked Priest is not one man but the Hasmoneans including their priests, the Pharisees and new Sanhedrin that was new to Yerusalem and neither faction ever mentioned in the entire Old Testament as they did not exist in Yerusalem until installed by the Hasmoneans around 165 B.C. These exiled the Aaronic, Levite Temple Priest leadership of antiquity to Qumran replacing them with a new unbiblical order in Yerusalem. That is the defiling of the Temple not Greece. They conquered as they maintained control of it and changed the religion to their Samaritan infusion of Persian basis with attempted worship of YHWH that He rejected then and rejects now. This is clear and indisputable and this is actual history from the First Century ignored and untold by the church generally as they maintain willing ignorance as 2 Peter 3 warned. Who do they listen to? The very ones who defiled the Temple.

*Excerpts from "The Complete Dead Sea Scrolls in English" by Geza Vermes [22]. One will notice multiple injections from Vermes and many scholars since of the Maccabees story as fact when these very writings of this community condemn the Hasmonean Revolt as the defiling of the Temple. That is dishonest and fraudulent!

# The Maccabees Did!

# FIRST TEMPLE FEAST OF DEDICATION:

*Feast of Tabernacles. 7th Hebrew Month (Ethanim)*
*Modern Calendar: Between Sept. 15 - Oct. 15*

1 Kings 8:63, 1 Kings 8:2, 2 Chronicles 5:3

# SECOND TEMPLE FEAST OF DEDICATION:

*Adar 3 or 23. 12th Hebrew Month (Not December)*
*Modern Calendar: Between Feb. 15 - Mar. 15*

Ezra 6:15-17, 1st Esdras 7:5-8 (Note: March 15 is still Winter)

The Second Temple stood until 70 A.D. Therefore, it's Feast of Dedication remained Late February to Early March. The history used to redefine this as a rededication proves to be fraud according to the Qumran community *(previous page)*. What the Maccabees did was celebrate their pagan, Persian Winter Solstice Festival and they called it Hanukkah which is the Hebrew word for dedication. However, they defiled the Temple on that date. It is a rather disgusting display in fraud. Some attempt to claim Messiah was celebrating the Hasmonean Hanukkah but that as well is a lie.

# EXPOSED IN 1st ESDRAS!

*Matthew 15:12-14 KJV*
*Then came his disciples, and said unto him, Knowest thou that the Pharisees were offended, after they heard this saying? But he answered and said, Every plant, which my heavenly Father hath not planted, shall be rooted up. Let them alone: they be blind leaders of the blind. And if the blind lead the blind, both shall fall into the ditch.*

Messiah Was In The Temple In Adar (February) NOT December!

*John 10:22 KJV*
*And it was at Jerusalem **the feast of dedication**, and it was **winter**. And Yahusha walked in the Temple in Solomon's porch.*

This is consistent with the Second Temple Feast of Dedication in the Winter in Late February to Mid-March. Messiah did NOT celebrate the Hasmonean Hanukkah nor does He ever embrace their story on any level. He rebukes their priests, their religion and even their lineage. It is time we correct this for good.

| "Vipers" | "Hypocrites" | "Expand the Word with Leaven" |
|---|---|---|
| Matt. 3:7, 12:34, 23:33<br>Luke 3:7 | Matt. 6:2, 6:5, 15:7, 16:3, 22:18, 23:13, 14, 15, 23, 25, 27, 28, 29, 24:51<br>Mark 7:6<br>Luke 11:44, 12:56 | Matt. 15:6, 16:6, 11<br>Mark 7:13, 8:15<br>Luke 12:1 |
| "Lead People to Hell" | "Operate Against His Commandments" | "Blind" "Vain" |
| Matt. 23:13, 23:15, 24:51<br>Luke 11:52 | Matt. 15:3-6, 23:4, 23<br>Mark 7:5-13<br>Rom. 2:17-20 | Matt. 15:12-14, 23:16-17, 23-26<br>Mark 7:7<br>John 9:39-41<br>Rom. 1:21, 2:17-20 |
| "Condemned to Hell Generally" | "Unclean" "Self-Righteous" | "Murderers" |
| Matt. 5:20, 23:13-15, 24:51 | Matt. 6:5, 23:5, 15, 23-27, 28<br>Luke 7:29-30, 36-50, 18:9-14<br>John 8:39-59, 12:42 | Matt. 12:14, 21:45-46, 23:31, 26:4<br>Luke 6:11, 11:47<br>John 8:44, 11:45-57<br>Acts 3:14-15, 7:52 |

"Pharisaism shaped the character of Judaism and the life and thought of the Jew for all the future."
—*Jewish Encyclopedia [60]*

# According to the Bible

**Why Ignore What the Bible Says to Support a False Paradigm?**

| "Seed/Synagogue of Satan" | "Devour Widow's Houses/Poor" | "Pray/Give to Be Seen" "Haughty" |
|---|---|---|
| John 8:44<br>Rev. 2:9, 3:9 | Matt. 23:14<br>Mark 12:40<br>Luke 7:36-50, 20:47, 21:1-6 | Matt. 6:2, 5, 16, 23:5-6, 14, 17-22<br>Mark 12:40<br>Luke 11:43,16:14, 20:45-47 |
| **"Don't Know Prophecy" "Seek Signs"** | **"Don't Know Scripture"** | **"Thieves" "Extort"** |
| Matt. 12:14-37, 16:1-4, 27:40-43<br>Mark 8:11-12<br>Luke 7:29-30, 11:29-32<br>John 5:18, 10:24-39 | Matt. 16:6-12, 21:23-27, 22:34-46, 23:23-24 , 26:62-68<br>Mark 3:6; Acts 1:6<br>Luke 7:29-30, 22:2<br>17:20-21<br>John 5:18, 10:24-39 | Matt. 21:13, 23:25<br>Mark 11:17<br>Luke 19:46 |
| **"Stand in the Way of Knowledge"** | **"Accusers and Liars"** | **"Fools"** |
| Matt. 23:34-35<br>Luke 11:52, 22:2<br>John 12:42 | Matt. 12:1-2, 13-17, 22-24, 22:15-22,<br>Mark 3:22<br>Luke 6:7, 7:39, 11:53, 19:39, 20:20-26<br>John 8:13; Rev. 2:9 | Matt. 23:17, 19<br>Luke 11:40, 24:25<br>Rom. 1:22, 2:17-20 |

**Pharisaism Became Rabbinic Judaism After 70 A.D.
Pharisees Are Modern Rabbis, Modern Jews.**

## *Page Number in Paranthesis.

| "Sons of Darkness" "Men of the Pit" | "Sons of Belial/ Satan" "Lot of Belial" | "Wicked Priests" |
|---|---|---|
| War Scroll, (165-182) | 4Q286 (394), 4Q386 (613) | |
| Dam. Doc. (134, 144) | Dam. Doc. (133) | 4Q394-9 (221) |
| 4Q548 (573) | Temple Scroll (212) | 4Q448 (340) |
| Comm. Rule (111) | War Scroll (176) | iQpHab (509-515) |
| 4Q258 (121) | Comm. Rule (99) | 4QpPsa (519) |
| Hymn 9 (265) | Hymn 7 (263) | |

| "Defilers of the Temple" | "Theives" "Rob the Poor" "Prey on Widows" | "Unclean" |
|---|---|---|
| iQpHab (513, 515) | iQpHab (509-515) | iQpHab (513) |
| Dam. Doc. | Dam. Doc. (134) | 4Q174 (525) |
| (133, 137, 148) | 4Q163 (499) | Dam. Doc. (133-134) |
| 4Q174 (525) | Hymn 13 (273) | 4Q286 (394) |
| Temple Scroll (212) | Comm. Rule (113) | |

| "Vain" | "Strangers" "Men of Perdition" | "Flouters of the Law" (Disregard, Despise) |
|---|---|---|
| iQpHab (514) | | |
| Dam. Doc. (134) | 4Q174 (525) | iQpHab (509-512) |
| 4Q174 (526) | 4Q501 (328) | Dam. Doc. (133) |
| Comm. Rule (103, 119) | Comm. Rule (113) | 4Q163 (499) |
| War Scroll (171, 176) | 4Q 171 (522) | 4Q174 (525) |
| Hymn 14 (276) | | 11Q13 (533) |

**"Pharisaism shaped the character of Judaism and the life and thought of the Jew for all the future."**
—Jewish Encyclopedia [60]

# According to the Dead Sea Scrolls

From "The Complete Dead Sea Scrolls in English, Revised Edition" By Geza Vermes. [22]

| "Liars" "Spouter of Lies" | "Those Who Seek Smooth Things" | "Scoffers" |
|---|---|---|
| 4QpPsa (37)<br>iQpHab (510-515)<br>Dam. Doc. (137)<br>4Q 171 (519, 522)<br>4Q501 (328)<br>Hymn 14 (278) | Dam. Doc. (129-130)<br>Thanksgiving Hymns (262-269)<br>4Q163, (499)<br>4Q169, (505-7)<br>4Q177, (536) | Dam. Doc. (129, 137)<br>iQH, 1Q36,4Q427-32<br>Hymn 6 (262)<br>4Q162 (499) |
| **"Abomination" "House of Guilt"** | **"Enemies"** | **"Oppressive" "Overbearing"** |
| iQpHab (511, 513)<br>Dam. Doc. (133)<br>4Q175 (528)<br>Temple Scroll (212)<br>4Q387 (603)<br>4Q389 (604) | iQpHab (514-515)<br>Dam. Doc. (133)<br>4Q174 (525)<br>War Scroll (176-177, 184)<br>Temple Scroll (215-217) | iQpHab (509-514)<br>4Q448 (341)<br>4Q508 (383)<br>4Q504 (378)<br>4Q 171 (522) |
| **"Unfaithful" "Rebellious"** | **"Vipers, Spiders, Serpents, Dragons"** | **"Men of Violence" "Instruments of Violence"** |
| iQpHab (509-510, 513)<br>Dam. Doc. (133)<br>4Q306 (243), 11Q13 (533)<br>Hymn 14 (278)<br>4Q332 (405)<br>Comm. Rule (99) | Dam. Doc. (133)<br>Hymn 14 (275)<br>Hymn 13 (273) | Hymn 14 (276, 278)<br>Hymn 7 (263)<br>4Q 171 (520-522)<br>Comm. Rule (113)<br>iQpHab (509-515)<br>4Q175 (528), 4Q379 (585) |

**Pharisais[...] Rabbinic Judaism After 70 A.D.
Pharisees Are Modern Rabbis, Modern Jews**

# JOHN THE BAPTIST
## IN QUMRAN ? He Likely Grew Up There *(Luke 1:80)*

"You may eat [the following] flying [insects]: every kind of great locust, every kind of long-headed locust, every kind of green locust, and every kind of desert locust." –The Temple Scroll, P. 207 [22]

## John's Rare Diet found there

"And as for locusts, according to their various kinds they shall plunge them alive into fire or water, for this is what their nature requires."
–The Damascus Document, P. 143 [22]

## Prophecy of John Blessing Messiah

*The Blessing of the Prince of the Congregation (100 B.C.) [22]*
"The *Master (John the Baptist) shall bless the Prince of the Congregation (Yahusha)* . . . and shall *renew for him the Covenant of the Community* that he may establish the *kingdom of His people for ever*, [that he may *judge the poor* with righteousness and] *dispense justice* with {equity to the oppressed} of the land, and that he may walk perfectly before Him in all the ways [of truth], and that *he may establish His holy Covenant* at the time of the affliction of those who seek Elohim. May the Lord raise you up to everlasting heights, and as a fortified tower upon a high wall! [May you *smite the peoples*] with the might of your hand and ravage the earth with *your sceptre*; may you *bring death to the ungodly with the breath of your lips*! ...The *rulers ... [and all the kings of the] nations shall serve you*. He shall strengthen you with *His holy Name* and you shall be *as a [lion*; and you shall not lie down until you have devoured the] prey which naught shall deliver"
–Calendars, Liturgies and Prayers, p. 389-390.

## Prepare the Way in the Wilderness...

Zacharias' prophecy at John's birth: *Luke 1:79*
### "To Give Light..."

Qumran Identification:
### "Sons of Light"
[22]

John baptized Yahusha in Qumran/ Bethabara fulfilling these 2 Qumran prophesies and Isaiah. These exiled Temple Priests knew their community would play such a role. This is the link between the Old and New Testaments.

And when these become members of the Community in Israel according to all these rules, they shall separate from the habitation of unjust men and shall go into the wilderness to prepare there the way of Him; as it is written, Prepare in the wilderness the way of..., make straight in the desert a path for our God (Isa. xl, 3). This (path) is the study of the Law which He commanded by the hand of Moses, that they may do according to all that has been revealed from age to age, and as the Prophets have revealed by His Holy Spirit.
–The Community Rule, P. 109. [22]

**Is the First Book of Enoch Scripture, Inspired and Canon?**

*Criteria set forth by Blue Letter Bible with our additions. [1]*

### 1. Prophetic Authorship

*"For a book to be considered canonical, it must have been written by a prophet or apostle or by one who had a special relationship to such (Mark to Peter, Luke to Paul). Only those who had witnessed the events or had recorded eyewitness testimony could have their writings considered as Holy Scripture."*

### 2. Witness of the Spirit, Quoted As Doctrine In Scripture

*"The appeal to the inner witness of the Holy Spirit was also made to aid the people in understanding which books belonged in the canon and which did not." BLB quotes Pinnock who claims the canon is a matter of "historical process" (Clark Pinnock, Biblical Revelation, Grand Rapids: Baker Book House, 1973, p. 104). [2] We would agree but Pinnock ignores the most obvious such history. The Levite Library or Bible canon found in Qumran serves as a time capsule for the Old Testament canon long before the Catholic Church nor councils. Every book in the modern Old Testament canon was found there except Esther. It is Levite Priests who were the keepers of scripture and the Qumran community identifies as such over 100 times.*

### 3. Acceptance

*"The final test is the acceptance of the people of God." BLB notes this is to accept Jesus and the Apostles which we agree for New Testament but this would also be to accept His people in the time of the Old Testament. First Enoch is both.*

### 4. In Agreement With the Whole of Scripture (Our Addition)

*Does it agree with scripture in whole? Even the Gospels have minor details to iron out in understanding, but how does it compare? The conclusion may surprise many.*

## 1. Prophetic Authorship: Who Wrote 1st Enoch?

The First Book of Enoch ascribes its authorship to the Prophet Enoch, the seventh from Adam many times, even written in the first person, and documented before and up to the Flood. This is affirmed by Noah in his writing in which we have fragments from the Dead Sea Scrolls, by Moses in the Book of Jubilees and by Jude which we will cover. Though there are prophetic references of great detail of future events, this book declares it written prior to the Flood which again Noah and Moses confirm in date. Could this be the case? This is where the scoffing scholar enters with many speculations as to how this was written much later and of course as usual, by a Pharisee and/or during Hellenism, from many inept scholars. This is a paradigm of stupid not scholarship.

Some such as Charles and Vanderkamp actually make the assertion that First Enoch had several authors. This is to justify their disbelief of First Enoch as scripture as they and most scholars are willing to accept fraud in claim that someone else wrote this book claiming to be Enoch. Somehow in modern scholarship, that is considered an acceptable paradigm. However, these inept scholars are leveling the very worst of charges at the Temple Priests who lived in Qumran/Bethabara who were not Essenes. They were the keepers of Bible Canon since the time of Moses – the exiled, Levite Priests, the sons of Zadok. Anyone calling themselves a Bible scholar claiming that those Temple Priests committed such fraud in creating a book in the Second Century B.C. purporting to be from before the Flood, is among the most illiterate of scholars and certainly, they are not Bible scholars. Some of the same will then use these materials they discredit in fraud which is also acceptable to them because they do not have a clue how the Bible works. The Temple Priests were not frauds, not plagiarists and were not in need of extra books to scare people. What a stupid paradigm modern scholarship has become in such thinking.

Imagine R.H. Charles and many actually claim that this very ancient Book of Enoch must be framed within the era of Hellenism as that is when the oldest copies have been found. These inept scholars ignorantly overlook the tradition of the scribe to copy over texts and these were found among Bible Canon not in some alternative library, but in the very library of the ordained keepers of scripture. How obtuse can any scholar be to pretend they even understand the paradigm to suggest something so illiterate.

We will cover the Book of Jubilees written by Moses as well as Jude both ascribe Enoch as the author of this First Book of Enoch. They not only identify him as author but quote it. We can find this throughout history in a historicity that is indisputable.

## 2. Witness of the Spirit: The Historical Process, Quoted As Doctrine In Scripture

The Book of Enoch is well recorded consistently throughout history not to 200 or so B.C. which is an illiterate lie of willing ignorance from a community of frauds. Even the scroll they attempt to date to such has not been scientifically tested which would hardly matter as following the scribal tradition, this scroll was copied over for thousands of years. They know this and apply it with those books from the modern Canon yet then forget that scribes practiced such in regards to any book found in Qumran that has not made it into their Pharisee Canon. This is a Canon of ignorance which turned a blind eye in the time of Messiah to several books from the Temple Library according to the Temple Priests. This is because that library was no longer kept in the Temple but in Qumran/Bethabara with the sons of Zadok exiled there from the Temple. These usurpers of the Temple and priesthood are the Pharisees who know nothing of Bible Canon nor the entire worship of Yahuah whom they do not worship but hide in doctrine. Messiah did not suggest such, he rebukes them many times very directly *(see chart pp. 30-34)*. Josephus, the Pharisee, Hasmonean and Essene trained, proves that when his list of supposed Bible Canon does not match that of the actual Biblical keepers of scripture which we found in Qumran/Bethabara. The Bible has nothing but rebuke of the Pharisee Canon and interpretation which has been continued in Rabbinic Judaism and the Catholic Church to this day.

We already proved in our Foreward that Moses affirms the Book of Enoch as the first writing among men period *(Jub. 4:16-19)*. There is no writing, rock carving, etc. which trumps Enoch except that of the Angel of the Presence in Heaven on the Heavenly Tablets. Portions of Enoch even derive from those same Tablets just as Moses was given to write Genesis and Jubilees. This again is confirmed by Luke and Paul *(Acts 7:53; Gal. 3:19)* as well as the Qumran exiled Temple Priests *(4Q180, p. 553 [22])*. However, the evidence is far more vast the First Book of Enoch existed prior to the Flood and since.


## BEFORE THE FLOOD, 4,000 B.C. *(approx.)*:

The First Book of Enoch itself as a scroll was written before the Flood. It was taught by Enoch to his son Methuselah who died just before the deluge erupted.

> **1 Enoch 76:14 *(Enoch to Methuselah)***
> *"...have I shown to thee, my son Methuselah."*
>
> **1 Enoch 79:1 *(Enoch to Methuselah)***
> *And now, my son, I have shown thee everything, and the law of all the stars of the heaven is completed.*
>
> **1 Enoch 81:5 *(Angels Instruct Enoch to Teach Methuselah and His Lineage)***
> *And those seven holy ones brought me and placed me on the earth before the door of my house, and said to me: 'Declare everything to thy son Methuselah, and show to all thy children that no flesh is righteous in the sight of Yahuah, for He is their Creator.*

Some would attempt to discount these passages because they originate in the First Book of Enoch. However, according to Moses in Torah, Methuselah, Lamech and Noah read and applied this First Book of Enoch before the Flood. Thus, for any modern Pharisee to date the origin of the First Book of Enoch to 200 B.C. is ludicrous especially without even attempting a scientific dating and clearly in willing ignorance.

**Jubilees 7:38** *(Noah, Methuselah and Lamech Read Enoch Before the Flood)*
*38 For thus did* **Enoch,** *the father of your father command* **Methuselah,** *his son, and Methuselah his son* **Lamech,** *and* **Lamech commanded me** *all the things which his fathers commanded him.*

However, Noah first learned of the Flood from reading Enoch's book according to Noah. Unfortunately, Charles and much of the scholarly dunderheads discount that this passage is not talking about Enoch's warning which is inept claiming it refers to Noah instead thus, Noah read Noah and learned? Really? Where else would Noah have read of the warning of the Flood? The word there is Enoch because it is Enoch's life in dating not Noah's. Yes, this is in the 500th year of Enoch's life in which Noah learned of the coming Flood. This is not talking about the time of the Flood yet which turns out to be similar but not in the 500th but 600th year of Noah's life. That's not a match and they are exhibiting illiterate interpretation to suggest this as a mistake when they are mistaken. Somehow, they also can't read that this is the 7th month on the 14th day and Noah's was the 2nd month on the 17th day thus not even the same day nor month. In other words, this is not a typo, scribal error or corruption as scoffers like to use to change texts. They call it textual criticism yet they can't even read the text. It was a different guy, off by a century in years, off by 5 months in months and off by days even. That is not logic. It demonstrates they do not believe the text nor understand it.

**1 Enoch 60:1 (A Noah Fragment)**
*In the year five hundred, in the seventh month, on the fourteenth day of the month in the* **life of Enoch.** *In that Parable I saw how a mighty quaking made the heaven of heavens to quake, and the host of the Most High, and the angels, a thousand thousands and ten thousand times ten thousand, were disquieted with a great disquiet.*

They don't know Him thus they dismiss the obvious to claim this must mean the 500th year of Noah yet this fragment is not beginning with the Flood start but when Noah learns of the coming doom. Unfortunately, scholarship is lined with such stupidity. This perfectly matches the timeline in Jubilees where Enoch was born in 522 Anno Mundi (from Creation). Enoch did not die so counting his days still makes sense even though this was after he was taken more than a century earlier. The 500th year of Enoch would be about 1022 A.M. and that is very appropriate as Noah, almost 300 years old at that time, would have learned about the coming Flood that year not long after Adam died in 930 A.M. as a new era had begun. This is before Noah's 3 sons are born from 1207-1212 A.M. in time to prepare and by that point, Noah is fully aware of the task at hand. Their ages would also fit the time in which they would be able to assist in building the ark. He builds the ark by 1307 A.M. and the Flood began 1308 A.M.

Just by reading 8 chapters later, Noah affirms he learned of the coming Flood in the First Book of Enoch specifically from the Book of Parables and later that day Michael spoke to him as well. Therefore, Charles and other scholars choose to ignore Enoch and change Noah's words. This is unacceptable and not scholarship. It is useless leaven and propaganda. What they are likely doing is protecting their false view that Noah built the ark for 120 years when Yahuah said and Jubilees especially clarifies, the 120 years has nothing to do with the ark timeline but Yahuah telling Noah He would reduce the lifespan of mankind. We prove this in our video titled "Is Man Limited to 120 Years of Life?" Science and Genesis agree with Jubilees which leaves no room for debate. If you look for it, you can see the motive behind many of these kinds of baseless claims and watch them try to cover their tracks. It is deplorable.

### 1 Enoch 68:1
*And after that* **my grandfather Enoch gave me the teaching of all the secrets in the book and in the Parables** *which had been given to him, and he put them together for me in the words of the book of the Parables.*

Even the New Testament Book of Jude quotes First Enoch multiple times but one time, he affirms the account of the Nephilim from before the Flood written and circulated by Enoch in the antediluvian era and written with Enoch in the story as an historical character. Jude is affirming this written account which he even names later in his chapter. Some try to maintain that Jude quoted Enoch from something else but not specifically this First Book of Enoch. It is dumfounding how obtuse such supposed scholars can behave in expressing themselves. They have the responsibility to prove their positions not just say "nuh uh" as a child. When Jude quotes Enoch's written prophecy from a book that matches the First Book of Enoch and no other, no one needs to wait another thousand years to see if another text turns up when it is right there – a direct quote and obvious to anyone who can think.

### Jude 1:6 KJV
*And the angels which kept not their first estate, but left their own habitation, he hath reserved in everlasting chains under darkness unto the judgment of the great day.*

## AFTER THE FLOOD, 3,600 B.C. *(approx.)*:

In Jubilees, Moses affirms that the First Book of Enoch survived the Flood and Noah still used it at that time to instruct his sons just as he affirms he, his father and grandfather were also instructed. Noah took this book with him on the ark.

**Jubilees 7:39 (Written By Moses, Noah Quotes Enoch After the Flood)**
*39 And I also will give you commandment, my sons, as* **Enoch** *commanded his son in the first jubilees: whilst still living, the seventh in his generation,* **he commanded and testified to his son and to his sons' sons until the day of his death.***"*

We know Enoch's commandments were put in writing and this refers to the First Book of Enoch. Noah is then, documented by Moses as continuing this practice learned from Enoch until the day of his death. Enoch is actually known as more righteous than Noah. Noah affirms Enoch's office as Prophet and the first Scribe among men having written a book Noah read and identifies as containing prophecy of the Flood all the way to the Day of Final Judgment in the End Times. This is the First Book of Enoch and really affirms all five sections existed at that time as we covered in our Foreward.

**Jubilees 10:17-18 (Until His Death, Noah Kept The Law of Enoch)**
*17 And in his life on earth he excelled the children of men save Enoch because of the righteousness, wherein he was perfect. For Enoch's office was ordained for a testimony to the generations of the world, so that he should recount all the deeds of generation unto generation, till the day of judgment.*

## TIME OF ABRAHAM, BEFORE 2000 B.C. *(approx.)*:

About 300 years later after Noah's death, Abraham was born according to Jubilees' timeline. Somehow, the Book of Enoch and the writings of Noah were passed down through Shem to Abraham. According to Moses in Jubilees, Abraham was reading the First Book of Enoch, following the commandments as Noah did and he taught Isaac, Ishmael and Jacob this Law all passed down from Enoch and Noah. There is no missing beat here. This is a continual history. Torah was not yet written by Moses for centuries.

**Jubilees 19:24 (Abraham to Jacob)**
*24 And in his seed shall my name be blessed, and the name of my fathers, Shem, and Noah, and Enoch,*

**Jubilees 19:27a (Abraham to Jacob)**
*27 "Jacob, my beloved son, whom my soul loveth, may Elohim bless thee from above the*

*firmament, and may He give thee all the blessings wherewith He blessed Adam, and Enoch, and Noah, and Shem;*

**Jubilees 21:10b-11 (Abraham's Final Words - Passing the Law of Enoch and Noah)**
*for thus I have found it* **written in the books of my forefathers,** *and in the words of* **Enoch,** *and in the words of* **Noah.** *11 And on all and let not the salt of the covenant be lacking in all thy oblations before Yahuah.*

How did Abraham know how to sacrifice? From the writings of First Enoch including Noah. How did he learn of covenant and Law?–From the same. We know Enoch was holy and righteous more so than even Moses and Noah. This concurs with Genesis and all of scripture. Of course, he had writings and they remain profound and in circulation.

**Genesis 5:22-24 KJV**
*And Enoch walked with God after he begat Methuselah three hundred years, and begat sons and daughters: And all the days of Enoch were three hundred sixty and five years: And Enoch walked with God: and he was not; for God took him.*

**Hebrews 11:5 KJV**
*By faith Enoch was translated that he should not see death; and was not found, because God had translated him: for before his translation he had this testimony, that he pleased God.*

## TIME OF MOSES, 1700 B.C. - 600 B.C. *(approx.)*:

In addition to the Jubilees 4, 7, 10, 19 and 21 passages we have reviewed, First Enoch is quoted by Moses in the modern accepted Torah as well. It cannot be the other way around as Abraham was reading and using the First Book of Enoch long before Moses as was Noah. You will find this similar quote in Habakkuk, Micah and Isaiah all originating in First Enoch which was in circulation before the Bible was written.

**Deuteronomy 33:2 KJV (Moses Quotes First Enoch)**
*And he said, The LORD came from Sinai, and rose up from Seir unto them; he shined forth from mount Paran, and he came with ten thousands of saints: from his right hand went a fiery law for them. Cf Hab. 3:3 (600 B.C.), Mic. 1:3(750-700 B.C.), Is. 26:21(700 B.C.)*

This is another tight quote of First Enoch used by Moses in Torah. Again, Abraham already used First Enoch and that is documented by Moses thus there is no debate that Enoch could be written after Torah whatsoever. They have no stance.

**1 Enoch 1:3-4**

*Concerning the elect I said, and took up my parable concerning them: The Holy Great One will come forth from His dwelling, And the eternal Elohim will tread upon the earth, (even) on Mount Sinai, [And appear from His camp] And appear in the strength of His might from the heaven [of heavens].*

One very prominent doctrine throughout scripture is that of the Fallen Angels *(Watchers)* who "left their first estate" *(Jude 1:6, 2 Pet. 2:4)* and came down to Earth first to teach. They decided to sin against the Law of Creation to reproduce after their kind. Angels, however, are not supposed to procreate. They are eternal and even Messiah is clear they are forbidden to do so in Heaven *(Matt. 22:30, Mark 12:25, Luke 20:35)*. However, when in human form, they could and did sin with the daughters of men. This is not strange doctrine but what the Bible has always taught. It originates in First Enoch as Moses quotes these two verses right out of 1 Enoch twice as he does it again in Jubilees.

**Genesis 6:1-2 KJV (Moses Quotes First Enoch)**

*And it came to pass, when men began to multiply on the face of the earth, and daughters were born unto them, That the sons of God saw the daughters of men that they were fair; and they took them wives of all which they chose.*

**1 Enoch 6:1-2**

*And it came to pass when the children of men had multiplied that in those days were born unto them beautiful and comely daughters. And the angels, the children of the heaven, saw and lusted after them, and said to one another: 'Come, let us choose us wives from among the children of men and beget us children.'*

Somehow, in the very next verse, Yahuah's reaction is that He will have to replenish the entire Earth due to this sin. For any scholar to miss this is gross negligence. Then, in verse 4, Moses is clear these were the Nephilim giants who were the product of this event mixing angels with humans. These are they that corrupted the orders of the Earth's Creation who would lead to Yahuah's salvation in the Flood. It is poor enough that scholars have missed this en masse for so long, but far worse, any layman can read this in comparison and see that these two passages are the same. You will find the very same in Jubilees 5:1-2 as well as the teachings of the Qumran/Bethabara community. This is the ancient understanding and the new strange doctrine is that that ignores this which we find in several denominations still in willing ignorance.

**TIME OF MOSES' JUBILEES, 1700 B.C.** *(approx.)*:

In our publishing of The Book of Jubilees: The Torah Calendar, we apply a very comprehensive Torah Test including historicity and we vet who lived in Qumran as we repeat such research in the Introduction of this book. Having even mapped the directions of Noah's Division of the Earth leading to monumental revelation, Jubilees holds firm in every test. This includes a direct endorsement by the exiled Temple Priests of Qumran/Bethabara labeling Jubilees as Torah and applying it as Torah. One cannot find a more ringing endorsement nor can they disprove that research which conclusion can only be that The Book of Jubilees was and remains Torah. Read it. However, Jubilees quotes 1 Enoch many times. R.H. Charles published these in his Introduction.

| **1 Enoch** | **Quoted in Jubilees:** |
|---|---|
| *19:1 sacrificing to demons as gods* | *1:11* |
| *10:16 the plant of righteousness and truth/ uprightness (Cf. 93:2, 93:5, 10; 84:6)* | *1:6, 16:26* |
| *25:3 the Lord of Glory... when He shall come down to visit the earth* | *1:26* |
| *40:2-3 four presences/angel of the presence* | *1:29* |
| *91:16 a new heaven shall appear, and all the powers of the heavens shall give sevenfold light* | *1:29* |
| *60:12-15 the spirit of the snow, rain, hoar-frost, thunder, lightning (Cf. 54:7-8)* | *2:2, 4* |
| *81:1-2, 93:2, 103:2 the heavenly tablets* | *3:10, 4:3* |
| *6:6 (the angels) descended in the days of Jared* | *4:15* |
| *1:5, 12:2-4 the Watchers* | *10:5* |
| *12:3-4, 15:1 Enoch the scribe (of righteousness)* | *4:17, 4:23* |
| *83-90 The Dream Visions* | *4:19 he saw in a vision of his sleep... until the day of judgement* |
| *1:2 placed the testimony on earth for all the children of men and for their generations (37:2 1,92:1,104:11-13)* | *4:19* |
| *85:3 Before I took..., Edna* | *4:20* |
| *12:1-2 he was hidden... and his activities had to do with the Watchers* | *4:21* |
| *82:13-20 the rule of the sun* | *4:21* |
| *12:3-6 testified to the Watchers (Cf. 13:1-12,14:3-7,15:2)* | *4:22* |

| **1 Enoch** | **Quoted in Jubilees:** |
|---|---|
| *6:2 sinned with the daughters of men* <br> *(Cf. 7:1,9:8,10:11,12:4,15:3-4)* | *4:22, 5:1* |
| *60:8 conducted him(Enoch) into the Garden of Eden* <br> *(Cf. 70:1-3)* | *4:23* |
| *18:7-8,24:3,25:3 Mount (s) of the East (of Eden)* | *4:26* |
| *7:2,15:3-8 they bare great giants* | *5:1* |
| *7:5 they began to sin against birds and beasts...* <br> *and to devour one another's flesh* | *5:2, 7:24* |
| *10:12 bind them fast in the valleys of the earth* | *5:6,10,10:7* |
| *10:9,14:5-6 Destruction of the angels'* <br> *children by the sword* | *5:7* |
| *10:9,12,88:1 that each should slay his neighbour* | *5:9* |
| *10:12 their fathers were witnesses (of their destruction)* <br> *(Cf. 12:6,14:6)* | *5:10* |
| *89:2 seven flood-gates of heaven* | *5:24* |
| *89:3,7 fountains were opened on the surface of* <br> *that great enclosure,* | *5:25,29,6:26* |
| *75:1-2 A year of 364 days, four being intercalary* <br> *days. (Cf. 82:4,6,11)* | *6:23,29-32* |
| *82:4-7 Warning against the use of any other calendar* | *6:32-38* |
| *10:2 The deluge due to the Watchers' sin* | *7:21, 4:22* |
| *15:3-7 against the law of their ordinances* | *7:21* |
| *8:2,9:6,10:8 they made the beginning of uncleanness* | *7:21* |
| *7:1 Giants, Nephilim, the Eliud (Eljo)* | *7:22* |
| *87:1 they devoured one another (Cf. 10:9,12,88:1)* | *7:22, 5:9* |
| *9:1 shed much blood... earth was filled with iniquity* | *7:23* |
| *103:7-8 their souls shall be made to descend into Sheol* <br> *...and into darkness* | *7:29, 22:22* |
| *60:8 the seventh from Adam* | *7:39* |
| *93:1-2 whilst still living he testified to his son* | *7:39* |
| *26:1 the middle of the earth (North Pole)* | *8:12* |
| *15:8,19:1 the giants shall be called evil spirits* | *10:1,11:5* |
| *101:2 withholds the rain and the dew from* <br> *descending on the earth* | *12:4* |
| *99:7 worship impure spirits and demons* | *22:17* |
| *5:9,10:17 future time of peace, joy, plenty, with long life* | *23:27-29* |
| *47:3 the book of life* | *30:22,36:10* |
| *95:3,96:1 The righteous rule and judge* | *32:18-19* |

| 1 Enoch | Quoted in Jubilees: |
|---|---|
| *20:5 Michael... set over the best part of mankind* | *35:17* |
| *89:12, 42, 49, 66 wild boars' (= Edom)* | *37:20* |

As we have already proven, Jubilees is Torah and written by Moses. Thus, Moses quoted First Enoch all of these times just in Jubilees alone. Why exactly are scholars even having this conversation when they do not bother to actually test nor do they know how? Their propaganda cards are showing indeed. It is not enough to be contrary, if they are supposedly educated and not miseducated, they should have been able to plow through these books a long time ago. The conclusion is obvious but not one they wish to see which is why they do not. Those who are awakening today, see through this facade and we are not entertaining foolishness disguised as scholarship.

## PROPHET ISAIAH, 720 B.C.:

With First Enoch legitimately dated in circulation long before his era, the Prophet Isaiah also quoted First Enoch with a direct quote. Actually, this is Yahuah speaking and Yahuah Himself is quoting First Enoch. Wow!!! Then Messiah quotes this same which origin is First Enoch.

> **Isaiah 66:1 (Cf. Mat. 5:35, Acts 7:49)**
> *Thus saith the LORD,* **The heaven is my throne, and the earth is my footstool:**

> **1 Enoch 84:2b**
> *And all* **the heavens are Thy throne for ever, And the whole earth Thy footstool** *for ever and ever.*

## PROPHETS DANIEL AND EZEKIEL, 600 B.C.*(approx.)*:

In Daniel 7, we find one of the most significant doctrines every scholar should understand yet few seem to think this through far beyond their box in which they are trapped in thought. Daniel puts forth two powers of Heaven — the Father and the Son. He does not equate the Holy Spirit though certainly His role significant. Daniel 7 labels the Father as "Ancient of Days" *(Dan. 7:9, 13, and 22)* and Messiah to come as the "Son of Man" *(Dan. 7:13)*. Notice 7:13 uses both titles together for the Father and the Son. No one else uses these terms in the modern Old Testament Bible Canon. Where did Daniel derive these two paramount titles?

Daniel was reading First Enoch as scripture for massively significant doctrine as Enoch refers directly to the Messiah in title as the "Son of Man" not just once as Daniel does, but 114 times in the R.H Charles publishing *(some commentary references)*. Daniel is the only to use the title in the modern Old Testament Canon and only once. Be careful not to confuse the "son of man" with a lower case "s" reference to men not Messiah in all other cases. No, Ezekiel and even Daniel never called themselves the Messiah. Then, Messiah picks up this same title throughout the Gospels about 82 times referring to Himself as the "Son of man." There is no doubt that He is quoting First Enoch here in similar weight as He is broadcasting He is the "Son of Man" of Enoch and Daniel, who is the Messiah. Then, in Revelation 1:13 and 14:14, prophecy invokes Messiah as the "Son of man" twice more coming from Heaven in His return. This is the same "Son of Man" of Heaven from First Enoch and Daniel who became flesh, ascended back to Heaven and returns in the End Times. All of these references originate in First Enoch.

Additionally, the Father in Enoch is titled "Head of Days" in the R.H. Charles publishing 26 times *(some commentary references)*. As one compares "Head of Days" or the First or Origin of Days really and "Ancient of Days," this is obviously the same connotation and the origin of Daniel's use just as Daniel picks up "Son of man" from Enoch.

However, that is not all Daniel derives from First Enoch. Regarding Daniel 7's origin, John Collins suggests:

> *"the scene as a whole belongs to the tradition of biblical throne visions, attested in such passages as 1 Kgs 22:19; Isaiah 6; Ezekiel 1; 3:22–24; 10:1 and paralleled in writings of the Hellenistic period such as 1 Enoch 14:18–23; 60:2; 90:20." – **J. J. Collins, Daniel (Hermeneia; Minneapolis: Fortress, 1993), 300.***

In essence in such Biblical tradition, First Enoch proves to be the origin of all of these references in Daniel 7 as well as Isaiah and Ezekiel as it was not written in the Hellenistic period which is illiterate. That was a copy and once again another scholar forgot the scribal tradition of copying scrolls which is rather elementary. It has been affirmed since Moses and in timing according to Moses, before the Flood in origin and Noah agrees. We will take Moses' and Noah's word over this and any scholar's on such matters. When they disagree with or willingly ignore Moses and Noah, they are not Bible experts but impertinent scoffers.

First Enoch is also quoted in the Testaments of the 12 Patriarchs at least 12 times, the Assumption of Moses 3 times and 2nd Baruch 21 times in Old Testament times. As we have not fully vetted these texts yet, we will not yet use them in comparison but only note they use First Enoch.

Also, in stride with the First Book of Enoch, we find the Prophet Ezekiel also appears to use 1 Enoch regarding its description of the Tree of Life after the Day of Judgment.

**Ezekiel 47:12 (After Judgment, Tree Of Life Description, 600 B.C.)**
*And* **by the river** *upon the bank thereof,* **on this side and on that side, shall grow all trees for meat,** *whose leaf shall not fade, neither shall the fruit thereof be*

*consumed: it shall bring forth new fruit according to his months, because* **their waters they issued out of the sanctuary:** *and the* **fruit thereof shall be for meat,** *and the* **leaf thereof for medicine.**

Then, 2nd Esdras from 400 B.C. adopts this same concept of the Tree of Life opening after the Day of Judgment including its fragrance, healing properties, planted next to a river, pouring from Heaven, etc. affirming Ezekiel but in origin, an even earlier source as this all originates in First Enoch in which Noah wrote that he read and Moses wrote that Noah and Abraham read.

**2nd Esdras 2:10-12 (After Judgment, Tree Of Life, 400 B.C.)**
*Thus says Yahuah unto Ezra, Tell my people that I will give them the kingdom of Yerusalem, which I would have given unto Israel. Their glory also will I take unto me, and give these the everlasting Tabernacles, which I had prepared for them. They shall have the* **Tree of Life for an ointment of sweet savor, they shall neither labor, nor be weary.**

**2nd Esdras 8:52 (After Judgment, Tree Of Life, 400 B.C.)**
*For* **unto you is Paradise opened,** *the* **tree of life is planted,** *the time to come is prepared, plentiousness is made ready, a city is built, and rest is allowed, yes perfect goodness and wisdom.*

We can follow this through to the Book of Revelation where it shares similar details regarding the Tree of life and themes, all predating Ezekiel and 2nd Esdras by far.

**Revelation 22:1-2, 14 (After Judgment, Tree Of Life, 90 A.D.)**
*And he shewed me a pure* **river of water of life,** *clear as crystal, proceeding* **out of the throne of God and of the Lamb.** *In the midst of the street of it, and on* **either side of the river,** *was there the* **tree of life,** *which* **bare twelve manner of fruits,** *and yielded her fruit every month: and the* **leaves of the tree were for the healing of the nations.**
*14 Blessed are they that do his commandments, that they may have right to the tree of life, and may enter in through the gates into the city.*

**Revelation 2:7 KJV (After Judgment, Tree of Life Reopened, 90 A.D.)**
*He that hath an ear, let him hear what the Spirit saith unto the churches; To him that overcometh will I give to eat of the tree of life, which is in the midst of the paradise of God.*

You can see the glaring similarities as all of these passages agree. However, Ezekiel, Ezra and John had a basis for their visions already a developed concept from an eyewitness observer of the Tree of Life from Enoch. The origin of Ezekiel, 2nd Esdras and Revelation, is the ancient text of First Enoch. The latter texts could certainly draw from Ezekiel but there is no replacing 1 Enoch as the origin of this significant doctrine.

> **1 Enoch 25:4-6 (After Judgment, Tree Of Life, Before the Flood)**
> *And as for this* **fragrant tree** *no mortal is permitted to touch it till the great judgment, when He shall take vengeance on all and bring (everything) to its consummation for ever. It shall then be* **given to the righteous and holy. Its fruit shall toe for food to the elect**: *it shall be transplanted to the holy place, to the temple of Yahuah, the Eternal King. Then shall they rejoice with joy and be glad. And into the holy place shall they enter; And its* **fragrance** *shall be in their bones, And they shall* **live a long life on earth**, *Such as the fathers lived: And in their days shall* **no sorrow or plague or torment or calamity touch them.** '

> **1 Enoch 28:2-3**
> **And water gushed forth from above.** *Rushing like a* **copious watercourse** *[which flowed] towards the northwest it caused clouds and dew to ascend* **on every side.**

## PROPHET EZRA'S BOOK OF 2ND ESDRAS, 400 B.C.*(approx.)*:

The Book of 2nd Esdras was written by the Prophet Ezra about 400 B.C which we fully vet and test in 2nd Esdras: The Hidden Book of Prophecy supported by a 26-week video series titled "Answers In 2nd Esdras." In assessing this book with First Enoch, we found much affinity. For instance, in 2nd Esdras, Ezra speaks with the Archangel Uriel who is not mentioned in the Bible Canon we have today but originates in First Enoch. 2 Esdras 4:41, further mentions the chambers within the Earth where the spirits/souls of the dead rest awaiting the Final Day of Judgment. This is throughout scripture really which we have covered in our "What Happens When We Die?" Video Series. However, the origin of the chambers in publishing is 1 Enoch 22. On this same topic of the earth giving back that which is entrusted to it meaning the souls of men, 2nd Esdras 7:32-33 also cites 1 Enoch 51:1 and 3. Then, again, we find a quotation in 2nd Esdras 7:37 originating in 1 Enoch 62:1 and 60:6 regarding those souls of men which dwell within the Earth as well as the Elect One, Messiah.

First Enoch 10:12 provides a dating of the time of man of about 7,000 years in which the Watchers will be locked away awaiting their judgment and this is affirmed in detail in Enoch's 7 Weeks*(not 10)* of Chapter 93 *(see chart)*. It appears the origin of Ezra's same 7,000-year timeline in 2nd Esdras 7:31. This also matches Daniel's 2,300 days prophecy *(Dan. 8, see chart Ch. 93)* when one understands the trigger point for such counting is the defiling of the Temple in 165 B.C. which calculates from Creation to that end as 7,000 years in total for mankind from Creation until the Day of Judgment. We published our research on that in full in "Daniel's 2,300 Days 1 and 2" on The God Culture YouTube, Rumble, Utreon, Odessy, as well as Podcast platforms and curated a chart in that chapter.

2nd Esdras 6:49-52 then picks up the stories of Leviathan and Behemoth even according to R.H. Charles *(Introduction)* from 1 Enoch 60:7-9. Finally, we already covered two references in 2 Esdras 2:10-12 and 8:52 regarding the Tree of Life which originate from First Enoch 25:4-6 and 28:2. Enoch was still being used as inspired scripture as it should be in 400 B.C.

## DEAD SEA SCROLLS, 200 B.C. *(approx.)*:

Several Aramaic fragments from numerous caves in Qumran are identified as the First Book of Enoch as well as the Book of Giants. Though overall ranked the third most found scrolls at Qumran, more than much of Torah, the only section of First Enoch not represented in these fragments is Section Two known as the Parables of Enoch. We will address the unintelligible logic some apply in then attempting to throw out this section as it most certainly is documented in use in the first century B.C. even tied to scripture used at Qumran which we will prove. The Book of Giants however, is missing from the Ethiopic translation which R.H. Charles translated prior to the Qumran find. We will discuss this in a separate publishing.

Essentially, all of the fragments found for 1 Enoch are suggested to 200 B.C. in date. We find that fraudulent even for copies. However, we have always noted this is not a scientific dating and based on an extremely poor guess ignoring the scribal tradition no scholar would apply to any portion of Torah found there but only to extra-biblical books in fraud. There is no dating of an original as 1 Enoch was written long before the Hellenistic era that these illiterates continue to force into these datings in willing ignorance. They have royally screwed up the entire narrative of the Qumran community.

Then, there are the usual propaganda lies they repeat setting false paradigms by which to test such as multiple authors which they do not know nor prove. When Enoch derives portions from the Heavenly Tablets as does Noah with Jubilees and Genesis especially, it does not mean Enoch nor Moses no longer wrote their books as they claim in writing. The notion is illiterate and essentially these supposed Bible scholars undermine Moses, Enoch and the true, holy Temple Priests as a result. Who exactly do they think they are?

Enoch especially was written over centuries and his style may have evolved in some ways. He was also far smarter than all of those scholars put together and likely capable of different writing styles and he was the first man to write even. Were they? Also, his accounts are based on encounters with different angels at different times. Additionally, the very nature of his five books in First Enoch are quite different in content topically. These same scholars would likely read memoirs of an historian and think that multiple people wrote them as well. They don't prove it yet stand by an untenable, illogical position they will never prove. This is a tactic to disrupt the process appearing communist in origin. It does not belong in scholarship. They lodge an objection one cannot overcome because they don't actually prove the objection valid nor can they. Their intention is to impede anyone from drawing a conclusion leaving a so-called scholarly seed of doubt though when broken down, it's simply stupid. It is time this is called out in scholarship as the fraud in practice that it represents. It is nonsense.

### *Complete Aramaic Enoch Found in Qumran Sold Secretly To Private Collector:*

We are told in the Qumran Scrolls only fragments of the First Book of Enoch were found. In fact, the only surviving complete copy was found in Ethiopia. Any scholar who has an issue with Yahuah preserving this text in the Ge'ez language is not following the Bible which never says Yahuah will preserve specifically in the original Hebrew language. That is just not there nor do they apply that in modern Canon texts necessarily so it is inconsistent and not a true measure. They make it up adding to the Word and apply it as a litmus test to discount obvious scripture because they do not wish to accept it. They ignore an awful lot and it sets a paradigm of stupid.

> *The most complete Book of Enoch comes from Ethiopic manuscripts, maṣḥafa hēnok (መጽሐፈ ሄኖክ), written in Ge'ez, which were brought to Europe by James Bruce in the late 18th century and were translated into English in the 19th century. – Wikipedia [35]*

However, in the case of the First Book of Enoch, what appears a complete manuscript in Aramaic is reported to have been found in Qumran by the Chief Editor even. It was sold off to a private collector in secret with no information available to the public. Some even attempt to deny this yet this was the Chief Editor not some busy body spreading rumors. If true, this appears nefarious. Former Chief Editor of the Dead Sea Scrolls, John Strugnell, granted two interviews to Biblical Archaeology Review where he claimed he witnessed a complete copy of the Book of Enoch from Cave 11. In a follow up interview, he also claimed he saw it on microfilm as well. This has not been made available to the public. Why?

*Regarding the scrolls, Strugnell claims at least four other scrolls have been found that have not yet come to light: "I've seen, with my own eyes, two." One of the two is a complete copy of the Book of Enoch. According to Strugnell, Israeli archaeologist Yigael Yadin is the reason these scrolls have still not come into scholarly hands. After the Six-Day war, Yadin confiscated the famous Temple Scroll a from a Bethlehem antiquities dealer known as Kando. Yadin paid Kando $250,000, according to Strugnell (according to Yadin, the sum was $105,000), to encourage anyone else with scroll materials to come forward. But this was not enough, says Strugnell: "Yadin gave Kando $250,000 where we'd offered Kando $1,000,000 five weeks earlier. When the owners of the manuscripts heard that, they just crossed the Jordan River." These scrolls, like the Temple Scroll, came from Cave 11 at Qumran, according to Strugnell. The manuscripts are now "somewhere in Jordan. Various people own them. Several of them have been sold to big bankers. They're investments for these people. There's no point in forcing a sale. If they really need cash—as one seems to now—I have the money."*
*As for the other two scrolls—the ones Strugnell has not seen—"[Lankaster] Harding [the director of Jordan's Department of Antiquities] on his death bed, told me he'd seen three, only one of which I've seen—so that makes four."* **– John Strugnell, former chief editor of the Dead Sea Scrolls, Biblical Archaeology Review, January/February 1991**

*"And then I, myself, saw one—the Enoch microfilm; but I must save that story for my memoirs."* **– John Strugnell, former chief editor of the Dead Sea Scrolls, Biblical Archaeology Review, July/August 1994**

If in fact, this book was recorded on microfilm, that is wonderful except where is it? Why is this not public? If a private collector has it, who is that and more so, where is the information? This is not some antique or rare book, it is scripture and  if true, how dare anyone allow that to be stolen away from the public eye. The good news is we have enough which survives to understand the First Book of Enoch in the Ethiopic Ge'ez supported by the other, though incomplete, Qumran scrolls we have. Whether one dates these fragments to 300-150 B.C. is of no consequence as they are copies and such dating is not actually based on science and ignores the scribal tradition no scholar would apply in discussing Genesis thus a false paradigm.

## THE SUPPOSED "MISSING SECTION" OF FIRST ENOCH:

The challenge presented is that of the five books or sections of First Enoch, only four were found in Qumran or essentially 80% of what is known today due to the Ethiopic preservation as First Enoch. Most of us hear that and realize this is pretty strong affirmation that the First Book of Enoch stands as Ethiopia preserved it. Imagine the illiterate arrogance of this small group of scholars, who hate Yahusha, claim the conclusion is then since only 80% of the texts were found in part in those Qumran fragments, that means we must throw out the other 20%. Essentially, the reason is because they are incapable of reason? That certainly defies reason and logic unless perhaps a clown circus. Do they suggest we throw out any portions of Exodus not found in Qumran? Or any other Modern Canon book? Of course not, that would be illiterate yet this is the exact rationale they use inconsistently with First Enoch which we have a complete publishing. However, let us not forget, it appears they too had a complete copy in Aramaic and it disappeared on their watch. Imagine that.

It is glaringly obvious when you understand the content of this second book or section of five has the first prophesies of Messiah in Heaven as the "Son of Man" where the term originates and Enoch met Him. This is an assault on Yahusha and on our intelligence by idiots and frauds who hate Him. These are not scholars nor experts and they are completely wrong as the Parables of Enoch known as the Second Section are most assuredly found and connected to the Temple Priests in 100 B.C. and we will take you much further back.

2nd Esdras can be dated to 100 B.C. at least in origin in use in Qumran, as we have proven though truly it was written by the prophet whom the book says wrote it in his time of 400 B.C. when he recorded. The problem for the inept scholars attempting to dismiss Enoch's 20% not found in the Dead Sea Scrolls in the Parables, is we have such evidence in the same timeframe as 2nd Esdras quotes the Parables of Enoch thus they were scripture back then still. These cannot be dismissed and for one calling themselves a scholar incapable of even reading R.H. Charles' Introduction of the First Book of Enoch, is inexcusable.

The supposed missing Second Section titled the Parables of Enoch are comprised of Chapters 37-71. They are not missing in the first century B.C. as the Parables of Enoch from the Second Section are quoted and preserved in date by 2nd Esdras 6 times even. 2nd Esdras is also quoted in the Dead Sea Scrolls in about 100 B.C. thus the connection is not difficult to assess. These are not scholars but scoffers bellowing ridicule in ignorance. In 2nd Esdras 6:49-52, the Prophet Ezra takes First Enoch 60:7-9 and expands on it even. That is a Parable in First Enoch from the supposed missing section about Leviathan and Behemoth being quoted in 100 B.C. or so at the very latest. Also, 2nd Esdras 7:32-33 cites 1 Enoch 51:1 and 3, 2 Esdras 7:37 quotes 1 Enoch 62:1 and 60:6, and 2nd Esdras 7:36 derives from 1 Enoch 48:9-10 and 27:3 even according to R.H. Charles*(Introduction)* in 1912. There has never been a point to this criticism yet many believe they should ignore these 40 plus Chapters of scripture documented in use in the first century B.C. because illiterate scoffers are only capable of textual criticism or scoffing without follow through in research. This is called gross negligence and any scholar who has maintained this position is no scholar and hates Yahusha.

We already covered 1 Enoch 68:1 where Noah, not Enoch, credits not just the First

Book of Enoch, but specifically the Book of Parables within. If this Second Section of the First Book of Enoch was around for Noah and read as scripture by him where he even credits his Great Grandfather Enoch as the writer of that specific Second Section, what exactly is there to discuss? When another fragment written by Noah in 1 Enoch 60:1 credits Enoch's Book of Parables again which is where Noah learned of the Flood, it would take uneducated propaganda to stand against this Book of Parables in willing ignorance. Realize, that is the First Book of Enoch twice quoting the Book of Parables as part of it thus Enoch's book included it all along. Who is so illiterate they can't figure this out? Of what exactly are they a scholar?

Then, there appears the oversight of an intellectual toddler in attempting to comprehend no actual scholar could possibly miss, demonstrating they only know their boxed paradigms. Enoch opens his entire First Book with a quote of His parable from Section 2: The Book of Parables *(Chapters 46-48)*. Frankly, only an uninformed blockhead could ever suggest Section 2 is not an allotment of this same book.

**1 Enoch 1:2**
*And he took up his parable and said—Enoch a righteous man, whose eyes were opened by* **Elohim, saw the vision of the Holy One in the heavens,** *[which] the angels showed me... (Cf. 46-48)*

Then, in Section 5: The Epistle of Enoch, he again quotes and endorsed his own Section 2: The Book of Parables where he saw the Son of Man *(Messiah)* in Heaven.

**1 Enoch 93:2b**
*And concerning the plant of uprightness, I will speak these things. Yea, I Enoch will declare (them) unto you, my sons: According to that which appeared to me in the heavenly vision. And which I have known through the word of the holy angels. And have learnt from the heavenly tablets.*

Finally, when the Book of Jubilees 7:38 also affirms Noah reading from the First Book of Enoch affirming these two fragments; 7:39 affirms Noah keeping the Law of Enoch from this same writing; 10:17 confirms Enoch's office of Prophet and Scribe including Enoch's written testimony of the ages all the way to the Day of Judgment; and 21:10-11 documents where even Abraham read the First Book of Enoch as did his fathers which would include Noah and Enoch who tell us that included the Book of Parables precisely even, then, there is no point here. There is no missing section from First Enoch period.

However, in addition to the Temple Priests exiled to Qumran/Bethabara, the First Book of Enoch was still being used as scripture in the New Testament.

## THE NEW TESTAMENT, FIRST CENTURY:

The First Book of Enoch is then quoted in the New Testament in the First Century still used as inspired scripture specifically, and in some cases very directly, by Messiah, Jude, Paul en masse, Luke in his Gospel and Acts, John in his Gospel, 1 John and especially a large showing in Revelation, Matthew, Peter, James, and Hebrews. Enoch, the seventh from Adam prophesied meaning he wrote it down just as Moses' Jubilees and Noah's fragments say he did. He had a scroll or book and we know exactly which Enoch this was, the one who was taken because he walked with Elohim. We know he wrote as the Great Scribe and that book survived over the ages. This is what scripture says. If your scholar does not, who exactly does he or she represent?

Just this portion alone discredits anyone attempting to throw out First Enoch as we are to follow the example of the Apostles as well as Messiah. How illiterate can a so-called scholar be to suggest that this ancient book written by a Prophet and quoted by Yahusha and the Apostles be censored or marginalized? First Enoch preceded all of these even in their fraudulent 200 B.C. dating of a copy. How could it possibly be viewed as anything but inspired scripture? Regarding Bible Canon, that is really simple because in the Bible, the sons of Zadok kept what was determined as the only Bible Canon up until that point*(Deut. 31:24-26, Jub. 45:16)*. They remained holy when Israel strayed*(Ez. 40:46, 44:15, 48:11)*. They kept First Enoch found as the third most numerous scroll in Qumran. Thus, this book was in circulation in the era of Yahusha still documented as written by Enoch himself.

Then, Messiah placed His endorsement launching His ministry right there among the community who grabbed ahold of the prophecy to prepare the way for Messiah in the wilderness of Judaea known as Bethabara or in modern fraud, as the Muslim name Qumran maintained*(The Community Rule, P. 109 [22])*. Thus, any scholar changing what was affirmatively Bible Canon is a deceiver whether knowingly or not. They do not represent scripture on the matter.

Understand that Peter's brother Andrew became a disciple. Andrew came from Qumran/Bethabara where he was a disciple of John the Baptist previously *(John 1:40)*. He met Yahusha at His baptism there and followed Him per John's revelation. The connection between Messiah and Bethabara/Qumran is firm. There is no separating that library from the worship of Yahuah and Yahusha and no other library in history serves as Bible Canon with authority as this one.

### Jude 1:14-16 KJV
***And Enoch also, the seventh from Adam, prophesied of these, saying,***
*Behold, the Lord cometh with ten thousands of his saints, To execute judgment upon all, and to convince all that are ungodly among them of all their ungodly deeds which they have ungodly committed, and of all their hard speeches which ungodly sinners have spoken against him.*

> *These are murmurers, complainers, walking after their own lusts; and their mouth speaketh great swelling words, having men's persons in admiration because of advantage.*

This is a direct quote from the written First Book of Enoch. The notion that Jude was a sucker who fell for a fraud created 200 years earlier is stupidity not to mention Messiah and the rest of the Apostles who quote First Enoch. He is quoting the ancient scroll of Enoch from the first chapter of Enoch even pretty closely and credits it as such. Jude knew the Temple Priests at Qumran/Bethabara did not manufacture scripture under false pretenses and he uses this passage and others as scripture. Why do we allow inept modern scholars to accuse Jude of being a fool and the true Levite Temple Priests as being frauds? They were not, Pharisees are. This is not a quote from any other book but the First Book of Enoch period and certainly not the opposite.

**1 Enoch 1:9** *(Cf. 5:4, 27:2)*
*And behold! He cometh with ten thousands of [His] holy ones to execute judgment upon all. And to destroy [all] the ungodly: And to convict all flesh of all the works [of their ungodliness] which they have ungodly committed, [And of all the hard things which] ungodly sinners [have spoken] against Him.*

Any scholar claiming the Final Judgment is an unimportant doctrine is an impertinent scoffer of no value. In fact, Jude is a pretty short book yet much of it relates directly from First Enoch. He even warns of these same scoffers today who crept in unawares. One can even note he opens his book four verses in with words right out of First Enoch which uses such terms multiple times.

**Jude 1:4 KJV**
*For there are certain men crept in unawares, who were before of old ordained to this condemnation, ungodly men, turning the grace of our God into lasciviousness, and* **denying the only Lord God, and our Lord Jesus Christ.**

**1 Enoch 48:10b** *(Cf. 38:2, 41:2)*
**...For they have denied Yahuah of Spirits and His Anointed.**

Then, Jude quotes the Watcher Fallen Angel narrative deriving from much of the First Section of 1 Enoch as well *(Cf. 12:4, 10:4, 6, 11-12)*. Even his use later in verse 13 of "wandering stars" originates in 1 Enoch 18:15, 21:2-3, 6.

**Jude 1:6 KJV**
*And the angels which kept not their first estate, but left their own habitation, he hath reserved in everlasting chains under darkness unto the judgment of the great day.*

Jude is not the only to quote Enoch as Peter uses this same account of the Watchers specifically from First Enoch as he even uses the Greek word **Tartaroō** which originates in the Hebrew word Tartarus directly from 1 Enoch 20:2.

**2 Peter 2:4 KJV**
*For if God spared not the angels that sinned, but cast them down to* **hell (Tartaroō: ταρταρόω: Tartarus), and delivered them into chains of darkness, to be reserved unto judgment;**

Peter, then, uses the foundation of 1 Enoch in the story of Messiah's death regarding the chambers enclosed within the Earth which Peter calls prisons. However, Messiah preached to the spirits of men there and this is the chamber where the souls of men sleep awaiting the Day of Judgment from 1 Enoch 22.

**1 Peter 3:19 KJV**
*By which also he went and preached unto the spirits in prison; Which sometime were disobedient, when once the longsuffering of God waited in the days of Noah, while the ark was a preparing, wherein few, that is, eight souls were saved by water.*

Though his word translations are terrific, somehow Charles could exhibit a profound disability in understanding this book. In all fairness, he did not have the Dead Sea Scrolls in his time. He is clearly steeped in a paradigm of extreme ignorance on a host of things. In his cross-reference of this passage in 1 Peter, he confuses this prison or chamber where Yahusha's spirit went within the Earth when he died with the Fallen Angel prison. Enoch has an entire chapter*(22)* dedicated to explaining these chambers and he does not leave room for such ignorance of scoffers. Charles even fails to site that chapter at all but chooses five references to Messiah evidently going to and preaching to Fallen Angels who are not redeemable with already certain judgment on the Day of Judgment. That notion is illiterate. It would be a waste of time.

Yahusha did not go to that portion of Sheol or Hades which Charles well knew was interpreted Hell in English including the chambers for men's souls and the Fallen Angel prison. He went into the chamber called Abraham's bosom *(Luke 16:22)* which he also referred to as Paradise to the thief on the cross *(Luke 23:43)*. He did not go to the Paradise of Heaven and did not lie to the thief. He also did not go to what we call a burning Hell as again, He would have then lied to the thief. When scholars manipulate in such fashion, they essentially may not realize they are calling Messiah a liar. He is also infusing occult doctrine into 1 Enoch now in addition which is inexcusable. This should not be a difficult foundation for a scholar to set when reading the Bible. Always assume Yahusha is not a liar. Instead, Charles makes himself a liar which is sad. It is Chapter 22 which deals with the chambers of man's spirit not the five Fallen Angel accounts

Charles weaves in in ignorance. If not ignorance, he did so with intention to deceive.

> **1 Enoch 22:3-4**
> *Then Raphael answered, one of the holy angels who was with me, and said unto me: 'These hollow places have been created for this very purpose, that* **the spirits of the souls of the dead should assemble therein,** *yea that* **all the souls of the children of men** *should assemble here. And these places have been made to* **receive them till the day of their judgment and till their appointed period** *[till the period appointed],* **till the great judgment (comes) upon them.** *'*

No men enter the Fall Angel prison and the reason Peter used the term prison referring to the chambers of men's souls is because they are enclosed, protected and locked up. Additionally, Peter rolls out an incredibly significant doctrine of Yahuah's promise of new heavens and a new Earth for the righteous after the Day of Judgment.

> **2 Peter 3:13 KJV**
> *Nevertheless we, according to his promise, look for new heavens and a new earth, wherein dwelleth righteousness.*

In ultimate origin, this derives from First Enoch who is first among men to write of this and he mentions it three times.

> **1 Enoch 45:4-5** *(Cf. 72:1, 91:16)*
> *Then will I cause Mine Elect One to dwell among them. And I will transform the heaven and make it an eternal blessing and light, And I will transform the earth and make it a blessing: And I will cause Mine elect ones to dwell upon it: But the sinners and evil-doers shall not set foot thereon.*

We will cover Revelation, the writings of Paul, the Gospels, Hebrews, etc. in large blocks as a massive amount of terms, concepts and direct quotes lead us to 1 Enoch in origin. It is not only Jude who provides a direct quote. However, 1 John lays out one of the bedrock principles of the character of Messiah and His role as our advocate. Did you know that originates in the antediluvian First Book of Enoch? Messiah was our advocate before He came in the Flesh from the beginning as He will be to the end. In willing ignorance, scholars would wish to discard especially this portion of 1 Enoch yet they are unqualified to render such opinion placing themselves above the Temple Priests who kept scripture and even above Messiah Himself.

**1 John 2:1 KJV**

*My little children, these things write I unto you, that ye sin not. And if any man sin, we have an advocate with the Father, Jesus Christ the righteous:*

**1 Enoch 53:6**

*And after this the Righteous and Elect One shall cause the house of his congregation to appear: henceforth they shall be no more hindered in the name of Yahuah of Spirits.*

1 John was written centuries after the oldest copies of 1 Enoch thus no matter what dating they attempt, Enoch becomes the origin of many concepts in the New Testament. John then refers to the Word as the true light which now shines and the darkness is now past. This is directly from Enoch's prophecy.  Understanding the heritage of our faith which comes from hearing the Word, is the Word. Yahusha is the Word and that is the context of both yet he quotes 1 Enoch as the Word.

**1 John 2:8 KJV**

*Again, a new commandment I write unto you, which thing is true in him and in you: because* **the darkness is past,** *and the true light now shineth.*

**1 Enoch 58:5**

*And after this it shall be said to the holy in heaven that they should seek out the secrets of righteousness, the heritage of faith: For it has* **become bright as the sun upon earth. And the darkness is past.**

We all know we are not to love the world and its trappings. However, this is yet another rather direct concept that 1 John derives from First Enoch in this regard.

**1 John 2:15 KJV**

*Love not the world, neither the things that are in the world. If any man love the world, the love of the Father is not in him.*

**1 Enoch 108:8**

*Who love Elohim and loved neither gold nor silver nor any of the good things which are in the world, but gave over their bodies to torture.*

**1 Enoch 48:7**

*And the wisdom of Yahuah of Spirits hath revealed him to the holy and righteous; For he hath preserved the lot of the righteous; Because they have hated and despised this world of unrighteousness, And have hated all its works and ways in the name of Yahuah of Spirits: For in his name they are saved, And according to his good pleasure hath it been in regard to their life,*

Before the Flood, the Prophet Enoch knew that we would be like Messiah in the end. We find this in 1 John yet its origin is 1 Enoch.

### 1 John 3:2 KJV

*Beloved, now are we the sons of God, and it doth not yet appear what we shall be: but we know that, when he shall appear, we shall be like him; for we shall see him as he is.*

### 1 Enoch 90:37-38

*And I saw that a white bull was born, with large horns, and all the beasts of the field and all the birds of the air feared him and made petition to him all the time. And I saw till all their generations were transformed, and they all became white bulls; and the first among them became a lamb, and that lamb became a great animal and had great black horns on its head; and Yahuah of the sheep rejoiced over it and over all the oxen.*

Finally, R.H. Charles noted *"The contrast between light and darkness in John's Epistles repeatedly enforced in 1 Enoch."* He references: *1 John 1:7: "But if we walk in the light, as he is in the light..."* which directly derives from 1 Enoch 92:4 with several such origins throughout First Enoch. John was clearly reading 1 Enoch as inspired scripture and this is common for the Apostles who quote Enoch either directly or in concept an incredible number of times. None of these were written prior to the copy of First Enoch at Qumran. The scholarly attempt to marginalize First Enoch is among one of the most outlandish and ridiculous of all attempts. There is no separating First Enoch as a fundamental source of New Testament doctrine.

James, as well, cites First Enoch in the profound characterization of the double-minded man who is unstable in all his ways. This reminds us of Pharisee scholars today. They have no compass because they have no foundation. They waffle to and fro clinging to any doctrine they can use to defile and profane the Word especially these books found at Qumran that the Pharisees had already ignored and the Catholic Church continued such ignorance. Neither have an opinion which counts.

### James 1:8 KJV

*A double minded man is unstable in all his ways.*

### 1 Enoch 91:4

*And draw not nigh to uprightness with a double heart. And associate not with those of a double heart, But walk in righteousness my sons. And it shall guide you on good paths, And righteousness shall be your companion.*

The entire paradigm of modern scholarship's textual criticism is exactly this. They are double minded hypocrites who are greatly challenged in understanding because they are not committed in foundation to the very basics. This includes R.H. Charles. They are like the baseball shortstop who failed to practice the basics because he only wanted to be seen hitting homeruns. The problem is when the game-ending ground ball barrels his way, he fails to remember the simple basic of bending his knees, the ball rolls between and the game is lost. If he had only sured up the fundamental basics, he would have saved the game and much embarrassment. Scholars have egg on their face when they stand firmly against First Enoch. They cannot successfully.

They do not approach things seeking the truth in most cases nor to restore scripture but they seek to marginalize it. They rip out fragments out of context and turn them into the opposite exactly as their Pharisee kind has since the days of Messiah *(Mark 7:9)*. They write of and offer opinion on a book they do not even believe. Many tee up holes left by these censored writings used as and considered Bible Canon by those who matter and the only who have such a say on the matter. This leaves room for scoffing occultists to slither in claiming to have found something wrong with the Bible. This is why we all must prove all things for ourselves or we will be deceived by this longstanding leaven.

James also launches into a dissertation on woes against riches in 5:1-6. These woes are mentioned largely in 1 Enoch 94:8-11,46:7, 63:10, 96:4-8, and 97:8-10.

However, in assessing the Book of Revelation, even R.H. Charles could not help but note significant amount of similarities to First Enoch. Calling the book Apocalyptic does not reclassify that as such a stupid classification anyway. He and many others attempt such. Charles writes: *"The writer or writers of this book are steeped in Jewish apocalyptic literature."*

There is so much false in this sentence and it lines modern scholarship. Since no Jewish Pharisee/Rabbi ever wrote any portion of the Bible, such a title is deceiving and false. Enoch never qualifies as Jewish anything as he lived before the Flood and Pharisee libraries are impertinent. Also, no Jews or Pharisees lived in Qumran/Bethabara. The word Jew is fraud and cannot be rendered in Ancient Hebrew even. It is Yahudim or Yah's for short, never Jew. How can one call themselves a Hebrew and then render their identification with a non-Hebrew word? The word does not belong in the Bible and anyone calling themselves such is not Hebrew. There is no J in Ancient Hebrew period. The Word is יהודי: (Y-H-U-D-I or IM plural) Yahudi or Yahudim. Though they did insert it in fraud many times just as they erased the name of YHWH 6,800 times in fraud, the word Jew is not Ancient Hebrew. This remains in seminaries, scholarship and most of the church today and it is a false paradigm in whole.

John certainly held First Enoch in high regard quoting it for scripture as much of the basis for the Book of Revelation. This cannot be ignored.

| **1 Enoch** | **Quoted in Revelation:** |
| --- | --- |
| *90:21 seven first white ones* | *1:4 Seven spirits before throne (Cf. 4:5, 8:2)* |
| *25:4-6 only elect eat of Tree of Life* | *2:7, 22:2, 14, 19* |
| *90:31 clothed in white* | *3:5 clothed in white raiment* |
| *37:5 those that dwell upon the earth* | *3:10, 6:10, 8:13, 11:10, 13:8, 14, 17:8* |
| *90:29 new house* | *3:12 New Jerusalem* |
| *97:8 we have become rich with riches and have possessions* | *3:17* |
| *62:14 with that Son of Man shall they eat lie down and rise up for ever and ever* | *3:20 I will come unto him and sup with him* |
| *108:12 seat each on the throne of his honour* | *3:21, 20:4 Sit with me on my throne* |
| *40:2 On the four sides of the Lord of Spirits I saw four presences* | *4:6 round about the throne were four living creatures* |
| *39:13 who sleep not... and say* | *4:8 who rest not... saying* |
| *14:22, 40:1, 71:8* | *5:11* |
| *47:2, 97:3-5, 99:3, 16, 104:3, 22:5-7* | *6:10 righteous souls cry out for vengeance* |
| *62:3,5* | *6:15-16* |
| *69:22 the spirits... of the winds* | *7:1 the four angels of the winds* |
| *45:4 I will cause Mine Elect One to dwell among them* | *7:15 He that sitteth on the throne shall dwell among them* |
| *48:1 fountain of righteousness... fountains of wisdom* | *7:17 Shall guide them unto fountains of waters of life* |
| *9:1-3,11,15:2,40:7,47:2,99:3 This intercession of the angels is found frequently in 1 Enoch (5:8 Elders also)* | *8:3-4 Angel with golden censer of incense offers it with the prayers of the saints before God.* |
| *86:1 I saw... and behold a star fell from heaven* | *9:1 I saw a star from heaven fallen unto the earth* |
| *66:1* | *9:14-15* |
| *99:7 idol worship as demon worship* | *9:20* |
| *16:1* | *10:5-7* |
| *40:7 fending off the Satans and forbidding them come... to accuse them who dwell on the earth* | *12:10 The accuser of our brethren is cast down* |
| *54:6 Leading astray those who dwell on the earth (Cf. 67:7)* | *13:14 Deceiveth them that dwell on the earth* |
| *18:9 The unrighteous 'burn before the face of the holy . . . sink before the face of the righteous'* | *14:9-10 The worshippers of the beast are tormented with fire and brimstone in presence angels... and the lamb* |
| *100:3 The horse shall walk up to the breast in the blood of sinners* | *14:20 Blood came out of the winepress even unto the horses' bridles* |

| **1 Enoch** | **Quoted in Revelation:** |
|---|---|
| *60:16 the spirit of the sea* | *16:6 Angel of the waters* |
| *9:4 Lord of lords . . . King of kings* | *17:14 Lord of lords and King of kings* |
| *90:20 took the sealed books and opened those books* | *20:12 And the books were opened and another book was opened which is* |
| *47:3 The books of the living* | *20:12 the book of life* |
| *51:1 in those days shall the earth also give back that which has been entrusted to it, and Sheol also shall give back that which it has received, and hell shall give back that which it owes (Cf. 61:5)* | *20:13 The sea gave up the dead which were in it, and death and Hades gave up the dead which were in them* |
| *90:26 Cast into this fiery abyss* | *20:15 Cast into the lake of fire* |
| *25:6 'no sorrow or plague or torment or calamity* | *22:3 no more curse* |

The Apostle Paul was one of the most prolific writers of scripture. His words have been under attack for 2,000 years according to Peter *(2 Pet. 3:15-16)*. He has in recent years been assaulted by those who ridicule even after being affirmed as an Apostle by Luke, Peter, Yahusha, and Ananias among others. Much of the church reads Paul in fragments pulling out whatever doctrine of men they wish to force. We have already dealt with many. However, Paul passes all such tests and when read in context, he is likely the best writer in the whole of scripture. One has to read him in context and in chapters, not verses, or they will never understand him.

In the tradition of the Apostles as a whole, Paul was well versed in First Enoch. They attempt to marginalize his quoting it because of a certain idiom he may have quoted from a Greek philosopher or the like. Paul never derived doctrine from Greek philosophy. This is another tactic to attempt to make Paul appear to favor the occult which is inept. His doctrine is sound as any. Though he, too, attempts to marginalize Paul's endorsement of First Enoch, R.H. Charles writes: *"We shall find that he(Paul) was well acquainted with and used 1 Enoch."* Notice the uses, however. Paul is not quoting First Enoch for poetry nor a quip. He does so as significant doctrine period. He viewed First Enoch as inspired scripture and so should all of us.

| **1 Enoch** | **Quoted By Paul:** |
|---|---|
| *61:10 angels of power and angels of principalities* | *Rom. 8:34 Neither angels, nor principalities, nor powers* |
| *77:1 He who is blessed for ever* | *Rom. 9:5 God blessed for ever* |
| *48:7 in his (i.e. the Messiah's) name they are saved* | *1 Cor. 6:11 Justified in the name of the Lord Jesus* |

| **1 Enoch** | **Quoted By Paul:** |
|---|---|
| *38:4 The Lord of Spirits has caused His light to appear on the face of the holy, righteous, and elect* | *2Cor. 4:6 To give the light of the knowledge of the glory of God in the face of Jesus Christ* |
| *62:15-16* | *2Cor. 5:2-4* |
| *77:1 He who is blessed for ever* | *2Cor. 11:31 He who is blessed for ever* |
| *48:7 this world of unrighteousness* | *Gal. 1:4 This present evil world* |
| *61:10 angels of power and angels of principalities* | *Eph. 1:21 Above all principality and power* |
| *49:4 according to His good pleasure* | *Eph. 1:9 According to His good pleasure* |
| *108:11 the generation of light* | *Eph. 5:8 Children of light* |
| *48:5 shall fall down and worship before Him (i.e. the Messiah)* | *Phil. 2:10 At the name of Jesus every knee should bow* |
| *61:10 angels of power and angels of principalities* | *Col. 1:16 Principalities and powers* |
| *46:3 the Son of man . . . who reveals all the treasures of that which is hidden* | *Col. 2:3 In whom are hid all the treasures of wisdom and knowledge* |
| *62:4 Then shall pain come upon them as on a woman in travail* | *1Th. 5:3 Then sudden destruction cometh upon them as upon a woman with child* |

**Both these passages refer to the sudden appearing of the Messiah.*

| **1 Enoch** | **Quoted By Paul:** |
|---|---|
| *108:11 the generation of light* | *1Th. 5:5 Sons of light* |
| *61:10 the angels of power* | *2Th. 1:7 the angels of His power* |
| *93:4 a law shall be made for the sinners* | *1Tim. 1:9 Law is not made for a righteous man but for the lawless (sinners)* |
| *94:1 worthy of acceptation* | *1Tim. 1:15 Worthy of all acceptation (Cf. 4:9)* |
| *39:1 elect and holy children... from the high heaven* | *1Tim. 5:21 The elect angels* |
| *9:4 Lord of Lords . . King of Kings* | *1Tim. 6:15 King of Kings and Lord of Lords* |
| *14:21 None of the angels could enter and could behold His face by reason of the magnificence and glory* | *1Tim. 6:16 Dwelling in the light which no man can approach unto, whom no man hath seen* |

Charles uses the term that these quoted 1 Enoch as scripture regarding the Book of Hebrews. *"As we have seen above this writer cites 1 Enoch as Scripture in the Epistle which goes by his name."* That is clear but then you will find in scholarly fashion, he distances himself from committing to such. The fact is they most certainly read and espoused the doctrines of First Enoch which is why they use it in their work. Either a scholar believes the Bible inspired or they don't. When they refuse to accept the endorsement and use of the Apostles which elevate this work to similar inspired scripture, they become fools and their opinions are moot. Hebrews is one of the most profound books of the New Testament and this writer uses First Enoch as scripture indeed.

| **1 Enoch** | **Quoted In Hebrews:** |
|---|---|
| *9:5 all things are naked and open in Thy sight, and Thou seest all things, and nothing can hide itself from Thee* | *4:13 There is no creature that is not manifest in His sight: but all things are naked and laid open before the eyes of Him with whom we have to do* |
| *90:29 God Himself builds the New Jerusalem* | *11:10 the city which hath foundations whose builder and maker is God (Cf. 13:14)* |
| *37:2 (over 100 times) Lord of Spirits* | *12:9 Father of spirits* |
| *90:29 The heavenly Jerusalem* | *12:22* |

Even the Book of Acts derives doctrines from First Enoch. None of this should be a surprise for a book documented in use and circulation from the antediluvian era forward. It matters not whether any scholar accepts that. They are unqualified.

| **1 Enoch** | **Quoted In Book of Acts:** |
|---|---|
| *53:6 the Righteous and Elect One (i. e. the Messiah)* | *3:14 The Righteous One, i.e. Christ. Cf. 7:52, 22:14* |
| *48:7 in His (i.e. the Messiah's) name they are saved* | *4:12 There is none other name under heaven... whereby we must be saved* |
| *99:3 raise your prayers as a memorial... before the Most High* | *10:4 Thy prayers . . . are gone up for a memorial before God* |
| *41:9 'He appoints a judge for them all and he judges them all before Him* | *17:31 He will judge the world in righteousness by the man whom He hath ordained* |

In the four Gospels, Yahusha is found quoting the First Book of Enoch as inspired scripture. If Messiah did so, how could any scholar or church dare oppose Him and His words? How can they not know of His endorsement of this very library including this book and that He was baptized and launched His ministry there. There is much deception in the modern church who would mostly warn us from even reading this book that was quoted in inspired scripture as inspired scripture.

| 1 Enoch | Quoted In The Gospels: |
|---|---|
| *89:51 Temple = house of 'the Lord of the sheep . But owing to sin of Israel it is said He forsook that their house* | *John 2:16 The temple is called 'God's house', but owing to sin of Israel 'your house'* |
| *69:27 the sum of judgement was given unto the Son of Man* | *John 5:22,27 He hath committed all judgement unto the Son* |
| *48:4* | *John 8:12* |
| *108:11 the generation of light* | *John 12:36 Sons of light (Cf. Luke 16:8)* |
| *39:4 dwelling-places of the holy and the resting-place of the righteous* | *John 14:2 Many mansions* |
| *46:4 shall raise up (Read 'put down') the kings . . . from their seats* | *Luke 1:52 He hath put down princes from their thrones* |
| *40:5 'the Elect One', i.e. the Messiah. Cf. 45:3-4 ('Mine Elect One), 49:2, 4.* | *Luke 9:35 This is My Son, the Elect One* |
| *63:10 unrighteous gains* | *Luke 16:9 Mammon of unrighteousness* |
| *47:1-2 prayer of the righteous... that judgement may be done unto them and that He is longsuffering over them (Cf. 2Pet. 3:9)* | *Luke 18:7 Shall not God avenge His elect which cry to Him day and night, and they may not have to suffer for ever* |
| *51:2 the day has drawn nigh that they should be saved* | *Luke 21:23 Your redemption draweth nigh* |
| *40:5 The Elect One* | *Luke 23:35 'The Christ of God, the Elect One* |
| *27:2, 90:26-27 where Gehenna first definitely appears as hell* | *Matt. 5:22,29,30 where Gehenna is the place of final punishment.* |
| *16:1* | *Matt. 8:20* |
| *98:3* | *Matt. 13:42* |
| *62:5 When they see that Son of Man sitting on the throne of his glory* | *Matt. 19:28 When the Son of Man shall sit on the throne of His glory* |
| *108:12 I will seat each on the throne of his honour* | *Matt. 19:28 Ye also shall sit on twelve thrones* |
| *40:9 inherit eternal life* | *Matt. 19:29 Inherit eternal life* |
| *51:4-5 chains . . . prepared for the hosts of Azazel* | *Matt. 25:41 Prepared for the devil and his angels* |
| *38:2 It had been good for them if they had not been born* | *Matt. 26:24 It had been good for that man if he had not been born* |
| *62:6 (the Son of man) who rules over all* | *Matt. 28:18 All authority hath been given to Me in heaven and on earth* |
| *89:54* | *Mark 11:17* |

In addition, the entire New Testament essentially follows Enoch's separation of the parts of the Inner Earth or underworld. Even Messiah many times is quoted using the word Gehenna in Greek which is where there will be gnashing of teeth and the Lake of Fire resides. This is the same Tartarus or Gehenna of Enoch which is the origin of Peter as no other Bible Canon references it. Of course, the Old Testament also differentiates that within Sheol there is a "lower Hell." This is extremely evident when one conducts a true word study of the word translated Hell which is different words in Hebrew and Greek. The notion that the underworld is all a burning Hell is a doctrine from the occult and Scientism, a religion in control of science today. There is no science which supports such occult religious view and the Bible most certainly does not.

This paradigm of Peter and the whole of the New Testament follows the Book of First Enoch and the Heavenly Tablets which is why it will never reconcile to the modern church doctrine of occult origin. This claims when we die, we face immediate judgment and enter Heaven or Hell. That is not Biblical at all but originates in occult writings such as the Egyptian Book of the Dead. Even Purgatory is a direct occult concept from the Egyptian Book of the Dead never the Bible. Enoch proves accurate to scripture, most church doctrines on this topic do not but originate in the occult. This is why we all must prove all things *(1 Thess. 5:21)* because if we do not in this age of strong delusion, we will be deceived. For overwhelming evidence, watch our video series "Where Do We Go When We Die? on YouTube, Rumble, Utreon, Odessy, or Podcast.

No man goes to Heaven or Hell when we die which requires immediate judgment from the doctrine of Osiris – a position never found in the whole of scripture. When our bodies die 1 Enoch 22:1-12 says, our spirits go into chambers to rest awaiting judgment on the Day of Judgment and never before. These are within the Earth which Enoch observed. All of these scriptures originate in First Enoch's first writing of these chambers where our spirits sleep awaiting the Day of Judgment from 1 Enoch 22:1-12:

*Messiah references the doctrine first found in First Enoch in John 5:28, Luke 16:22-23 (Abraham's Bosom & Chamber for sinners), Luke 23:42 (Paradise=Abraham's Bosom); Paul in Eph. 4:7-10, 1 Thess. 5:9-10; Peter in 1 Peter 3:18 (Prison=Chamber); Ezra in 2 Esdras 2:29 and 4:41; and Isaiah in Isaiah 14:9-11.*

This concept of our spirits sleeping awaiting the Day of Judgment deriving from First Enoch is repeated:

*By Messiah in Matt. 22:28-32, Mark 5:39, John 5:28, 11:11-14; by Luke in Acts 7:59-60, 13:36; by Paul in 1 Cor. 15:17-22, 1 Thess. 4:13-18, 5:9-10; and by Peter in 1 Peter 3:18 and 2 Peter 3:4. This is also documented in the Old Testament by Moses in Deuteronomy 31:16; by Job in Job 14:12; by Jeremiah in 2 Samuel 7:12, 1 Kings 1:21; by David in Psalm 13:3; by Daniel in Daniel 12:2; and by Ezra in 2 Esdras 2:31.*

There are many more such quotes and all originate in concept in First Enoch which lines the foundation of the Old and New Testaments as it should because Enoch was the first Great Prophet indeed. How any scholar could attempt to marginalize the significance of this man and his work is unimaginable.

The resurrection of the dead is first recorded in 1 Enoch 22:4 and this concept is also a bedrock of the New and Old Testaments.

*By Messiah in Matthew 22:28-32, Luke 20:34, John 5:28, 11:23-27; By Paul in 1 Thess. 4:14-18, 1 Cor. 15:20-22, 2 Cor. 15:52; By Hebrews in Hebrews 9:26; By Daniel in Daniel 12:2; By Solomon in Eccl. 9:5, 12:7-8; By Ezra in 2 Esdras 2:31, 4:42; and By Isaiah in Isaiah14:9-11.*

Our spirits our raised on the Day of Judgment also first found in 1 Enoch 22:4 and 11. This concept serves as foundation for the New and Old Testaments as well.

*By Paul in 1 Thess. 4:15-17, 1 Cor. 15:23-24, 1 Cor. 15:52, 2 Cor. 5:1-10; By Hebrews 9:26; By Daniel in Daniel 12:2; and By Ezra in 2 Esdras 2:31.*

We have all referred to Yahusha as the "King of Kings" of scripture indeed. However, Enoch is the first to use the term and we find it used in 1 Timothy 6:15; Revelation 17:14, and 19:16. The origin of this term in publishing is 1 Enoch 9:4 and 84:2.

These are some of the most significant doctrines in all of scripture and they originate being first published on Earth in the First Book of Enoch. This first among men to write, wrote the most profound of doctrines and if your seminary is not teaching them, they lack such profundity. The most ancient Biblical source and many ignore it.

This is the reason we continue to find residual quotes from the so-called "early church fathers." One must assess each one as to which church they belonged however, as imposters were already infiltrating in the days of Jude and Paul. Any of these representing a church no longer following the example of the Apostles is meaningless. However, even they still quoted First Enoch. This is far too late for debate on the Canonicity of a book from before the Flood. Such conversation is incredibly inept when the Temple Priests kept this as inspired scripture and Bible Canon in the only Bible Canon ever found in that era. That precedence cannot be challenged nor explained away in willing ignorance no matter how much scholarly consensus there may be. Truly, this is one of the ways one can tell whether a scholar is honest or just another Pharisee scoffer.

## QUOTED BY "EARLY CHURCH FATHERS" (150-380 A.D.):

**150 A.D.: Minucius Felix, Octavius,** *xxvi (1 En. 8,15:8-12,16:1,19:1)*

**150 A.D.: Clement of Alexandria,** *Ecloyae Prophet, (ed. Dindorf). iii. (1 En. 8:1-3,16:3,19:3)*

**154 A.D.: Bardesanes,** *Book of the Lav.s of Countries. (1 En. 6)*

**160 A.D.: Tatian,** *Oratio adv. Graecos 8. (1 En. 8:3)*

**165 A.D.: Justin Martyr,** *Apol. ii. 5 (1 En. 9:8-9, 15:8-9).*

**170 A.D.: Atlienagoras,** *Legatio pro Christianis,24(1 En. 6:6-7,13:5, 14:5,15:8-10)*

**202 A.D.: Irenaeus** *(1 En. 10:13-14,5:4,8:1,3,12:4,6,13,14:3-7,15,16, 10:2, 99:7, 19:1)*

**210 A.D.: Tertullian, regards Enoch as Scripture, Apol. xxii.** *(1 En. 15:8-9) De Idol. iv.(1 En.19:1,8:1,99:6-7) De Cultu Femin. i. 2.(1 En. 8:1) De Idol. ix. De Virg. Veland. vii (1 En. 6,14:5)*

**220 A.D.: Hippolytus,** *Or. adv. Graecos (ed. Bxmsen, Analecta Anfe-Nicaena, i. 393). (1 En. 22:3,21:1)*

**237 A.D.: Julius Africanus,** *Chronographia. (1 En. 7:1,8)*

**250 A.D.: Commodianus,** *Instructiones (ed. Migne, P.L. V. 203, 204), i. 3. (1 En. 6:1-2,7:2,8:1,1:9,13:2,14:5,10:4,12,19:1,15:6,19:1)*

**250 A.D.: Zosimus of Panopolis,** *quoted in Syvoellus (Dindorf, i, 1829, p. 24). (1 En. 6,7,8)*

**250 A.D.: Cyprian,** *De Hah. Virg. 14 (Hartel, i, p. 197). (1 En. 8:1)*

**250 A.D.: Pseudo-Cyprian,** *Ad Novatianum (ed. Hartel, Cyprian, in, p. 67). (1 En. 1:9)*

**269 A.D.: Anatolius** *appointed* **Bishop of Laodicea** *in 269. Quoted in Euseb. Hist. Tied, vii, 32. 19.*

**300 A.D.: Clementine Homilies,** *Yiii. 12-18. (1 En. 19:1,8:1,3,6:1-2,7:1-3,10:4,13:1,14:5,15:2,8,16:1)*

**300 A.D.: Clem. Recog.** *iv. 26, 27 (ed. Cotelier, i, p. 543). (1 En. 19:1,15:3,6,7,7:1,8:2-3,10:2,106:13-15)*

**320 A.D.: Lactantius,** *Imtit. (Migne, P. L. vi. 330-332; Brandt and LaubmanUj i, pp. 162 sqq.). (Long passage with 1 Enoch as main feature.) Instit. ii. 14 (1 En. 14:5-7,69:4,7:1,54:6,15:8-11,16:1,19:1) Inst. iv. 27, V. 18. (1 En. 19:1). vii. 7. (1 En. 22). vii. 16.(1 En. 80:2). vii. 19.(1 En. 90:19,91:12, 90:25, 54,63). vii. 24. (1 En. 10:17). vii. 26.(1 En. 48:9).*

**360 A.D.: Cassianus,** *CoUatio VIIT. xxi. (1 En. 8:1).*

**380 A.D.: Priscillian,** *De Fide et de Apocnjphis (Schepss, 1889, p. 44). Tied 1 Enoch as source of Jude and Heb. 11:5)*

**1011 A.D.: Carmen Apologeticum.** *(1 En. 18:13-16)*

**1070 A.D.: Pseudo-Tertullian,** *Five Books against Marcion, iii. ch. ii (Migne, ii. 1070).*

At this point, there is no scholar who can go backwards and change the Bible Canon which the Temple Priests who were ordained to keep such compiled. It does not matter if the Pope himself makes such declaration nor an Emperor as neither had such authority. Yahusha is the Word and he approved the Bible Canon at Qumran/Bethabara kept by the sons of Zadok from the Temple endorsing it having launched His ministry there and not the Jerusalem Temple. This is because the Temple was defiled and the Temple Priests and worship system were relocated by exile to Qumran/Bethabara. Messiah visited there again according to scripture. Any Canon not kept by the Temple Priests is not one of the Bible.

It matters not what Pharisees did or did not perceive as scripture as their worship system rejects the son of Yahuah and he rebuked them many times for it especially in Mark 7 accusing them of turning Torah against Torah. They still do and they are hiding it in fraud. Josephus, the Pharisee, Hasmonean and Essene is among the sons of darkness rebuked by the Temple Priests in their Qumran writings. The cult in Egypt, likely Essene, who translated the Septuagint also were not Aaronic Temple Priests thus they have no opinion as to what is Bible Canon or not. Only the Temple Priests up until the first century can record such and here, they did so with Messiah's endorsement. Thus, no one can change it. These books in Qumran are what we call Bible Canon and nothing else qualifies. Modern Bibles today are Pharisee Canons typically.

When one reviews the objections of so-called "early church fathers" of the false church, it is no surprise they did not like First Enoch especially when the tide turned to change the Bible and they went along. These were a cursed lot as you do not change what the true Temple Priests already kept as Bible Canon. They do not like Yahuah and did not actually serve Him which is obvious in their church foundation. Certainly, one can read of Origen's *(200 A.D.)* or Augustine's *(400 A.D.)* hatred of the book. They did not prefer the truth but the lies of their false church who demonstrated a preference for occult roots instead which they would replace. Enoch exposes them. A false church who abandoned the practice of the Apostles and persecuted the true ekklesias in Turkey is the wrong measure to assess what is inspired scripture. They are not even an inspired church nor entire system. They are the men Jude *(1:4)* warned crept in unawares before launching into several quotes from the First Book of Enoch.

We have well covered the response of the ekklesias who followed the Apostles example, though not perfect, who are mentioned in Revelation versus these liars who were working hard to change the structure of Yahusha's ekklesia. Anatolius *(269 A.D.)*, Bishop of Laodicea, one of the 7 ekklesias of Revelation, quoted Enoch thus used it. Unfortunately, not much survives of those 7 as their bishops were typically martyred and their message hijacked by frauds who were profaning the Sabbath and chipping away at every tenet of the fabric of the Bible they could. Of course, they would not like a book at its very foundations.

For instance, Chrysostom *(350 A.D.)* was already trashing the Fallen Angel narrative though that is in Genesis 6 thus the guy did not even believe the Bible and did not represent what Paul, Jude, Peter and John taught whether alone Enoch. He was not one of any authority to oppose what the Temple Priests taught which we now have in their Qumran writings as well affirming they did. He was representing new and strange doctrine never taught by the Apostles. We were warned about his type and they often label them "early church fathers" erroneously? They were early church infiltrators and deceivers called out by Jude, Yahusha and Paul. You can tell by their doctrine. Who cares if Jerome *(400 A.D.)* regarded Enoch as apocryphal. He was in a false church who did not know how to even assess scripture whether alone prophecy. He was no authority over the original keepers of scripture. These are all frauds who claim authority and are given weight they do not deserve. They also did not have the Qumran scrolls.

However, in the fifth century or so, history would then witness the rise of a church that declares its leader above Yahusha on Earth. It even led to a doctrine of infallibility where they claim when the Pope disagrees with the Bible, the Bible is wrong, not the Pope. That is idiotic. His office has attacked the sanctity of scripture and forgotten just about all of it in application because his false church never knew it. It is occult from its very roots as evidenced in its oldest writings which demonstrate it operated against scripture while the true early ekklesia in Turkey kept the Biblical traditions handed down to them by the Apostles in the commandments including the Sabbaths and Feasts which we document historically in REST: The Case For Sabbath.

Thus, it is useless to then follow this false church to see what it did or did not change in scripture. The point is they dared to change it and never had authority. They are illegitimate and their changes void. Even with that said, they still continued to use First Enoch until at least 380 A.D. with latter references still proving they knew the Temple practice of keeping Enoch as scripture which they abandon not Messiah nor any Apostle. They are caught and exposed as they are guilty of continuing the Pharisee Bible over the Temple Priests further proving they are not the ekklesia of Messiah. They don't know Him, especially not His ways and they do not represent Him thus they do not get an opinion.

## ETHIOPIAN ORTHODOX TEWAHDO CHURCH, 300 A.D. *(approx.)* - PRESENT:

Remember, in Acts 8:25-40, essentially the Treasurer of the nation of Ethiopia met Philip. He was already reading Isaiah without understanding it. Philip explained to this man the story of Messiah and the man accepted Yahusha that day. He would return to his country knowing the traditions at least in part of the ekklesia of Messiah. It is there we find the continuation of the First Book of Enoch as Bible Canon.

Somehow, and no one truly documents how, the Ethiopian Orthodox Tewahdo Church included the First Book of Enoch and The Book of Jubilees in it's Bible Canon around 300 A.D. until today. One must wonder if the true origin of this decision might really be that Treasurer that day who learned some from Philip and likely many others before leaving to return to his country with a message in which he would have amassed a following. We are aware there are churches that attempt to take credit for taking Jesus there but let's be clear, the Bible already makes such connection and none of them are the likely origin. In this case, clearly this community followed a precedence from somewhere and not from any other Orthodox Church really. The others do not use these books and they are known as the oldest ekklesia outside of the near Middle East.

Though no written history truly appears to identify this firmly, we believe they continued that tradition especially regarding First Enoch and Jubilees directly from the Apostles and exiled Temple Priests not from any other church and certainly not from Pharisees who practice differently. Around 300 A.D., the Ethiopian Orthodox Tewahdo Church was established and chose to continue these two books as Bible Canon which does not match any other Bible Canons really except that of the Apostles and Temple Priests in regards to these two books. We are not addressing their entire Canon. We know this because we find the Apostles quoting Jubilees and Enoch as inspired scripture many times. This continues in their Bible to this day.

Thus, First Enoch and Jubilees have essentially always been Bible Canon. It is this book which R.H. Charles, as well as others, were able to acquire copies by which to translate into English a century ago restoring this for all of us. We applaud his translation which has passed the test of time. However, his foot notes identify him as another scoffer who clearly has an obsession with Rabbinical writings and the Talmud as he attempts to inject their thinking. He did not understand what this book represents which is the opposite of Rabbinic thinking as did Messiah.

This is why they reject it and they did even in the days of Messiah as the Temple Priests specifically record Israel (the Pharisee worship system at that time) turned a "blind eye" to Jubilees. With the publishing of Josephus' Canon missing many books and adding Esther, it is very clear the Pharisees already manipulated the Bible Canon at that time in 90 A.D. It is also evident that the Catholic Church compiled nothing concerning the Old Testament but copied the Pharisee Canon largely with changes.

In time, some would move over into a category of stupid called Apocrypha or books outside of the Pharisee Canon. Essentially that says nothing. Only the sons of Zadok kept Canon so there is no category of Apocrypha in true Bible Canon history. It was manufactured and remains a fraud. For the Old Testament, there are the books kept by the Temple Priests who were ordained by Moses, and really Jacob, to curate scripture as their calling. No Pharisee had such ever and there is no such thing as Apocrypha. It was either in their Bible Canon or not scripture and not used period. They make no mention in their community writings of anything such as an Apocrypha which is a ridiculous term. A Pharisee Apocrypha has no Biblical authority and is fraud even in beginning any discussion.

## 3. Acceptance

First Enoch was written before the Flood. At that time, there were no Hebrews nor what we call the New Testament ekklesia. However, even with that said, we find Enoch fully prophesying of the People of Israel and much of their history up until the time of Messiah. We then find not only mentions of Messiah coming in the flesh but Enoch met Yahusha in Heaven in spirit before the Flood and before He came in the flesh. He clearly identifies Him as the coming Messiah. He then, in prophecy speaks of the Second Coming in part including the Day of Judgment and his work is the origin of such. Even in antiquity, this book fully qualifies as maintaining the acceptance of the coming Israel as Yahuah's people as well as Messiah and the End Times Ekklesia. This book passes in this regard in every aspect.

## 4. In Agreement With the Whole of Scripture (Our Addition)

As demonstrated in Part 2 of this Torah Test, the First Book of Enoch agrees with the whole tone and tenor of the Old and New Testaments serving as the foundational basis in several parts we have identified. In this publishing, we will address the recent movement of those who believe in a Flat Earth as Enoch most certainly did write from such perspective but anyone saying the rest of scripture is not, is clueless and cannot read. We have seen several such dunderhead responses claiming that a circle is sphere or ball when very clearly Bible writers knew the difference and when they use circle they mean a 2-dimensional shape not a ball. Those scholars are simply not honest.

From Enoch's journey around the surface of the Earth, the interior of the Earth and Heaven, we find agreement with the whole of scripture. Though not every detail is there in scripture as Enoch provides much, understand Heaven does not have a whole lot of true eyewitnesses. In fact, it is very telling that most accounts of those claiming to go to Heaven do not match scripture and especially have a major issue as we do not get judged upon death and go immediately to Heaven or Hell. No one has seen Hitler nor a Pope in either place. Perhaps they had a strong dream or vision but they most certainly do not represent the Biblical paradigm. The Bible agrees with Enoch as you will see.

We find the First Book of Enoch passes in each regard as inspired scripture and Bible Canon as only the exiled Temple Priests held such an authoritative library until the first century. Its historicity cannot be questioned and it is the undeniable foundational origin of many doctrines in scripture in the Old and New Testaments as it should be. We find Messiah's endorsement there and we do not need any scholar's.

### 1. Prophetic Authorship

*Enoch, the Prophet wrote First Enoch. As he was a prophet and this vets as inspired scripture, there is ample history in use for this book to be dated in origin before the Flood. Methuselah, Lamech and Noah had this book and Noah quotes from it including the supposed missing book, the Second Section titled The Book of Parables. Abraham as well received and read copies of First Enoch as well. Moses records this multiple times. Enoch is the only author other than fragments by Noah included. No one else authored this book and Temple Priests did not follow such fraudulent practices as Rabbis do.*

### 2. Witness of the Spirit, Quoted As Doctrine In Scripture

*It is indisputable that the historicity of First Enoch can be established all the way back to the tie before the Flood. Noah brought it with him on the ark and it survived after as Noah used and quoted it. In fact, this is how Noah learned of the Flood. Abraham also used and taught First Enoch as scripture. Moses affirms all of this and continues to use Enoch in his writings especially Jubilees many times. Prophets quote First Enoch and we see it used for significant doctrine through the Old Testament. In the New Testament, it is almost as if First Enoch is reinvigorated into the hearts of the Apostles especially Paul, John, Peter, Luke and Jude. Jude especially offers direct quotes from this written book of Enoch, as does Messiah. However, the End Times view of Enoch is prevalent throughout the New Testament and it does not differ.*

### 3. Acceptance

*One cannot find a more accepting view of the Messiah even before the Flood in Heaven where Enoch met Him. He speaks of His coming in the flesh as well as the Day of Judgment. Israel and the New Testament Ekklesia are all predicted and seen as holy in First Enoch.*

### 4. In Agreement With the Whole of Scripture (Our Addition)

*There truly is no scripture that disagrees with the First Book of Enoch. There are only paradigms and when tested, it is clear they are not Biblically based even. We have not found anything that truly presents an issue along these lines.*

The first Messianic prophesies of Enoch are the most significant in history. First Enoch severs as the foundation for the attributes of Messiah found throughout scripture.

In Chapter 46, Enoch sees the coming Messiah in Heaven in spirit known as the "**Son of Man**" whom he describes as:

> *"...countenance had the appearance of a man..."*
> *"...his face was full of graciousness, like one of the holy angels..."*
> *"...who hath righteousness with whom dwelleth righteousness..."*
> *"...who revealeth all the treasures of that which is hidden..."*
> *"...Yahuah of Spirits hath chosen him..."*
> *"...whose lot hath the pre-eminence before Yahuah of Spirits in uprightness for ever..."*
> *"...Shall raise up the kings and the mighty from their seats..."*
> *"...shall loosen the reins of the strong..."*
> *"...break the teeth of the sinners..."*
> *"...shall put down the kings from their thrones and kingdoms..."*
> *"...shall put down the countenance of the strong, and shall fill them with shame..."*

In Chapter 48, Enoch continues to sound like the book of Revelation not written yet.

> *"...shall be a staff to the righteous..."*
> *"...shall be the light of the Gentiles..."*
> *"...the hope of those who are troubled of heart..."*
> *"All who dwell on earth shall fall down and worship before him..."*

Yahusha calls Himself **"Son of Man"** 82 times in the Gospels and twice he is referenced as such in Revelation. The notion that this originates in Daniel's *(7:13)* one mention of the term is ludicrous when Enoch mentions him many times first and is the true origin of Daniel. These are not scholars. They do not believe the Bible.

Enoch identifies this is He who was before the world was formed.

**1 Enoch 48**
**2** *And at that hour that **Son of Man** was named in the presence of Yahuah of Spirits, And his name before the Head of Days.* **3 Yea, before the sun and the signs were**

*created. Before the stars of the heaven were made. His name was named before Yahuah of Spirits*.

**6** *And for this reason* **hath he been chosen and hidden before Him, before the creation of the world** *and for evermore.*

**1 Enoch 62**

**7** *For from the beginning the* **Son of Man was hidden. And the Most High preserved him in the presence of His might**.

For this is Yahusha by whose name all shall be saved. **1 Enoch 48:7 ...For in his name they are saved...**

First Enoch continues as it references this **"Son of Man"** who will resurrect the dead, judge the wicked consuming with eternal fire, and the righteous will rest with Him for eternity. This is long before the New Testament even in fraudulent datings.

**1 Enoch 48**

**9** *And I will give them over into the hands of Mine elect* **as straw in the fire so shall they burn** *before the face of the holy; As lead in the water shall they sink before the face of the righteous, And* **no trace of them shall any more be found.**
**10** *For they have* **denied Yahuah of Spirits and His Anointed.**

**1 Enoch 47**

**3** *In those days I saw the Head of Days when He seated himself upon the throne of His glory, And the* **books of the living** *were opened before Him.*

**1 Enoch 62**

**5** *And one portion of them shall look on the other. And they shall be terrified. And they shall be downcast of countenance, And pain shall seize them, When they see that* **Son of Man sitting on the throne of his glory.** 6 *And the kings and the mighty and all who possess the earth shall bless and glorify and extol him who rules over all, who was hidden.*
**14** *And Yahuah of Spirits will abide over them.* **And with that Son of Man shall they eat and lie down and rise up for ever and ever.**

Enoch knew Messiah long before the New Testament and really before the Old Testament was written. This is undeniable.

# EYE WITNESS TO MESSIAH IN HEAVEN BEFORE THE FLOOD.

*For those who have heard the unscholarly opinion regarding "THE SUPPOSED "MISSING SECTION" OF FIRST ENOCH," please refer to our test disproving this shallow, unsupported claim on page 51.*

# LORD OF SPIRITS

**104 Times**

**Yahuah:** יהוה *(H3068) only name of God interpreted erroneously 6,800+ times in modern Bibles as the LORD. (used 298 times as "The Lord" in R.H. Charles publishing)*

**rûaḥ:** רוח *(h7307): wind; by resemblance breath, i.e. a sensible (or even violent) exhalation; figuratively, life, anger, unsubstantiality; by extension, a region of the sky; by resemblance spirit, but only of a rational being (including its expression and functions):—air, anger, blast, breath, × cool, courage, mind, × quarter, × side, spirit(-ual), tempest, × vain, (whirl-) wind(-y).*

In certain sections especially describing Heaven, Enoch calls the Creator the Lord of Spirits as it is translated into English 104 times. However, though Charles used the Ethiopic Geez full edition, when one takes this back to the original Hebrew, it would read as the very name of Yahuah (YHWH: יהוה) with the Hebrew Ruah (רוח) which would identify Yahuah of Breath or Spirits as He breathed life into Adam and man became a living soul *(Gen. 2:7)*. Jubilees 2, the record of Creation from the Heavenly Tablets given to Moses on Sinai, documents Yahuah Created the Angels and all spirits of man and beast on Day 1 of Creation. He already knew the end of our current era and exactly how many spirits or souls He would need. He breathed this spirit into Adam on the 6th Day as he became a living soul or spirit. Note, Enoch says multiple times:

39:7 "...And their lips extol **the name of the Lord of Spirits**..."
39:9 "In those days I praised and extolled **the name of the Lord of Spirits**..."
40:6 "...pray and intercede for those who dwell on the earth and supplicate in **the name of the Lord of Spirits**..."
41:2 "...sinners being driven from thence which deny **the name of the Lord of Spirits**..."

This is His name, Yahuah Ruah, not a title. Charles knew that and then ignored it to claim it is a title due to his Pharisee education hiding the name of YHWH really, one of the most illiterate doctrines of all time. It is when you mistranslate Yahuah as the Lord indeed. That is a fraudulent practice of Pharisees and the modern church in our modern Pharisee-leavened Bibles.

However, though Lord of Spirits or Yahuah of Spirits does not appear in the modern Canon, "Elohim of Spirits" does and that is a title indeed. Hebrews uses in Greek "Father of Spirits." This proves a Biblical practice and not strange in Enoch.

**Numbers 16:22 KJV**
*And they fell upon their faces, and said, O God, the* **God of the spirits of all flesh**, *shall one man sin, and wilt thou be wroth with all the congregation?*
**Numbers 27:16 KJV**
*Let the LORD, the* **God of the spirits of all flesh**, *set a man over the congregation,*
**Jubilees 10:3**
*3 And he prayed before Yahuah his Elohim, and said:* **Elohim of the spirits of all flesh**, *who hast shown mercy unto me,*

**ĕlōhîm:** אלהים *(H430)* **rûaḥ:** רוח *(h7307)*

**Hebrews 12:9**
*Furthermore we have had fathers of our flesh which corrected us, and we gave them reverence: shall we not much rather be in subjection unto the* **Father of spirits**, *and live?*

**patēr:** πατήρ: *father (G4151)*
**pneuma:** *πνεῦμα: a current of air, i.e. breath (blast) or a breeze; by analogy or figuratively, a spirit, i.e. (human) the rational soul , (by implication) vital principle, mental disposition, etc., or (superhuman) an angel, demon, or (divine) God, Christ's spirit, the Holy Spirit:—ghost, life, spirit(-ual, -ually), mind.*

The fact is Enoch was using the very name of YHWH, Yahauh, and even includes Yahuah of the Mighty *(63:2)*, Yahuah of Kings *(63:2)*, Yahuah of Riches (resources) *(63:2)*, Yahuah of glory *(63:2)*, Yahuah of Wisdom *(63:2)*. He also uses "Head of Days" *(46:2)* or first of days really, which we see expressed in Daniel similarly as "Ancient of Days" *(Dan. 7:9,13,22)*. These are consistent with the whole of scripture and not a new character nor title. This is the very name of YHWH, Yahuah used many times by Enoch. This should be no surprise to scholarship, however, who should learn how to read the Bible as Enos, son of Seth called upon the name of Yahuah *(Gen. 4:26)* as did Seth, Adam and the others living with Adam in Havilah at that time thus Enoch certainly knew the name YHWH, Yahuah. All knew and pronounced the name of YHWH, Yahuah. So did Abraham many times and even Yahuah tells His name is Yahuah, multiple times *(see chart pp. 80-81)*. The Pharisee doctrine Charles espouses, as most scholars, claiming we are to hide and not pronounce this name is utterly stupid and unsupported in the whole of scripture.

## The Name Of God in Enoch

We learn from Jubilees Hebrew is the language of Creation thus it must be simple and somehow for thousands of years, it was written with just consonants yet spoken without ever needing vowel points. Those were added in about 1000 A.D. by the Masoretes and at times serve to offer more confusion than clarity as they clearly were not honest about the name of Yahuah since it was their practice to hide His name. Therefore, this must be a phonetic language requiring no vowels and no fancy rules especially those changing even within a word illogically. What we call Hebrew today is Yiddish-infused not Ancient Hebrew.

Phonetically, YH is simple. H is AH *(see chart to right)*. That's YAH. The next combination is HW which we know by the names of the prophets is HU. Thus, it's YAHU as with the prophets. Finally, we add the last H or AH for YAHUAH.

We recognize there is a whole church out there which stakes it's claim on the name Jehovah. Here's the largest problem with that word. It is not Ancient Hebrew, Aramaic, Greek, Latin, Old French, Old German nor Old English. In other words, every language in which the Bible has been interpreted through in origin cannot render J nor V until the Renaissance *(1500s or so)*. The Bible was already thousands of years old and never used J nor V in any ancient text. There is a Pharisee out there deceiving many by trying to make this fit, but we have the Dead Sea Scrolls dating to as early as 300 B.C. with even entire books such as the Isaiah scroll of about 25 feet in length which never renders a J nor a V even once. There is no overturning that. One may ignore it but let us not pretend they would be interested in the truth.

This leads us to the name of Messiah as the same first 3 letters YHW or YAHU as set by Yahuah. Yes, He literally meant He came in His Father's name. His name ends with SH - SHIN, A - AYIN which is SHA. He is Yahusha with Yahushua also appearing as a variant in scripture. Joshua has this same name in Hebrew. His people are the YAHUdim never Jews but YAH's.

Finally, some focus on the one time in scripture that Yahuah says His name is HYH, HAYAH as His only name ignoring the 6,800 times it is recorded as YHWH, Yahuah. However, modern Yiddish renders this as EHYEH and similar in fraud. Ancient Hebrew is HA YAH or THE YAH. It is the same name. Yahuah is being specific in saying I am The Yah not to be confused with any other. He is still invoking His name Yahuah in that passage which matches. In fact, YAH is rendered in the Old Testament 45 times on a standalone basis.

| | | |
|---|---|---|
| **PHOENICIAN** | ∃Y∃⅃ | 1100 B.C. |
| **PALEO-HEBREW** | ∃ヨ∃ｚ | 1000 B.C. |
| **HEBREW** | יהוה | 300 B.C. - TODAY |

# YAHUAH

**FATHER**

## יהוה

HEY     WAW     HEY     YAD

## HᴀU HᴀY

### YAHUAH

---



### Ancient Semitic/Hebrew

| Early | Middle | Late | Name | Picture | Meaning | Sound |
|---|---|---|---|---|---|---|
| | | א | El | Ox head | Strong, Power, Leader | ah, eh |
| | | ב | Bet | Tent floorplan | Family, House, In | b, bh(v) |
| | | ג | Gam | Foot | Gather, Walk | g |
| | | ד | Dal | Door | Move, Hang, Entrance | d |
| | | ה | Hey | Man with arms raised | Look, Reveal, Breath | h, ah |
| | | ו | Waw | Tent peg | Add, Secure, Hook | w, o, u |
| | | ז | Zan | Mattock | Food, Cut, Nourish | z |
| | | ח | Hhet | Tent wall | Outside, Divide, Half | hh |
| | | ט | Tet | Basket | Surround, Contain, Mud | t |
| | | י | Yad | Arm and closed hand | Work, Throw, Worship | y, ee |
| | | כ | Kaph | Open palm | Bend, Open, Allow, Tame | k, kh |
| | | ל | Lam | Shepherd Staff | Teach, Yoke, To, Bind | l |
| | | מ | Mem | Water | Chaos, Mighty, Blood | m |
| | | נ | Nun | Seed | Continue, Heir, Son | n |
| | | ס | Sin | Thorn | Grab, Hate, Protect | s |
| | | ע | Ghah | Eye | Watch, Know, Shade | gh(ng) |
| | | פ | Pey | Mouth | Blow, Scatter, Edge | p, ph(f) |
| | | צ | Tsad | Trail | Journey, chase, hunt | ts |
| | | ק | Quph | Sun on the horizon | Condense, Circle, Time | q |
| | | ר | Resh | Head of a man | First, Top, Beginning | r |
| | | ש | Shin | Two front teeth | Sharp, Press, Eat, Two | sh |
| | | ת | Taw | Crossed sticks | Mark, Sign, Signal, Monument | t |
| | | | Ghah | Rope | Twist, Dark, Wicked | gh |

Ancient Hebrew Research Center    26

**AH**   **U**   **Y**

---

# YAHUSHA

**"YAHU IS SALVATION"**

## יהושע

AYIN    SHIN    WAW    HEY    YAD

## AᴴS U HᴀY

### YAHUSHA

NO "J"

NO "V"

NO VOWEL POINTS

---

**YAHUdim** יהודים
Yah's People (Never Jews, Yah's)

**YAHUdah** יהודה
"Yahu Be Praised" (Tribe of Judah)

**Ha YAH** היה
I AM or THE YAH

**EliYAHU** אליהו
"My God Is Yahu"

## Yahuah Told Us His Name Is YHWH, Yahuah Many Times:

**Isaiah 42:8**: I am YHWH (יהוה): that is my name...

**Exodus 20:2-4**: I am YHWH (יהוה) thy God...

**Exodus 6:6**: I am YHWH (יהוה)

**Leviticus 19:12**: I am YHWH (יהוה)

**Jeremiah 16:21**: ...and they shall know that my name is YHWH (יהוה)

**Exodus 3:15**: And God said... YHWH (יהוה) God of your fathers, the God of Abraham, the God of Isaac, and the God of Jacob, hath sent me unto you: this is my name for ever, and this is my memorial unto all generations.

**Zechariah 13:9**: "They will call on My name, And I will answer them; I will say, 'They are My people,' And they will say, 'YHWH (יהוה) is my God.'"

**Ezekiel 39:6**: And I will send a fire on Magog, and among them that dwell carelessly in the isles: and they shall know that I am YHWH (יהוה)

## YHWH Pronounced in the Bible As a Practice:

**Genesis 4:26**: And to Seth, to him also there was born a son; and he called his name Enos: then began men to call upon the name of YHWH (יהוה)"

**1 Samuel 7:5-9**: Then Samuel said, "Gather all Israel to Mizpah and I will pray to YHWH (יהוה) for you."

**1 Kings 18:36-37**: At the time of the offering of the evening sacrifice, Elijah the prophet came near and said, "O YHWH (יהוה), the God of Abraham, Isaac and Israel..."

**Jonah 2:2** and he said, "I called out of my distress to YHWH (יהוה)

**Genesis 12:8**: ...he builded an altar unto the Lord, and called upon the name of YHWH (יהוה)

**Genesis 26:24-25**: And YHWH (יהוה) appeared unto him the same night, and said, I am the Elohim of Abraham thy father: fear not, for I am with thee, and will bless thee, and multiply thy seed for my servant Abraham's sake. And he builded an altar there, and called upon the name of YHWH (יהוה)

**1 Chronicles 16:8**: Give thanks unto YHWH (יהוה), call upon his name...

**Psalm 105:1**: O give thanks unto YHWH (יהוה); call upon his name:

**Zephaniah 3:9**: For then will I turn to the people a pure language, that they may all call upon the name of YHWH (יהוה), to serve him with one consent.

**Lamentations 3:55**: I called upon thy name, O YHWH (יהוה)

**2 Samuel 22:4**: I call upon YHWH (יהוה), who is worthy to be praised...

**Psalm 18:3**: I call upon YHWH (יהוה), who is worthy to be praised...

**1 Kings 18:24**: "Then you call on the name of your god, and I will call on the name of YHWH (יהוה)

**2 Kings 5:11**: ...Naaman was furious and went away and said, "Behold, I thought, 'He will surely come out to me and stand and call on the name of YHWH (יהוה) his God...

**Psalm 18:6**: In my distress I called upon YHWH (יהוה)

**Psalm 28:1-2**: To You, O YHWH (יהוה), I call...

**Psalm 55:16**: As for me, I shall call upon God, And YHWH (יהוה) will save me.

**Psalm 120:1**: In my trouble I cried to YHWH (יהוה), And He answered me.

**Isaiah 58:9**: Then you will call, and YHWH (יהוה) will answer...

**Joel 1:19**: To You, O YHWH (יהוה), I cry...

**Joel 2:32**: "And it will come about that whoever calls on the name of YHWH (יהוה)

**Psalm 99:6**: Moses and Aaron were among His priests, And Samuel was among those who called on His name; They called upon YHWH (יהוה) and He answered...

**Numbers 21:7**: So the people came to Moses and said, "We have sinned, because we have spoken against YHWH (יהוה) and you; intercede with YHWH (יהוה)

**1 Samuel 12:19**: Then all the people said to Samuel, "Pray for your servants to YHWH (יהוה) your God...

**Genesis 13:4**: ...to the place of the altar which he had made there formerly; and there Abram called on the name of YHWH (יהוה)

**Exodus 32:11-13**: Then Moses entreated YHWH (יהוה) his God, and said, "O YHWH (יהוה)

**Deuteronomy 9:26-29**: "I prayed to YHWH (יהוה) and said, 'O YHWH (יהוה) GOD do not destroy Your people...

**Numbers 14:13-19**: But Moses said to YHWH (יהוה), "Then the Egyptians will hear of it, for by Your strength You brought up this people from their midst, and they will tell it to the inhabitants of this land. They have heard that You, O YHWH (יהוה), are in the midst of this people, for You, O YHWH (יהוה), are seen eye to eye... *(and there are many more as this name appears over 6,800 times)*

## YHWH Will Be Restored in the Last Days Says YHWH:

**Isaiah 52:6**: Therefore my people shall know my name: therefore they shall know in that day that I am he that doth speak: behold, it is I.

**Jeremiah 16:21**: Therefore, behold, I will this once cause them to know, I will cause them to know mine hand and my might; and they shall know that my name is YHWH (יהוה)

**Ezekiel 39:7**: So will I make my holy name known in the midst of my people Israel; and I will not let them pollute my holy name any more: and the heathen shall know that I am YHWH (יהוה), the Holy One in Israel.

*All passages from the KJV.*

THE
Levite
BIBLE
THE. Levite
BIBLE
LeviteBible.com

# THE FIRST BOOK OF ENOCH

## THE OLDEST BOOK IN HISTORY

### WITH THE RESTORED NAME OF YAHUAH

# SECTION 1:

# THE BOOK OF THE WATCHERS

# 1-5
# PARABLE OF ENOCH

Only the Final Judgment
coalesces with Enoch's Vision.

## ON THE FUTURE LOT OF THE WICKED AND THE RIGHTEOUS

# CHAPTER 1:

*Cf. Deut. 33:1 "The blessing of Moses."*

*Cf. 38:2-4, 39:6-7, 48:1, 58:1-2, 61:13, 62:12-13, 15, 70:3. "elect and righteous."*

*Cf. 5:7, 25:5, 41:2, 48:1, 56:6-8, 58:3, 61:4,12, 62:7-11, 93:2. elect = End Times remnant.*

*Cf. Mt. 24:24, 31; Lk. 18:7; Rom. 8:33; Col. 3:12; Tit. 1:1.*

*The Holy One in this context is Messiah whom the angels revealed to Enoch in Heaven. Cf. 46-48.*

*Cf. Jub. 4:19. "placed the testimony on earth for all children of men and their generations."*

*Cf. 92:2, 97:6, 98:6, 104:9, 10:1, 14:1, 25:3. "Holy Great One," "Great Holy One," "Holy and Great One." is Yahuah.*

*Cf. Mic. 1:3; Is. 26:21; As. of Moses 10:3. "come forth from His dwelling."*

*Cf. Gen. 21:33; Rom. 16:26; As. of Moses 10:17. "The eternal God."*

*1-5. Parable of Enoch on the Future Lot of the Wicked and the Righteous.*

1 The words of **the blessing of Enoch**, wherewith he blessed the **elect [and] righteous**, who will be living in the **day of tribulation**, when all the wicked [and godless] are to be removed, 2 And he took up his parable and said—Enoch a righteous man, whose eyes were opened by Elohim, saw the vision of **the Holy One** in the heavens, [which] the angels showed me, and from them I heard everything, and from them I understood as I saw, but not for this generation, but for a remote one which is for to come, 3 Concerning the elect I said, and took up my parable concerning them: **The Holy Great One** will come forth from His dwelling, 4 And the eternal Elohim will tread upon the earth, (even) on **Mount Sinai**, [And appear from His camp] And appear in the strength of His might from the heaven [of heavens]. 5 And all shall be smitten with fear; And the Watchers shall quake, And great fear and trembling shall seize them unto the ends of the earth. 6 And the high mountains shall be shaken, And the high hills shall be made low, And shall **melt like wax before the flame**. 7 And the earth shall be **[wholly] rent in sunder**, And all that is upon the earth shall perish. And there shall be a judgment upon all (men). 8 But with the righteous He will make peace, And will protect the elect, And mercy shall be upon them. And they shall all belong to Elohim, And they shall be prospered, And they shall [all] be blessed. [And He will help them all], And **light shall appear unto them**, [And He will make peace with them]. 9 And behold! **He cometh with ten thousands of [His] holy ones to execute judgment upon all**. And to destroy [all] the ungodly: And to convict all flesh of all the works [of their ungodliness] which they have ungodly committed, [And of all the hard things which] ungodly sinners [have spoken] against Him.

*Cf. 10:9, 35, 12:4, 13:10, 14:1, 15:2, 16:-2, 91:15. Gen. 6:1, Jub. 10:5; Jude 1:6; 2 Pet. 2:4; Dan. 4:13, 17, 23; "Watchers" corrupted fallen angels.*

*Cf. Ps. 97:5; 2 Pet. 3:7. Only the Final Judgment is by fire not the Flood. This is for a remote generation to come, not the Flood. Mountains during the Flood were carved but not moved.*

*Cf. Deut. 33:2; Dan. 7:10; Jude 1:14-15. Jude quoted 1 En. directy and specifically by name.*

*Holy ones are angels.*

# CHAPTER 2:

1 Observe ye every thing that takes place in the heaven, how **they do not change their orbits**, [and] the luminaries which are in the heaven, how they all rise and set in order each in its season, and **transgress not against their appointed order**. 2 Behold ye the earth, and give heed to the things which take place upon it from first to last, [how steadfast they are], how [none of the things upon earth] change, [but] all the works of Elohim appear [to you]. 3 Behold the summer and the winter, [how the whole earth is filled with water, and clouds and dew and rain lie upon it].

*Cf. Ps. 8:3; Is. 40:26; Jer. 31:35 "and the ordinances of the moon and of the stars..." Fixed orders.*

*Cf. Sir. 16:26-29. "neither labour, nor are weary, nor cease... never disobey."*

*Cf. Gen 2:5. Prior to the Flood, rain would be from the mist that went up from the Earth. Enoch does not change that.*

# CHAPTER 3:

1 Observe and see how (in the winter) all the trees [seem] as though they had withered and shed all their leaves, except **fourteen trees, which do not lose their foliage** but retain the old foliage from two to three years till the new comes.

*Though species would number far greater, Enoch classifies evergreen trees into 14 categories. This actually matches Wikipedia today which renders 14 families of evergreens. Enoch's science is accurate and this serves as evidence that Noah succeeded in the transport of tree families over the Flood. [61]*

# CHAPTER 4:

1 And again, observe ye the days of summer how **the sun is above the earth** over against it. And you seek shade and shelter by reason of the heat of the sun, and the earth also burns with glowing heat, and so you cannot tread on the earth, or on a rock by reason of its heat.

# CHAPTER 5:

1 Observe ye how the trees cover themselves with green leaves and bear fruit: wherefore give ye heed [and know] with regard to all [His works], and recognize how He that liveth forever hath made them so. 2 And [all] His works go on [thus] from year to year [forever], and all the tasks [which] they accomplish for Him, and [their tasks] change not, but according as [Elohim] hath ordained so is it done. 3 And behold how the sea and the rivers in like manner accomplish [and change not] their tasks [from His commandments]. 4. But ye— ye have not been steadfast, nor done the commandments of Yahuah, But ye have turned

*The sun is above the Earth. Enoch did not observe a sphere Earth with a sun 93 million miles away nor has any modern scientist. That is not science by any definition but an ancient, occult religion placing the sun within their worship as the center of all. It requires extreme faith to believe such a theory without a single photo but computer generated images and animations in sorcery. Rev. 18:23 "for by thy sorceries were all nations deceived."*

*Cf. Sir. 18:1. "He that liveth... them so."*

*Cf. 2nd Esd. 4:13-21. Parable of the Forest and the Sea.*

*Cf. 27:2, 101:3. Jude 1:15; Ps. 12:4; Dan. 7:11, 14, 23; Rev. 13:5.*

*In 6-7, Charles breaks these out into sub-verses to reorder in translation. We have represented this order without the confusion.*

*Cf. Ps. 102:9; Is. 65:16, Jer. 29:22.*

*Cf. Jn. 8:12; 9:5. "I am the light of the world."*

away and spoken **proud and hard words** with your impure mouths against His greatness. Oh, ye hard-hearted, ye shall find no peace. 5 Therefore shall ye execrate your days. And the years of your life shall perish. And [the years of your destruction] shall be multiplied in eternal execration. And ye shall find no mercy. 6 In those days ye shall make your names an eternal execration unto all the righteous. And by you shall [all who curse] curse. [And all the sinners [and godless] shall imprecate by you, And for you the godless there shall be a curse. 7 "And all the... shall rejoice, And there shall be forgiveness of sins, And every mercy and peace and forbearance: There shall be salvation unto them, a goodly light. And for all of you sinners

*Cf. Matt. 5:14; Jn. 8:12. "Ye are the light..."*

*Cf. Ps. 25:13, 37:9, 11, 22; Matt. 5:5. "they shall inherit the earth."*

*Cf. Jn. 5:24. "does not come unto judgment."*

*Cf. Jub. 23:27-29; Jn. 3:16, 4:14, 5:11, 24, 10:27-28, 11:25-25; Ps. 37:18*

there shall be no salvation, But on you all shall abide a curse. But for the elect there shall be light and grace and peace, And they shall inherit the earth. 8 And then there shall be bestowed upon the elect wisdom, And they shall all live and never again sin, Either through ungodliness or through pride: But they who are wise shall be humble, 9. And they shall not again transgress, Nor shall they sin all the days of their life. Nor shall they die of (the divine) anger or wrath. But they shall complete the number of the days of their life. And **their lives shall be increased in peace**. And the years of their joy shall be multiplied, in **eternal gladness and peace**. All the days of their life.

# The Fall of the Angels:

the Demoralization of Mankind: the Intercession of the Angels on behalf of Mankind. The Dooms pronounced by Elohim on the Angels: the Messianic Kingdom (a Noah fragment)

## CHAPTER 6:

*Cf. Gen. 6:1; Jub. 5:1.* 1 And it came to pass when the children of men had multiplied that in those days were born unto them beautiful and comely daughters. 2 And the angels, the children of the *Cf. Gen. 6:2; Jub. 5:2.* heaven, saw and lusted after them, and said to one another: 'Come, let us choose us wives *Cf. Gen. 6:2; Jub. 4:22, 5:1. "sinned with the daughters of men."* from among the children of men and beget us children.' 3 And Semyaza, who was their leader, said unto them: 'I fear ye will not indeed agree to do this deed, and I alone shall have to pay the penalty of a great sin.' 4 And they all answered him and said: 'Let *Cf. Jub. 4:15. "days of Jared." As Nephilim spirits are the origin of demons, all theories of Serpent Seed, Lilith or any demon/ Nephilim prior to that is fiction not Bible.* us all swear an oath, and all bind ourselves by mutual imprecations not to abandon this plan but to do this thing.' 5 Then swore they all together and bound themselves by mutual imprecations upon it. *North Israel. Noto: Boforo the Flood, Israel was a defiled land as ground zero for the Watchers and the Nephilim. It was not holy ground Yahuah's I holy of Holies made it so. .* 6 And they were in all **two hundred**; who descended **in the days of Jared** on the summit of **Mount Hermon,** and they called it Mount Hermon because they had sworn and bound themselves by mutual imprecations upon it. 7 And these are the names of their leaders: Semiazaz, their leader Arakiba, Rameel, Kokabiel, Tamiel, Ramiel, Danel, Ezeqeel, Baraqiyal, Asael, Armaros, Batarel, Ananel, Zaqiel, Samsapeel, Satarel, Turel, Yomyael, Sariel. 8 These are their chiefs of tens.

## CHAPTER 7:

1 And all the others together with them took unto themselves wives and each chose for himself one, and they began to go in unto them and to defile themselves with them, and they taught them **charms** and **enchantments**, and the **cutting of roots**, and made them acquainted with plants. 2 And they became pregnant, and **they bare great giants, whose height was three thousand ells**: 3 Who consumed all the acquisitions of men. And when men could no longer sustain them, 4 The giants turned against them and devoured mankind. 5 And they began to sin against birds, and beasts, and reptiles, and fish, and to devour one another's flesh, and drink the blood. 6 Then the earth laid accusation against the lawless ones.

*Cf. Gen. 6:2; Jub. 4:22, 5:1. "sinned with the daughters of men."*

*Cf. Gen. 6:4; Jub. 5:1. "they bare great giants."*

*Cf. Jub. 7:22. Giants, Nephilim, the Eliud(Eljo).*

*Ell means arm which is similar to the manner of a cubit (18" or 45 cm). Before the Flood, no one knows exactly what this measure was. Could be the forearm for that matter. Either wav, some were Titans of epic proportions.*

*Cf. Jub. 5:2, 7:24. "they began to sin against birds and beasts and to devour one's flesh."*

# CHAPTER 8:

*Cf. Gen. 4:22. Tubalcain from Cain's lineage was an instructor in metalwork. He learned from Azazel and this is a direct tie to Cain and the Nephilim. His sister, Namaah was known as a Nephilim breeder and she did not marry Noah which is an occult lie.*

1 And **Azazel** taught men to make swords, and knives, and shields, and breastplates, and **made known to them the metals (of the earth) and the art of working them**, and bracelets, and ornaments, and the use of antimony, and the **beautifying of the eyelids**, and all kinds of costly stones, and all coloring tinctures.

*Cf. Jub. 7:21. They made the beginning of uncleanness.*

*This is occult doctrine still today deriving from these Fallen Angel teachings. All these things are against Yahuah's ways and the opposite of the Bible. Anyone trying to use these doctrines in Bible interpretation is a deceiver knowingly or not. i.e. Witchcraft, freemasonry, sorcery, sun and moon worship, earth worship, astrology, etc.*

2 And there arose much godlessness, and they committed **fornication**, and they were led astray, and became corrupt in all their ways. 3 **Semyaza** taught **enchantments**, and root-cuttings, **Armaros** the resolving of enchantments, **Baraqiyal** (taught) **astrology**, **Kokabel** the **constellations**, **Ezeqeel** the knowledge of the **clouds**, (**Araqiel** the signs of the **earth**, **Shamsiel** the signs of the **sun**), and **Sariel** the course of the **moon**. 4 And as men perished, they cried, and their cry went up to heaven...

# CHAPTER 9:

*Cf. Jub. 7:23. Shed much blood... earth filled with iniquity.*

1 And then Michael, Uriel, Raphael, and Gabriel looked down from heaven and saw much blood being shed upon the earth, and all lawlessness being wrought upon the earth.

*Cf. 9:11,15:2, 40:7, 47:2, 99:3; Rev. 8:3-4 "Angel with golden censer of incense."*

2 And they said one to another; 'The earth made without inhabitant cries the voice of their crying up to the gates of heaven. 3 And now to you, the holy ones of heaven, the souls of men make their suit, saying, Bring our cause before the Most High.' 4 And they said to Yahuah of the ages: 'Lord of lords, El of Elohim. King of kings (and Elohim of the ages), the throne of Thy glory (standeth) unto all the generations of the ages, and Thy name holy and glorious and blessed unto all the ages!

*Cf. 84:2 "King of Kings." 1Tim. 6:15; Rev 17:14, 19:16.*

*Cf. Heb. 4:13. "There is no creature that is not manifest in His sight: but all things are naked and laid open before the eyes of Him with whom we have to do."*

5 Thou hast made all things, and power over all things hast Thou: and all things are naked and open in Thy sights and all things Thou seest and nothing can hide itself from Thee.

6 Thou seest what Azazel hath done, who hath taught all unrighteousness on earth and revealed the eternal secrets which were (preserved) in heaven, which men were striving to learn: 7 And Semyaza, to whom Thou hast given authority to bear rule over his associates. 8 And they have gone to the daughters of men upon the earth, and have slept with the women, and have defiled themselves, and revealed to them all kinds

*Cf. Jub. 7:21. They made the beginning of uncleanness.*

*Cf. Gen. 6:2; Jub. 4:22, 5:1. "sinned with the daughters of men."*

of sins. 9 And the women have borne giants, and the whole earth has thereby been filled with blood and unrighteousness. 10 And now, behold, the souls of those who have died are crying and making their suit to the gates of heaven, and their lamentations have ascended: and cannot cease because of the **lawless deeds** which are wrought on the earth.

11. And Thou knowest all things before they come to pass, and Thou seest these things and Thou dost suffer them, and Thou dost not say to us what we are to do to them in regard to these.'

Cf. 22:5-7; Gen. 4:10. Yahuah hears the blood of the martyred innocent cry out.

Cf. 9:1-3,15:2, 40:7, 47:2, 99:3; Rev. 8:3-4 "Angel with golden censer of incense."

Cf. Jub. 7:21, 4:22. Deluge due to Watchers' sin, not an angry God who hates mankind which is inept.

# CHAPTER 10:

1 Then said the Most High, the Holy and Great One spake, and sent Uriel to the son of Lamech, and said to him: 2 '(Go to Noah and) tell him in my name "Hide thyself!" and reveal to him the end that is approaching: that the whole earth will be destroyed, and a deluge is about to come upon the whole earth, and will destroy all that is on it. 3 And now instruct him that he may escape and his seed may be preserved for all the generations of the world.'

Cf. Gen. 6:13; Jub. 5:19-21.

4 And again Yahuah said to Raphael: 'Bind Azazel hand and foot, and cast him into the darkness: and make an opening in the desert, which is in **Dudael**, and cast him therein. 5 And place upon him rough and jagged rocks, and cover him with darkness, and let him abide there for ever, and cover his face that he may not see light. 6 And on the day of the great judgment he shall be cast into the fire. 7 And heal the earth which the angels have corrupted, and proclaim the healing of the earth, that they may heal the plague, and that all the children of men may not perish through all the secret things that the Watchers have disclosed and have taught their sons. 8 And the whole earth has been corrupted through the works that were taught by Azazel: to him ascribe all sin.' 9 And to Gabriel said Yahuah 'Proceed against the bastards and the reprobates, and against the children of fornication: and destroy [the children of fornication and] the children of the Watchers from amongst men: [and cause them to go forth]: send them one against the other that they may destroy each other in battle: for length of days shall they not have. 10 And no request that they (i. e. their

Cf. Dudael (Heb. דודאל, compd. of dud דוד "kettle", "cauldron", "pot" + El אל "deity", "divinity" — lit. "cauldron of God"). [24] It is the same place as Duidain from 60:8 on the East of the Garden where the righteous (Adam's generations) dwelt until the Flood[6]. Havilah, Philippines. The world's largest caldera where Raphael once opened the earth is located just to the East of the Philippines in the Benham Rise known as "Apolaki Caldera." It is "a volcanic caldera with a diameter of ~150 km (93 miles), twice the size of Yellowstone." [23]

Raphael: רפה רפא ':(rapa'), to heal, El אל: "Healing of Elohim." [7] Cf. Jub. 7:21. They made the beginning of uncleanness. Cf. Jub. 5:7, 9, 7:22.. Destruction of the angels' children by sword. Cf. Gen. 6:3. Cf. Gen. 6:2; Jub. 4:22, 5:1. "sinned with the daughters of men."

Nephilim lifespans limited to 500 years. Eternal life and salvation is not available to them.

Cf. Jub. 5:6, 10, 10:7. Watchers bound within the earth.

Cf. Jub. 5:7, 9, 7:22. each slay his neighbor.

Cf. Jub. 5:10. their fathers witness their destruction.

Cf. 93, 2Esd. 7:31; Dan. 8. "70 generations... to end of all generations (14) = 7,000 years. See charts Ch. 93. The Watchers are not released until the Day of Judgment in which they are destroyed. They don't return and such narrative has never fit Enoch. Cf. Jude 1:6, 2 Pet. 2:4. Jude and Peter knew this. Cf. Rev. 20:11-15, Jn. 5:24.

Cf. Jub. 1:6, 16:26.

Messiah, not Israel. Cf. 93:2, 5, 10; Jub. 16:26, 21:24, 36:6.

fathers) make of thee shall be granted unto their fathers on their behalf; for they hope to live an eternal life, and that each one of them will live five hundred years.' 11 And Yahuah said unto Michael: 'Go, bind Semyaza and his associates who have united themselves with women so as to have defiled themselves with them in all their uncleanness.

12 And, when their sons have slain one another, and they have seen the destruction of their beloved ones, bind them fast for **seventy generations** in the valleys of the earth, until the day of their judgment and of their consummation, until the judgment that is for ever and ever is consummated.

13 In those days they shall be led off to the abyss of fire: (and) to the torment and the prison in which they shall be confined for ever. 14 And whosoever shall be condemned and destroyed will from thenceforth be bound together with them **to the end of all generations.**

15 And destroy all the spirits of the reprobate and the children of the Watchers, because they have wronged mankind.

16 Destroy all wrong from the face of the earth and let every evil work come to an end: and let the **plant of righteousness** and truth appear: and it shall prove a blessing: the works of righteousness and truth shall be planted in truth and joy for evermore. 17 And then shall all the righteous escape, And shall live till they beget thousands of children, And all the days of their youth and their old age shall they complete in peace. 18 And then shall the whole earth be tilled in righteousness, and shall all be planted with trees and be full of blessing.

Cf. Jub. 23:27-29; Jn. 10:28-30; 1 Jn. 2:17; Heb. 7:25.

Cf. Rev. 2:7; 22:1-5; Is. 51:3; Ez. 35:35.

19 And all desirable trees shall be planted on it, and they shall plant vines on it: and the vine which they plant thereon shall yield wine in abundance, and as for all the seed which is sown thereon each measure (of it) shall bear a thousand, and each measure of olives shall yield ten presses of oil. 20 And cleanse thou the earth from all oppression, and from all unrighteousness, and from all sin, and from all godlessness: and all the uncleanness that is wrought upon the earth destroy from off the earth.

21 'And all the children of men shall become righteous, and all nations shall offer adoration and shall praise Me, and all shall worship] Me. 22 And the earth shall be cleansed from all defilement, and from all sin, and from all punishment, and from

all torment, and I will never again send (them) upon it from generation to generation and for ever.

## CHAPTER 11:

1 And in those days I will open the store chambers of blessing which are in the heaven, so as to send them down upon the earth over the work and labor of the children of men. 2 And truth and peace shall be associated together throughout all the day's of the world and throughout all the generations of men.'

# 12-16 DREAM VISION OF ENOCH:

# CHAPTER 12:

# CHAPTER 13:

1 Before these things Enoch was hidden, and no one of the children of men knew where he was hidden, and where he abode, and what had become of him. 2 And his activities had to do with the Watchers and his days were with the holy ones. 3 And I Enoch was blessing Yahuah of majesty and the King of the ages, and lo! the Watchers called me—Enoch the scribe—and said to me: 4 'Enoch thou scribe of righteousness, go, declare to the Watchers of the heaven who have left the high heaven, the holy eternal place, and have defiled themselves with women, and have done as the children of earth do, and have taken unto themselves wives: "Ye have wrought great destruction on the earth:

5 And ye shall have no peace nor forgiveness of sin: and inasmuch as they delight themselves in their children,

6. The murder of their beloved ones shall they see, and over the destruction of their children shall they lament, and shall make supplication unto eternity, but mercy and peace shall ye not attain."

*Cf. Jub. 4:21.*

*Cf. Jub. 10:5. "Watchers."*

*Cf. Jub. 4:21. "testified to Watchers."*

*Cf. Jub. 4:17, 23. "Enoch the scribe."*

*Cf. Gen. 6:2; Jub. 4:22, 5:1. "sinned with the daughters of men."*

*Cf. Jub. 5:10. their fathers witness their destruction.*

1 And Enoch went and said: 'Azazel, thou shalt have no peace: a severe sentence has gone forth against thee to put thee in bonds: 2 And thou shalt not have toleration nor request granted to thee, because of the unrighteousness which thou hast taught, and because of all the works of godlessness and unrighteousness and sin which thou hast shown to men.'

3 Then I went and spoke to them all together, and they were all afraid, and fear and trembling seized them. 4 And they besought me to draw up a petition for them that they might find forgiveness, and to read their petition in the presence of Yahuah of heaven. 5 For from thenceforward they could not speak (with Him) nor lift up their eyes to heaven for shame of their sins for which they had been condemned. 6 Then I wrote out their petition; and the prayer in regard to their spirits and their deeds individually and in regard to their requests that they should have forgiveness and length.

7 And I went off and sat down at the waters of Dan, in the **land of Dan, to the south of the west of Hermon:**

*Cf. Jub. 4:21. "testified to Watchers."*

*Note: The Watchers did not war in Heaven neither have any angels in all of scripture until the future event in Rev. 12.*

*Cf. Gen. 6:3. Notice how, this is the place where Daniel 8 predicted an enemy would rise to defile and usurp the Temple and its practice, the Pharisees. Same as Modi'in where the Maccabees originated who fulfilled that and Ps. 83 from this place of the Watchers.*

I read their petition till I fell asleep. 8 And behold a dream came to me, and visions fell down upon me, and I saw visions of chastisement, and a voice came bidding (me) to tell it to the sons of heaven, and reprimand them. 9 And when I awaked, I came unto them, and they were all sitting gathered together, weeping in **Abelsjail, which is between Lebanon and Seneser**, with their faces covered, 10 And I recounted before them all the visions which I had seen in sleep, and I began to speak the words of righteousness, and to reprimand the heavenly Watchers.

*Abelsjail. This is what would become Northern Israel, a defiled and unholy land before the Flood. Abel never lived there. This is named in a negative fashion as Cain's lineage mingled with the Watchers who taught how to kill men in fact. Perhaps this areas was named for either training ground for soldiers or prisons for men.*

# CHAPTER 14:

1 The book of the words of righteousness, and of the reprimand of the eternal Watchers in accordance with the command of the Holy Great One in that vision. 2 I saw in my sleep what I will now say with a tongue of flesh and with the breath of my mouth: which the Great One has given to men to converse therewith and understand with the heart. 3 As He has created and given to man the power of understanding the word of wisdom so hath He created me also and given me the power of reprimanding the Watchers the children of heaven. 4 I wrote out your petition, and in my vision it appeared thus, that your petition will not be granted unto you throughout all the days of eternity, and that judgment has been finally passed upon you: yea (your petition) will not be granted unto you" 5 And from henceforth you shall not ascend into heaven unto all eternity, and in bonds of the earth the decree has gone forth to bind you for all the days of the world. 6 And (that) previously you shall have seen the destruction of your beloved sons and ye shall have no pleasure in them, but they shall fall before you by the sword. 7 And your petition on their behalf shall not be granted, nor yet on your own: even though you weep and pray and speak all the words contained in the writing which I have written. 8 And the vision was shown to me thus: Behold, in the vision clouds invited me and a mist summoned me, and the course of the stars and the lightnings

*Cf. Jub. 4:21. "testified to Watchers."*

*Imagine the faith of Enoch who stood rebuking 200 powerful angels.*

*Cf. Jub. 5:10. their fathers witness their destruction.*

*Cf. Jub. 5:7. Destruction of the angels' children by sword.*

sped and hastened me, and the winds in the vision caused me to fly and lifted me upward, and bore me into heaven.

9 And I went in till I drew nigh to a wall which is built of crystals and surrounded by tongues of fire: and it began to affright me. 10 And I went into the tongues of fire and drew nigh to a large house which was built of crystals: and the walls of the house were like a tessellated floor (made) of crystals, and its groundwork was of crystal. 11 Its ceiling was like the path of the stars and the lightnings, and between them were fiery cherubim, and their heaven was (clear as) water. 12 A flaming fire surrounded the walls, and its portals blazed with fire. 13 And I entered into that house, and it was hot as fire and cold as ice: there were no delights of life therein: fear covered me, and trembling gat hold upon me. 14 And as I quaked and trembled, I fell upon my face. And I beheld a vision. 15 And lo! there was a second house, greater than the former and the entire portal stood open before me, and it was built of flames of fire. 16 And in every respect it so excelled in splendor and magnificence and extent that I cannot describe to you its splendor and its extent. 17 And its floor was of fire, and above it were lightnings and the path of the stars, and its ceiling also was flaming fire. 18 And I looked and saw therein a lofty throne: its appearance was as crystal, and the wheels thereof as the shining sun, and there was the vision of cherubim. 19 And from underneath the throne came streams of flaming fire so that I could not look thereon. 20 And the Great Glory sat thereon, and His raiment shone more brightly than the sun and was whiter than any snow. 21 None of the angels could enter and could behold His face by reason of the magnificence and glory, and no flesh could behold Him. 22 The flaming fire was round about Him, and a great fire stood before Him, and none around could draw nigh Him: ten thousand times ten thousand (stood) before Him, yet He needed no counsellor. 23 And the most holy ones who were nigh to Him did not leave by night nor depart from Him. 24 And until then I had been prostrate on my face, trembling; and Yahuah called me with His own mouth, and said to me: 'Come hither,

*Cf. 60:2, 90:20; Dan. 7; 1 Ki. 22:19; Is. 6; Ez. 1, 3:22-24, 10:1. Biblical throne visions that match.*

*Cf. 1 Tim. 6:16. "Dwelling in the light which no man can approach unto, whom no man hath seen."*

*Cf. 40:1, 71:8; Rev. 5:11.*

Enoch, and hear my word.'
25 And one of the holy ones came to me and waked me, and He made me rise up and approach the door: and I bowed my face downwards.

# CHAPTER 15:

Cf. Jub. 4:17, 23. "Enoch the scribe of righteousness."

Cf. Jub. 4:21. "testified to Watchers."

Cf. 9:1-3,11, 40:7, 47:2, 99:3; Rev. 8:3-4 "Angel with golden censer of incense."

Men do not pray to or for angels. Cf. Gen. 6:3; Jude 1:6; 2 Pet. 2:4. Cf. Gen. 6:2; Jub. 4:22, 5:1. "sinned with the daughters of men."

Cf. Gen. 6:4; Jub. 5:1. "they bare great giants."

Cf. Jub. 7:21. Against the law of their ordinances.

1 And He answered and said to me, and I heard His voice: 'Fear not, Enoch, thou righteous man and scribe of righteousness: approach hither and hear my voice. 2 And go, say to the Watchers of heaven, who have sent thee to intercede for them: You should intercede for men, and not men for you: 3 Wherefore have ye left the high, holy, and eternal heaven, and lain with women, and defiled yourselves with the daughters of men and taken to yourselves wives, and done like the children of earth, and begotten giants (as your) sons. 4 And though ye were holy, spiritual, living the eternal life, you have defiled yourselves with the blood of women, and have begotten (children) with the blood of flesh, and, as the children of men, have lusted after flesh and blood as those also do who die and perish. 5 Therefore have I given them wives also that they might impregnate them and beget children by them, that thus nothing might be wanting to them on earth. 6 But you were formerly spiritual, living the eternal life, and immortal for all generations of the world. 7 And therefore I have not appointed wives for you; for as for the spiritual ones of the heaven, in heaven is their dwelling. 8 And now, the giants, who are produced from the spirits and flesh, shall be called evil spirits upon the earth, and on the earth shall be their dwelling. 9 Evil spirits have proceeded from their bodies; because they are born from men, and from the holy watchers is their beginning and primal origin; they shall be evil spirits on earth, and evil spirits shall they be called. [10 As for the spirits of heaven, in heaven shall be their dwelling, but as for the spirits of the earth which were born upon the earth, on the earth shall be their dwelling.] 11 And the spirits of the giants afflict, oppress, destroy, attack, do battle, and work destruction on the earth, and cause trouble: they take no food, but nevertheless hunger and thirst, and cause offences. 12 And these spirits shall rise up against the children of men and against the women, because they have proceeded from them.

Cf. Gen 1:28.

Cf. Matt. 22:30; Mark 12:25. Angels are not to marry. They do not in Heaven but can in human form. This is what Luke 17:27 refers as well.

Origin of demons. Cf. Jub. 10:1, 11:5. Giants called evil spirits. Yahuah did not create them.

Unlike men, there are no chambers for Nephilim evil spirits to rest. They crawl the dry places of the Earth hoping to possess a mankind if invited.

These are demons.

Cf. Eph 6:12.

# CHAPTER 16:

**1** From the days of the slaughter and destruction and death of the giants, from the souls of whose flesh the spirits, having gone forth, shall destroy without incurring judgment—thus shall they destroy until the day of the consummation, the great judgment in which the age shall be consummated, over the Watchers and the godless, yea, shall be wholly consummated." **2** And now as

*Demons are among us until the Day of Judgment. The Flood did not end the damage of the Watchers. Their offense has ruined the Earth once and will bring it to ruin again.*

*The Watchers were not all-knowing and their "Golden Age" was that of incomplete knowledge from Heaven. They were epic failures and their doctrines worthless.*

to the Watchers who have sent thee to intercede for them, who had been aforetime in heaven, (say to them): 3 **"You have been in heaven, but all the mysteries had not yet been revealed to you, and you knew worthless ones**, and these in the hardness of your hearts you have made known to the women; and through these mysteries women and men work much evil on earth." 4 Say to them therefore: "You have no peace."

# Enoch's Journeys through the Earth and Sheol

**Jude 1:9 KJV** And the angels which kept not their first estate, but left their own habitation, he hath reserved in **everlasting chains under darkness unto the judgment of the great day**.

## 17-19 The First Journey: Inner Earth

# CHAPTER 17:

*Enoch enters the interior of the Earth.*

*Angels can take on the form of man throughout the Bible.*

*Heavenly Mt. Zion at the North Pole. Enoch's perspective remains from within the Earth.*

*Cf. Job 37:3.*

*Pacific Ocean region. Perhaps the International Date Line or close. The West gates.*

*This appears the Ring of Fire and the sea or large body of water likely the Pison River from Eden.*

*Cf. Gen. 2:10. Before the Flood, there were 5 great rivers. The River From Eden itself is the greatest or largest.*

*"No flesh walks" within the Earth.*

*Fountains of Great Deep flow down into the Earth.*

**1** And they took and brought me to a place in which those who were there were like flaming fire and when they wished, they appeared as men. **2** And they brought me to the place of darkness, and to a mountain the point of whose summit reached to heaven. **3** And I saw the places of the luminaries and the treasuries of the stars and of the thunder, and in the uttermost depths, where were a fiery bow and arrows and their quiver, and a fiery sword and all the lightnings. **4** And they took me to the living waters, and to the fire of the west, which receives every setting of the sun. **5** And I came to a river of fire in which the fire flows like water and discharges itself into the great sea towards the west. **6** I saw the great rivers and came to the great river and to the great darkness and went to the place where no flesh walks. **7** I saw the mountains of the darkness of winter and the place whence all the waters of the deep flow. **8** I saw the mouths of all the rivers of the earth and the mouth of the deep.

# CHAPTER 18:

*Cf. Ps 104:5, 75:3, 93:1; 1 Sam. 2:8; 1 Chr. 16:30; Is. 40:22 (Circle is 2D not a ball; Job 26:7-10 Enoch saw a cornerstone and foundations.*

*Cf. Job 9:8, 22:14; 1 Sam. 2:8; Jer. 51:15.*

*Cf. 1 Sam. 2:8; "...for the pillars of the earth are the LORD'S, and he hath set the world upon thom." Job 9:6, 26:11; Ps. 75:3.*

*Cf. Sun and moon move. Ps. 19:4-6; Jos. 10:13; Hab 3:11.*

*Cf. Gen 1:6-20; Ps. 19:1; Job 37:18. The Bible has always had only this paradigm.*

*Cf. Jub. 4:26. "Mount of the East." 4Q529, 6Q23.*

*Cf. Gen. 2:12-13. Ancient Havilah, land of Havah, Eve is defined by gold, pearl and the onyx stone The modern Philippines in the Far East.*

**1** I saw the treasuries of all the winds; I saw how He had furnished with them the whole creation and the firm foundations of the earth. **2** And I saw the cornerstone of the earth: I saw the four winds which bear [the earth and] the **firmament** of the heaven. **3** And I saw how the winds **stretch out the vaults of heaven**, and have their station between heaven and earth: these are the **pillars of the heaven**. **4** I saw the winds of heaven which turn and bring the circumference of the sun and all the stars to their setting. **5** I saw the winds on the earth carrying the clouds: I saw the paths of the angels: I saw **at the end of the earth the firmament of the heaven above**. **6** And I proceeded and saw a place which burns day and night, where there are **seven mountains of magnificent stones, three** towards the **east**, and **three** towards the **south. 7** And as for those towards the east (one) was of **colored stone**, and one of **pearl**, and one of **jacinth** and those towards the south of red stone. **8** But the **middle one reached to heaven like the throne of Elohim**, of **alabaster**, and the summit of the throne was of sapphire. **9** And I saw a flaming fire. And beyond these mountains **10** Is a region the end of the great earth: there the heavens were completed. **11** And I saw a deep abyss, with columns of heavenly fire, and among them I saw columns of fire fall, which were beyond measure alike towards the height and towards the depth. **12** And beyond that abyss I saw a place which had no firmament of the heaven above, and no firmly founded earth beneath it: there was no water upon it, and no birds, but it was a waste and horrible place.

**13** I saw there **seven stars** like great burning mountains, and to me, when I inquired regarding them, **14** The angel said: 'This place is the end of heaven and earth: this has become a prison for the stars and the host of heaven. **15** And the stars which roll over the fire are they which have transgressed the commandment of Yahuah in the beginning of their rising, because they did not come forth at their appointed times. **16** And He was wroth with them, and bound them till the time when their guilt should be consummated (even) for ten thousand years.

# CHAPTER 19:

**1** And Uriel said to me: 'Here shall stand the angels who have connected themselves with women, and their spirits assuming many different forms are defiling mankind and shall lead them astray into sacrificing to demons as gods, (here shall they stand), till the day of the great judgment in which they shall be judged till they are made an end of. **2** And the women also of the angels who went astray shall become sirens. **3** And I, Enoch, alone saw the vision, the ends of all things: and no man shall see as I have seen.



---

**PETER READ 1 ENOCH AS INSPIRED SCRIPTURE:**

**2 Peter 2:4 KJV** For if God spared not the angels that sinned, but **cast them down to hell** (Tartaroō: ταρταρόω: Tartarus), **and delivered them into chains of darkness, to be reserved unto judgment;**

# 20 NAMES AND FUNCTIONS OF THE SEVEN ARCHANGELS

## CHAPTER 20:

Cf. "Uriel" 2 Esd. "Raphael" Tobit.

**1** And these are the names of the holy angels who watch.

Cf. 2 Pet. 2:4. ταρταρόω Tartarus = lowest Hell. G5020

Spirits/Souls of men are in the chambers not Tartarus.

Luminaries have a separate judgment.

**2 Uriel**, one of the holy angels, who is *over the world and over Tartarus*. **3 Raphael**, one of the holy angels, who is over the *spirits of men*. **4 Raguel**, one of the holy angels who *takes vengeance on the world of the luminaries*. **5 Michael**, one of the holy angels, to wit, he that is *set over the best part of mankind and over chaos*. **6 Saraqael**, one of the holy angels, who is *set over the spirits, who sin in the spirit*. **7 Gabriel**, one of the holy angels, who is *over Paradise and the serpents and the Cherubim*. **8 Remiel**, one of the holy angels, whom Elohim *set over those who rise*.

Cf. Dan. 10:13,21, 12:1, Jude 1:9, 2Th. 2:6-8, Rev. 12:7. Michael , the restrainer, guards the righteous from chaos. Cf. Jub. 35:17. Michael set over best part of mankind.

Garden of Eden. Serpents = Angels.

Cf.40:9. Remiel = Phanuel.

## QUMRAN SCROLLS MENTION ANGELS BY NAME ALSO:

In addition to scripture, the local community writings also mention four of these archangels:
"Michael, Gabriel, Sariel, and Raphael" - The War Scroll, p. 174, The Book of War p. 188 [Vermes]
"Michael" - The War Scroll P. 183, Words of the Archangel Michael, p. 556. A Zedekiah Apocryphon p. 591 [Vermes]
"Gabriel" in the Garden of Eden in the East. - Words of the Archangel Michael, p. 556. [Vermes]

Thus, 5 of these 7 are mentioned outside of Enoch as Uriel is the main angel in 2nd Esdras. Raguel is out of view for everyone but Enoch who saw the chamber where he disciplines the lumary angels. Remiel is also in a hidden role not one Israel would encounter.

## GABRIEL, ANGEL OF THE EAST FROM THE GARDEN OF EDEN

Enoch places the Garden of Eden in the Far East with Gabriel in charge now. This is consistent with scripture in Revelation 7:2-3 "And I saw another angel ascending from the east, having the seal of the living God: and he cried with a loud voice to the four angels, to whom it was given to hurt the earth and the sea, Saying, Hurt not the earth, neither the sea, nor the trees, till we have sealed the servants of our God in their foreheads." Only an Archangel would have such authority. Notice Gabriel ascended out of the Earth from the Garden in which he is in charge. He is also in the very presence of Yahuah there not in Heaven but within the Earth. In Luke 1:19 "And the angel answering said unto him, I am Gabriel, that stand in the presence of God;" Gabriel is not in Heaven but in the Garden of Eden in Yahuah's Holy of Holies within the Earth just as Enoch witnessed affirmed by the Book of Jubilees.

# 21-36
# THE SECOND JOURNEY OF ENOCH: INNER EARTH

## 21
## PRELIMINARY AND FINAL PLACE OF PUNISHMENT OF THE FALLEN ANGELS (STARS)

### CHAPTER 21:

**1**. And I proceeded to where things were chaotic. **2** And I saw there something horrible: I saw neither a heaven above nor a firmly founded earth, but a place chaotic and horrible.

*Cf. Deut. 32:22 and Ps. 86:13. Lowest Sheol within the Earth.*

**3**. And there I saw **seven stars** of the heaven bound together in it, like great mountains and burning with fire. **4** Then I said: 'For what sin are they bound, and on what account have they been cast in hither?'

*Cf. 18:13. Same stars. See margin note.*

*Cf. 18:15; Jude 1:13. 'Wandering stars."*

**5**. Then said Uriel, one of the holy angels, who was with me, and was chief over them, and said: 'Enoch, why dost thou ask, and why art thou eager for the truth? **6** These are of the number of the stars of heaven which have transgressed the commandment of Yahuah, and are bound here till ten thousand years, the time entailed by their sins, are

*Cf. 20:2. Uriel, chief over Tartarus, "lowest Hell." Also, Gehenna in Greek.*

*Cf. 19:3. See margin note.*

consummated." **7**. And from thence I went to another place, which was still more horrible than the former, and I saw a horrible thing: a great fire there which burnt and blazed, and the place was cleft as far as the abyss, being full of great descending columns of fire: neither its extent or magnitude could I see, nor could I conjecture. **8** Then I said: 'How fearful is the place and how terrible to look upon! **9**. Then Uriel answered me, one of the holy angels who was with me, and said unto me: 'Enoch, why hast thou such fear and affright?' And I answered: 'Because of this fearful place, and because of the spectacle of the pain.' **10**. And he said unto me: 'This place is the prison of the angels, and here they will be imprisoned for ever.'

*The Watchers do not return nor escape. That doctrine never came from Enoch.*

# 22
# SHEOL OR THE UNDERWORLD

## CHAPTER 22:

*Enoch leaves Tartarus/ Gehenna where there were only fallen angels and no men. No men go to that Hell until the Day of Judgment in ALL of scripture.*

*Cf. Luke 16:24. This is the fountain from which the Rich Man requested water from Lazarus. He was not in Gehenna and only awake on the Day of Judgment.*

*Spirit and soul are one in application. Body is separate. Man is a 2-part being not 3.*

*Al l = all.*

**1** And thence I went to another place, and he showed me in the west "another" great and high mountain [and] of hard rock. **2** And there were four hollow places in it, deep and very smooth: three of them were dark and one bright and there was a fountain of water in its midst. And I said: 'How smooth are these hollow places, and deep and dark to view.' **3** Then Raphael answered, one of the holy angels who was with me, and said unto me: 'These hollow places have been created for this very purpose, that the **spirits of the souls of the dead should assemble** therein, yea that **all the souls of the children of men** should assemble here. **4** And these places have been made to receive them **till the day of their judgment and till their appointed period** [till the period appointed], **till the great judgment** (comes) upon them.' **5** I saw (the spirit of) a dead man making suit, and his voice went forth to heaven and made suit. **6** And I asked Raphael the angel who was with me, and I said unto him: 'This spirit which maketh suit, whose is it, whose voice goeth forth and maketh suit to heaven? **7** And he answered me saying: 'This is the spirit which went forth from Abel, whom his brother Cain slew, and he makes his suit against him till his seed is destroyed from the face of the earth, and his seed is annihilated from amongst the seed of men. **8** Then I asked regarding all the hollow places: 'Why is one separated from the other? **9** And he answered me saying:

*Cf. 47:2, 97:3-5, 99:3, 16, 104:3; Rev. 6:10 "Righteous souls cry out for vengeance."*

*Martyr's chamber. Cf. Gen. 4:10-11. Yahuah heard Abel's blood cry out from within the Earth from this same chamber. "..earth, which hath opened her mouth to receive thy brother's blood." Abel's spirit was already within the Earth. Heb 11:4 "by it he being dead yet apeaketh." Abel speaks from the grave. His spirit cries out even still.*

'These three have been made that the spirits of the dead might be separated. And this division has been made for the spirits of the righteous in which there is the bright spring of water. **10** And this has been made for sinners when they die and are buried in the earth and judgment has not been executed upon them in their lifetime. **11** Here their spirits shall be set apart in this great pain, till the great day of judgment, scourgings, and torments of the accursed for ever, so that (there may be) retribution for their spirits. There He shall bind them for ever. **12** And this division has been made for the spirits of those who make their suit, who make disclosures concerning their destruction, when they were slain in the days of the sinners. **13** And this has been made for the spirits of men who shall not be righteous but sinners, who are godless, and of the lawless they shall be companions: but their spirits shall not be punished in the day of judgment nor shall they be raised from thence.' **14** Then I blessed Yahuah of Glory and said: 'Blessed art Thou, Yahuah of righteousness, who rulest over the world.'

*3 chambers for the spirits of the dead: 1. Martyrs, 2. Holy 3. Wicked. Cf. 1 Pet. 3:18. These are separated by walls and enclosed as Peter calls them "prisons." Cf. 22:1-2. They are within a mountain.*

*Cf. Luke 16:24. These chambers and the fountain are confirmed by Messiah.*

*Sinners' spirits in pain knowing their judgment. They are not burning yet.*

*Sinners are not bound or burning yet. Just in their chamber sleeping.*

*Martyrs' spirits cry out making suit in their sleep. They are still resting. Yahuah desires to hear their accusation for the innocent blood shed.*

# WHAT IS HELL? BIBLE TERMS AND USAGE:

Many scholars confuse the term Hell when they see it only in English without qualifying it's use and the actual Hebrew or Greek word employed. When one conducts such a word study, it becomes obvious there is a general term for the Inner Earth which can be used for the entire underworld or sometimes specific to the chambers where spirits sleep or the angel prison known in Enoch as Tartarus repeated by Peter. In the Greek, the Lake of Fire which resides in the "lowest hell" or "the pit" is typically rendered as Gehenna not Hades. This is because the Inner Earth is far more complex just as Enoch describes in his tour of it. He is the only to take such tour thus this is called science. Your professor nor any scientist, academic nor scholar has not. Scripture agrees with Enoch not their occult world.

**General Underworld or Inner Earth:**
**Sheol:** שאול: *sheol, underworld, grave, hell, pit: H7585.*
*Deut. 32:22 and Psa. 86:13 define a "lowest Sheol" which is the Fallen Angel Prison (Tartarus) with the Lake of Fire not the entire underworld. Many passages which refer to Sheol and the lowest Hell as one are referencing the timing of the Day of Judgment when the chambers of sleeping souls are resurrected and the underworld then, opens and becomes the Lake of Fire. Cf. Isa. 5:13 "hell hath enlarged herself, and opened her mouth without measure."*
**Hadēs:** ᾅδης: *unseen, i.e. "Hades" or the place (state) of departed souls:—grave, hell. G86. (General term)*

**The Lake of Fire:**
**Géenna:** γέεννα: *Hell is the place of the future punishment called "Gehenna" or "Gehenna of fire". G1067.*
**Tartaroō:** ταρταρόω: *(the deepest abyss of Hades); to incarcerate in eternal torment:—cast down to hell. G5020. Specifically, the Fallen Angel prison in 2 Pet. 2:4 which is the same Hebrew Tartarus of Enoch.*

# INNER EARTH (SHEOL/HADES) CHAMBERS

Note: The Hebrew Sheol (שאול) or Greek Hades (ᾅδης) is not a reference to only what we call Hell but this entire Inner Earth. In fact, the Hell of Sheol is not for men but Fallen Angels and their progeny. David *(Ps. 139:8)* and Luke are not telling us Messiah went into Hell *(Acts 2:31)* nor that they would *(Acts 2:27)* but into the Inner Earth into these chambers Enoch observed on his journey.



The Garden Of Eden is Yahuah's Holy of Holies on Earth *(Jub. 8:19)* thus, these chambers are in His presence just as Paul says they are *(2Cor. 5)*. The spirits of the dead are with Him but not in Heaven nor Hell. That modern church doctrine originates in the Egyptian Book of the Dead NOT the Bible. Watch "Where Do We Go When We Die?" (YouTube, Rumble, Utreon, Odyssey: The God Culture).

# MESSIAH'S DEATH AND RESURRECTION AFFIRM 1 ENOCH

Prior to His death, Yahusha defines that no man has ascended to Heaven to reside prior to Him *(John 3:12)*. This includes Enoch and Elijah *(Gen. 5:24; 2 Ki. 1:1, 11)*. Jubilees reports Enoch was conducted into the Garden of Eden to reside *(Jub. 4:23-26)*, and Enoch saw prophetically Elijah would join him in the Garden *(1 Enoch 89:52)*. To live this long without death requires eating of the Tree of Life which remains in the Garden. Neither are in Heaven. We prove Enoch is still alive in our YouTube, Rumble, Utreon or Odyssey video "Where Did Enoch Go?"

Upon Messiah's death, Yahusha went into the chamber called Abraham's Bosom inside the Earth *(Eph. 4:7-10)*. There, He awakened and preached to the spirits of the dead *(1 Peter 3:18)*. When resurrected, He took 500 of these spirits He had awakened with Him to Jerusalem not Heaven *(1 Cor. 15:6, Matt 27:52-53)*. Previously, he had already awakened Moses who appeared on the Mount of Transfiguration *(Matt. 17)*. Also, Abraham knew of Moses likely having then met him in the spirit which is how he would know in the story of Lazarus and the Rich Man of the writings of Moses and the prophets *(Luke 16)*. Who else but these patriarchs would be among those awakened by Yahusha?

In Daniel 12:13, the prophet is told in the Last Days, he, too, will line up with his lot to be judged. The souls in these chambers did not go to Heaven but returned to sleep awaiting the Day of Judgment. When sleeping, our spirits are not conscious as the dead know nothing *(Eccl. 9:5)*. We don't pray to nor for them.

In addition to this miraculous exception, there will be two multitudes in Heaven during the Great Tribulation. This is another exception for an End Times purpose not the norm as men do not go to Heaven nor Hell when they die but our spirits into these chambers awaiting judgment. In all of the activity around the time of Yahusha's death and resurrection, He demonstrated His power to awaken and raise these spirits from these chambers. This is a foreshadowing of his great work to come when He resurrects all souls of all men who ever lived on the Day of Judgment. His work was not finished at the cross and the Bible never says so but much is yet to come.

# INNER EARTH: THE BIBLICAL PARADIGM

*This concept of Enoch's Inner Earth is fully affirmed and assists in explaining the mindset of the Prophets and Apostles throughout scripture. These references are massive in number. We have curated charts to demonstrate this. You will find a full series on this topic on The God Culture YouTube, Rumble, Utreon or Odyssey titled "Where Do We Go When We Die?"*

## SPIRITS/SOULS GO INTO INNER CHAMBERS

| | |
|---|---|
| 1 Enoch 22:1-12 | Eph. 4:7-10 |
| John 5: 28 | 1 Thess. 5:9-10 |
| Luke 16:22-23 | 2 Esd. 2:29 |
| *(Abraham's Bosom &* | 2 Esd. 4:41 |
| *Chamber for sinners)* | Is. 14:9-11 |
| Luke 23:42 | 1 Pet. 3:18 |
| *(Paradise=Abraham's Bosom)* | *(Prison=Chamber)* |

*Lazarus & Rich Man occurs on the Day of Judgment as these chambers have walls prior (1 Pet. 3:18) and spirits are asleep. It fits Enoch's description perfectly.*
*The thief was promised he would be in Paradise that day with Messiah. That is Abraham's Bosom as well which is the chamber for the righteous. Paul tells us Messiah did not go to Heaven at death but into the lower parts of the Earth (Eph. 4:7-10).*

## SPIRITS RAISED ON JUDMENT DAY

| | |
|---|---|
| 1 Enoch 22:4,11 | Dan. 12:2, 13 |
| 1 Th. 4:15-17 | 2 Cor. 5:1-10 |
| 1 Cor. 15:23-24 | Is. 14:5-11 |
| 1 Cor. 15:52 | Luke 20:34 |
| Heb. 9: 26 | |

## WICKED CONSUMED

| | |
|---|---|
| John 5:28 | Phil. 3:18 |
| 1 Cor. 15:20-24 | Dan. 12:2 |
| Rev. 2:11, | Ez. 18:4 |
| 20:6,14, 21:8 | 2 Esd. 15:22 |

## NEW JERUSALEM COMES DOWN FROM HEAVEN

| | |
|---|---|
| 1 Th. 4:14-18 | Rev. 3:12, 21:2 |
| 2 Cor. 15:52 | 2 Esd. 2:31 |

*My Father's house with many mansions is a reference to New Jerusalem and man does not dwell there until it comes to Earth in the End.*

## SPIRITS SLEEP UPON PHYSICAL DEATH

| | |
|---|---|
| 1 Enoch 22:1-12 | 1 Peter 3:18 |
| 1 Cor. 15:17-22 | 2 Pet. 3:4 |
| 1 Th. 4:13-18, | Deut. 31:16 |
| 5:9-10 | 2 Sam. 7:12 |
| Matt. 22:28-32 | 1 Ki. 1:21 |
| Mark 5:39 | Job 14:12 |
| John 5: 28, | Ps. 13:3 |
| 11:11-14 | Dan. 12:2 |
| Acts 7:59-60, | 2 Esd. 2:31 |
| 13:36 | and many more... |

## RESURRECTION OF THE DEAD

| | |
|---|---|
| 1 Enoch 22:4 | John 5:28, 11:23-27 |
| 1 Th. 4:14-18 | Heb. 9: 26 |
| 1 Cor. 15:20-22 | Dan. 12:2 |
| 2 Cor. 15:52 | Eccl. 9:5,12:7-8 |
| Matt. 22:28-32 | 2 Esd. 2:31, 4:42 |
| Luke 20:34 | Is. 14:9-11 |

## RIGHTEOUS RECEIVE NEW BODIES

| | |
|---|---|
| 1 Cor. 15:53-54 | Dan. 12:2 |
| 1 Cor. 15:20-22 | Esd. 2:31 |
| John 5:28 | 2 Cor. 5:1-10 |
| Phil. 3:21 | |

*Notice the many references to our receiving new bodies and not new spirits on the Day of Judgment. Our spirits continue and the wicked are consumed. However, Enoch's paradigm is the accurate one for such*

# THE BIBLE NEVER SAYS WE GO TO HEAVEN NOR HELL WHEN WE DIE! THE OCCULT DOES!

# 23
# THE FIRE THAT DEALS WITH THE LUMINARIES OF HEAVEN

## CHAPTER 23:

**1** From thence I went to another place to the **west of the ends of the earth**. **2** And I saw a burning fire which ran without resting, and paused not from its course day or night but (ran) regularly. **3** And I asked saying: 'What is this which rests not?' **4** Then Raguel, one of the holy angels who was with me, answered me [and said unto me]: 'This course of fire which thou hast seen is the fire in the west which persecutes! all the luminaries of heaven.'

*Cf. 20:4. Raguel is the archangel who "takes vengeance on the world of the luminaries." This is his domain. Luminaries are stars which are angels.*

# 24-25
# THE SEVEN MOUNTAINS

## AND THE
## TREE OF LIFE

## INNER EARTH CONTINUED

# CHAPTER 24:

*Cf. Jub. 8:22. These are the Mountains of Fire Noah used on the surface as Shem's SE border in Indonesia. Gunung Gunung Api in Javanese. [34] Enoch views them here from within the Earth.*

**1** And from thence I went to another place of the earth and he showed me a **mountain range of fire which burnt day and night**. **2** And I went beyond it and **saw seven magnificent mountains** all differing each from the other, and the stones (thereof) were magnificent and beautiful,

*Cf. Jub. 4:26. "Mount of the East." 4Q529, 6Q23.*

magnificent as a whole, of glorious appearance and fair exterior: three towards the east, one founded on the other, and three towards the

*The 7 Mountains of Eden or the Garden of Eden are Visayas, Philippines. This is a description from within the Earth and Enoch also locates them on the surface.*

south, one upon the other, and deep rough ravines, no one of which joined with any other. **3** And the seventh mountain was in the midst of these, and it excelled them in height, resembling the seat of a throne:

*Islands before the Flood were mountains. Visayas has 7 major islands/ ancient mountains. These stones as well as the spices on the surface match the Philippines.*

and fragrant trees encircled the throne. **4** And amongst them was a tree such as I had never yet smelt, neither was any amongst them nor were others like it: it had a fragrance beyond all fragrance, and its leaves and blooms and wood wither not for ever: and its fruit is beautiful, and its fruit resembles the dates of a palm. **5** Then I said: 'How beautiful is this tree, and fragrant, and its leaves are fair, and its blooms very delightful in appearance.'

**6** Then answered Michael, one of the holy and honored angels who was with me, and was their leader.

# CHAPTER 25:
# The Tree Of Life

**1** And he said unto me: 'Enoch, why dost thou ask me regarding the fragrance of the tree, and why dost thou wish to learn the truth? **2** Then I answered him saying: 'I wish to know about everything, but especially about this tree.'

*Cf. Jub. 1:26.*

**3** And he answered saying: 'This high mountain which thou hast seen, whose summit is like the throne of Elohim, is His throne, where the Holy Great One, Yahuah of Glory, the Eternal King, will sit, when He shall come down to visit the earth with goodness.

*Cf. Jub. 4:26. "Mount of the East." 4Q529, 6Q23.*

*There is no physical mountain which raches Heaven today. However, this is before the Flood.*

**4** And as for this fragrant tree no mortal is permitted to touch it till the great judgment, when He shall take vengeance on all and bring (everything) to its consummation for ever. It shall then be given to the righteous and holy. **5** Its fruit shall be for food to the elect: it shall be transplanted to the holy place, to the temple of Yahuah, the Eternal King.

*Cf. Rev 2:7, 22:2, 14, 19. The Tree of Life remains in the Garden of Eden and will be opened to believers after the Day of Judgment.*

*Cf. 28:2-3. Ez. 47:12; 2 Esd. 2:10-12, 8:52; Rev. 2:7, 22:1-2, 14. New Jerusalem comes down. It moves not the Tree of Life.*

**6** Then shall they rejoice with

Cf. 2 Esd. 8:52. Garden of Eden.
joy and be glad. **And into the holy place** shall they enter; And its fragrance shall be in their bones, And they shall live a long life on earth, Such as the fathers lived: And in their days shall no sorrow or plague

Cf. Rev. 22:3. "No more curse."

Cf. 2 Esd. 2:12.

or torment or calamity touch them.' **7** Then blessed I the Elohim of Glory, the Eternal King, who hath prepared such things for the righteous, and hath created them and promised to give to them.

# 26
# NORTH POLE AND THE MOUNTAINS, RAVINES, AND STREAMS: EXITING INNER EARTH

## CHAPTER 26:

Cf. Jub. 8:12. "The middle of the earth (North Pole)." Enoch exits Inner Earth.

**1** And I went from thence to **the middle of the earth**, and I saw a blessed place in which there were trees with branches abiding and blooming [of a dismembered tree]. **2** And there I saw a **holy mountain**, and underneath the mountain to the east there was **a stream and it flowed towards the south**. **3** And I saw towards the east another mountain higher than this, and between them a deep and narrow

There are only 3 Holy Mountains on Earth. At the North Pole, is the original Mt. Zion and Heavenly Jerusalem for which the ones in Israel will be named after.

Cf. Gen. 2:10-14. Stream that flows out of Eden = The River from Eden. Starts at the North Pole flowing South.

ravine: in it also ran a stream underneath the mountain. **4** And to the west thereof there was another mountain, lower than the former and of small elevation, and a ravine deep and dry between them: and another deep and dry ravine was at the extremities of the three mountains. **5** And all the ravines were deep and narrow, (being formed) of hard rock, and trees were not planted upon them. **6** And I marveled at the rocks, and I marveled at the ravine, yea, I marveled very much.

There is no physical mountain which reaches Heaven today. However, this is before the Flood. In history, there are actual renderings of the North Pole based on legends which offer a visualization of this layout Enoch saw (see next spread).

# THE ANCIENT PERSPECTIVE:

## "MIDDLE OF THE EARTH"

Oldest surviving
world map.
(c. 6th century BCE) [5]

In Chapters 26 and 27, Enoch travels to "the middle of the earth." Many Pharisee scholars including R.H. Charles have attempted to claim that is Israel, yet geographic Israel is never in the middle, center or navel of the earth in any sense in the ancient perspective they ignore. They attempt to stretch one passage to claim such in which that is not even talking of the whole earth but the middle of the land of Israel specifically and impertinent. The ancient paradigm of Earth's cosmology is one of a flat round disc with the North Pole at the very center.

This is evident in the Book of Jubilees when it maps the Earth in Noah's Division *[The Book of Jubilees: The Torah Calendar, Ch. 8-9]* and places Heavenly Mt. Zion, Heavenly Jerusalem and Eden (not to be confused with the Garden of Eden planted East of Eden) in its original location in the North Pole at the center of the navel of the Earth. Certainly, these names were copied in Israel, but this should be no surprise as the entire Temple was not an original but a replica of the Garden of Eden where Yahuah's physical, permanent Holy of Holies on all of Earth resides. This is why Solomon sought the gold of Ophir for the Temple walls especially. In Israel, that was temporary and so are the names of Mt. Zion and Jerusalem in Israel. We prove the Garden of Eden resides under the modern Philippines which is the ancient land of gold – Ophir *[The Search For King Solomon's Treasure, Ch. 18]*. The Rivers from Eden also prove this out *[The Search For King Solomon's Treasure, Ch. 17]*.

This is why even ancient maps are created and recreated as a flat round disc with the North Pole typically in the center. The East to West directions travel in a circular pattern not straight. The South Pole or Antarctica is known as the edge of the earth in this perspective at the very South surrounding the entire Earth in a circle. Regardless of the modern view of Scientism which propagates a religion not based on observable science and is not a scientific paradigm, this has always been the perspective of the writers of the Bible.

The challenge with Enoch is that he did not merely assume this paradigm. He traveled it and is the only eyewitness of the entire Earth and all its innerworkings to this day. He viewed the Earth from Heaven, from inside and traveled all over it. No scientist has and no NASA satellite has either.

Enoch is the only scientific observer of all of Earth and he records it. This book is far more accurate as a science textbook than any modern concoction when it comes to geography and the cosmology and structure of the Earth. Many try to make this book fit modern science and it never will.

That is a problem for modern science which is not based on observation and experiment but math in a vacuum and fraudulent occult tales. Whether you agree with the flat earth perspective or not is meaningless. If you are reading the Bible and the ancients, even much of ancient history, without understanding the world generally believed Enoch's cosmology or similar, then, you will misread and never understand the meaning of these ancient writings. These were "flat earthers" as they are labeled in ridiculous ridicule and demeaned because essentially, they believe Enoch over modern sorcerers who call themselves scientists.

It does not take much research to realize that when they tell us the earth has a magma core and sea which they have never seen nor proven in any sense. They are representing their occult paradigm of the underworld as a burning hell of sort. Though there is a chamber for Fallen Angels which burns in the "lowest Hell," the Earth's interior most certainly does not generally according to the Bible as there are other chambers, the Garden of Eden, etc. We know there are pockets of oil, water, magma, other resources and even hallow chambers within. We also know the deepest boreholes in history have proven to produce water flowing through rock. Again, Enoch witnessed this. No scientist ever has and they are propagating an occult paradigm in their religion which is not science. They even ignore and manipulate their own science in attempt to make their failed theories work.

One can see the concept of Enoch's representation of the ancient North Pole prior to the Flood in maps and legends such as Mercator's 1595 map of the Arctic. No one ever saw the Arctic like this after the Flood as it would be similar to what we see today. Most of the North Pole is covered by ice much of the year and underwater. Notice, how the ancient Holy Places of Yahuah are hidden from men today and in this case, really by the Flood. However, Enoch traveled here before the Flood and this map appears to be based on Enoch's observation. Note, there is a tall mountain at the North Pole which would be the holy mountain, Mt. Zion. Mercator's map is not based on observation but legend. Then, there are 2 mountains East and West and a stream flowing to the South with multiple ravines similar to what Enoch described. It is not a perfect representation but this appears to originate in legend that has true roots in the Book of Enoch. This cannot be seen today because this is before the Flood. We find multiple legends however, that there is an entrance to the Inner Earth in the North Pole. We haven't been there and we have no way to authenticate those legends but Enoch was an eyewitness. Left: Mercator's 1595 Map of the Arctic. Mercator, Gerhard, 1512-1594. "Septentrionalium Terrarum Descriptio" [1595]. First state, from his posthumously published atlas, Atlantis pars altera. Wikimedia Commons.

# THE PURPOSE OF THE ACCURSED VALLEY IN THE NORTH POLE: EARTH'S SURFACE

## CHAPTER 27:

1 Then said I: 'For what object is this blessed land, which is entirely filled with trees, and this accursed valley between? 2 Then Uriel one of the holy angels who was with me answered and said: 'This accursed valley is for those who are accursed for ever: **here shall all the accursed be gathered together who utter with their lips against Yahuah** unseemly words and of His glory speak hard things. Here shall they be gathered together and here shall be the place of their habitation. 3 In the **last times**, in the **days of the true judgment in the presence of the righteous for ever**: here shall the godly bless Yahuah of Glory the Eternal King. 4 In the days of judgment over the former, they shall bless Him for the mercy in accordance with which He has assigned them (their lot)." 5 Then I blessed Yahuah of Glory and set forth His glory and lauded Him gloriously.

*Cf. 90:26-27; Matt. 5:22,29,30. "Where Gehenna is the place of final punishment."*

*Cf. Rev 16:16; 2 Esd. 13:1-38. This is the Biblical valley of Megiddo, Har Megiddo, or Armageddon, not Israel.*

# ARMAGEDDON: THE FINAL BATTLE
# (NOT IN ISRAEL)

הר: har: "mountain" | מגדון: Mᵉgiddôwn, meg-id-done: "place of crowds"
Armageddon: "the hill or city of Megiddo" *(Note: Where the wicked gather.)*

The first use of Megiddo in the Bible is a place named by Canaanites in Joshua 12:21 of which, Nephilim were among them referring to the valley in Israel which would continue such name. This is now known as the Jezreel Valley in Northern Israel. However, Enoch wrote of this thousands of years before as the "accursed valley" in the North Pole from which the nations of the world will curse and fight Yahusha when He returns. Once again, as with Heavenly Mt. Zion next to it, Heavenly Jerusalem, and Ancient Eden, these are the North Pole, not Israel. That is where Enoch is located in offering these directions. Israel has many names that have ancient roots. In fact, there are 70 places named Eden on Earth today, yet there is only one Eden and only one Garden of Eden.

In the time of his writing, Enoch experienced the days of the Watcher Fallen Angels and their progeny, the Nephilim giants, specifically in what would become Israel long after the Flood. Enoch records that as the very place where the Watchers formed an oath in the days of his grandfather Jared to break Yahuah's Law of Creation to defile themselves with women on Mt. Hermon, Israel *(6:6)*. At the time of this writing, Israel was a defiled Nephilim stronghold which is why they wanted it back so badly after the Flood. It returned to such during its being called Canaan.

However, the origin of this name is the accursed valley in the North Pole where the nations of the Earth will gather to fight Yahusha in the End Times battle. That is the Mt. Zion of the beginning and the end. The one in Israel is named for it just as the Temple was a replica of Yahuah's Holy of Holies in the Garden of Eden. These Holy places remain significant to the end. It is through Mt. Zion that the Earth will be sanctified *(Jub. 4:26)*.

Regarding the technology of the time, it is very likely the cold will have no effect on these armies gathering not to mention it will likely occur in September or so near the Fall Feasts when it is warmer. Also, In 2nd Esdras 13, Messiah builds up this mountain or perhaps rebuilds Mt. Zion to its original state from before the Flood as Enoch saw it. Ezra does not recognize the place *(2 Esd. 13:1-38)*. This accursed valley is next to Mt. Zion and in Israel, Megiddo (Jezreel Valley) is not near Mt. Zion but 150 km away. Why such distance is not even considered in scholarly logic that does not connect, escapes us. That is not the staging area for an attack on Mt. Zion there because it does not fit Israel but the North Pole.

# FURTHER JOURNEY TO THE EAST: EARTH'S SURFACE

## CHAPTER 28:

*East begins in Asia in the ancient perspective.*

*The next Holy Place, Mt. Sinai.*

*Wilderness of Sin.*

*Cf. 25:4-6. Ez. 47:12; 2 Esd. 2:10-12, 8:52; Rev. 2:7, 22:1-2, 14. Water from above.*

**1** And thence I went **towards the east**, into the midst of the **mountain range of the desert**, and I saw a wilderness and it was solitary, full of trees and plants. **2** And water gushed forth from above. **3** Rushing like a copious watercourse [which flowed] **towards the northwest** it caused clouds and dew to ascend on every side.

## CHAPTER 29:

**1** And thence I went to **another place in the desert**, and approached to the **east of this mountain range**. **2** And there I saw **aromatic trees** exhaling the fragrance of **frankincense and myrrh**, and the trees also were **similar to the almond tree**.

*The next large desert further to the East fits the Great Indian Desert. These trees are found in India as well.*

*The frankincense tree with a nut like an almond is the Pili Tree from Oriental regions which produces Manila elemi known in ancient times and archaeology as frankincense as well as myrrh. There are 2 different resin varieties scientifically from this tree which also yields the pili nut like an almond (background). The Bible frankincense and myrrh was elemi affirmed in Egyptian archaeology not the fradulent Rabbi claim of a tree in Ethiopia and Arabia. Frankincense and myrrh must be in the Land of Creation as they were used in the first sacrifice of Adam when exiled from the Garden in the Far East [The Search For King Solomon's Treasure, Ch. 15]. However, prior to the Flood, its distribution was likely broader but this tells us we have entered the Orient and these directions form such indisputably as they are about to cross beyond the Erythraean Sea which is the Indian Ocean, as you will see, meaning Enoch is currently in that region. The Garden is Northeast once one exits the Indian Ocean.*

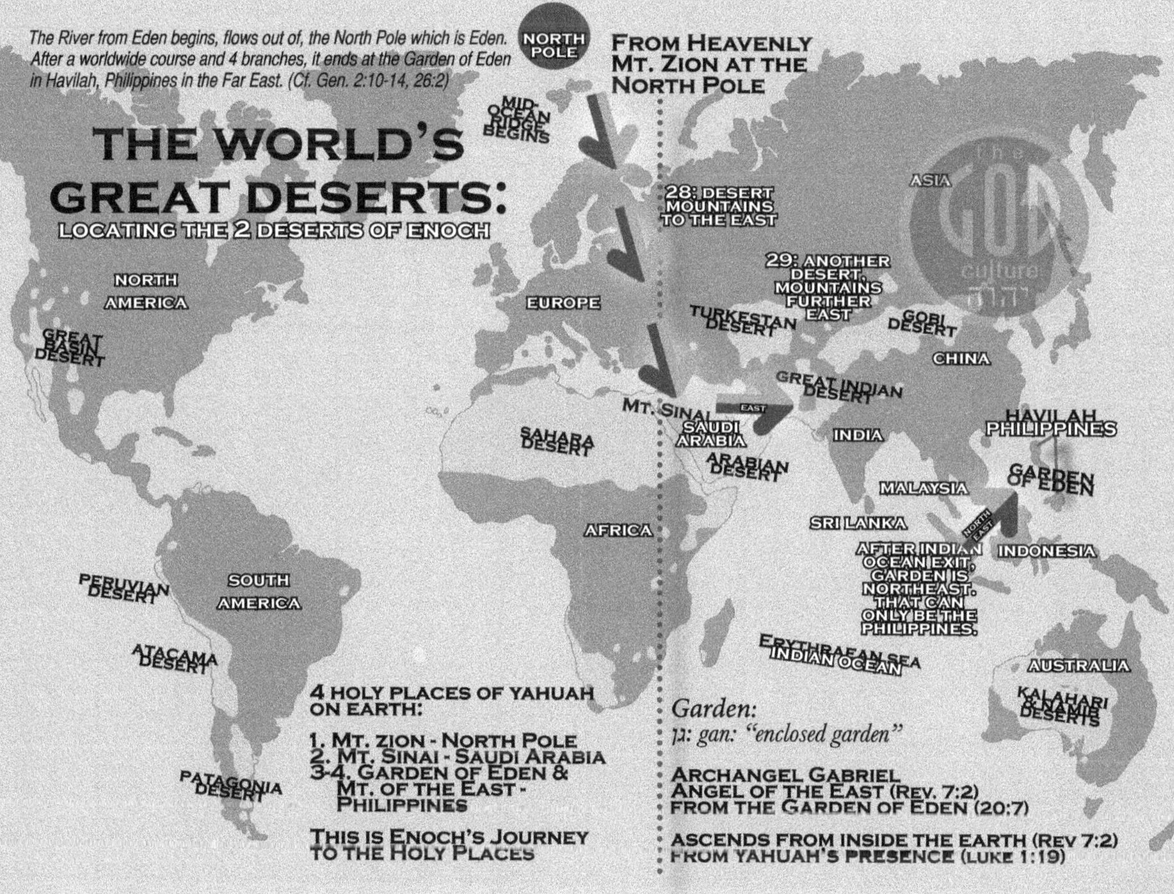


*Jubilees 8:19:* *And he knew that the* **Garden of Eden is the holy of holies, and the dwelling of Yahuah,** *and* **Mount Sinai the centre of the desert,** *and* **Mount Zion--the centre of the navel of the earth:** *these* **three** *were created as* **holy places facing each other.** *(These make up the border of Shem's territory)*

*Jubilees 4:26:* *For* **Yahuah hath four places on the earth,** *the* **Garden of Eden, and the Mount of the East,** *and this mountain on which thou art this day,* **Mount Sinai,** *and* **Mount Zion (which) will be sanctified in the new creation for a sanctification of the earth; through it will the earth be sanctified** *from all (its) guilt and its uncleanness throughout the generations of the world.*

In history and even in today's mindset, the Near East begins East of the Mediterranean. From Heavenly Mt. Zion in the North Pole, Enoch exits the Earth's interior and begins his journeys on the surface. From the North Pole, he travels East but to the desert. Notice, one cannot travel from the North Pole without heading South as well, of course. This is the Arabian Desert and for good reason. Mt. Sinai, His Holy Mountain is there. This would eliminate the Sahara and the deserts of the Americas. The Prophet, then, is taken to another mountainous desert East of Arabia in India. He will continue to the East until he exits the Indian Ocean to the Northeast and reaches the Garden of Eden in the Philippines. This is an exact match to Noah's Division of the Earth in the Book of Jubilees.

# CHAPTER 30:

*Far East or Orient. Enoch has not passed the Indian Ocean yet.*

*Famous for cinnamon, perhaps Sri Lanka which has the Hiddekel River flowing between India and Sri Lanka with basins that would form antediluvian lakes/seas such as the Bay of Bengal. Mastic = Indian Dammer.*

1 And beyond these, I went **afar to the east**, and I saw another place, **a valley (full) of water**. 2 And therein there was a tree, the color(?) of fragrant trees such as the mastic. 3 And on the sides of those valleys I saw fragrant **cinnamon**. And beyond these I **proceeded to the east**.

# CHAPTER 31:

*East of India and Sri Lanka is the East Indies rich in all of these spices throughout history. Again, mountains in this perspective before the Flood were what we call islands now. Note: aloe does not originate in Egypt because one drew it there. It has always been in the Far East as well.*

1 And I saw other mountains, and amongst them were groves of trees, and there flowed forth from them nectar, which is named sarara and **galbanum**. 2 And beyond these mountains I saw another mountain to the **east of the ends of the earth**, whereon were aloe trees, and all the trees were full of **stacte**, being **like almond trees**. 3 And when one burnt it, it smelt **sweeter than any fragrant odor**.

*NE of Indian Ocean is the Philippines. 7 Mountains of Visayas: Panay, Masbate, Samar, Leyte, Negros, Cebu and Bohol.*

# CHAPTER 32:

1 To the **northeast** I beheld **seven mountains** full of choice **nard** and **mastic** and **cinnamon** and **pepper**. *All spices native to Philippines.*

2 And thence I went over the summits of all these mountains, **far towards the east of the earth**, and **passed above the Erythraean sea**, and went **far from it**, and passed over the **angel Zotiel**. *To the Far East. Indian Ocean. Guardian cherub of the Garden.* 3 And I came to the **Garden of Righteousness**, and from afar off trees more numerous than these trees and great— *Garden of Eden.* **fruit trees there**, very great, beautiful, and glorious, and magnificent, and the **tree of knowledge**, whose holy fruit they eat and know great wisdom. *In the Garden of Eden.* 4 That **tree is in height like the fir**, and its **leaves are like (those of) the Carob tree**: and its fruit is like the **clusters of the vine**, very beautiful: and the **fragrance** of the tree penetrates afar. *i.e. Lanzones Tree (right). Fruit like clusters of grapes, leaven and bark look like a Carob Tree, height of a fir, beautiful and penetrating smell. It also has at least 3 legends described as beign poison yet purified. Lason in Tagalog is poison.* 5 Then I said: 'How beautiful is the tree, and how attractive is its look!' 6 Then Raphael, the holy angel who was with me, answered me and said: 'This is the **tree of wisdom**, of which thy father old (in years) and thy aged mother, who were before thee, **have eaten, and they learnt wisdom and their eyes were opened**, and they knew that they were naked and they were driven out of the garden.' *Adam. Havah, Eve. Tree of the Knowledge of Good and Evil. The forbidden fruit.*

### The Legend of Lanzones (Ang Alamat ng Lansones)

"Lansones is actually derived from the word lason, which is Tagalog for "poison." There was once a time when the pale yellow globes lived up to their sinister name.

The cream-colored clusters were said to have originated from Paete, Laguna. They were so poisonous that even the ants on it's branches died on the spot. But all that changed when a kindly old man named Mang Selo paused to rest under a shady tree while passing through the thick Paete forest, only the notorious Lansonses trees were nearby.

Faint from hunger, Mang Selo fell asleep and dreamt of a beautiful angel who plucked a fruit from the lansones tree for him to eat. Sensing his reluctance, the heavenly being pinched the tiny fruit to draw out the poison. Mang Selo awakened to find fruit peelings on the ground next to him. His curiosity and hunger soon overcame his fear of the lansones, and he cautiously peeled one and bit into it.

His gamble paid off, and he ended up relishing the fruit's sweet, refreshing taste. In gratitude to the angel who had saved him from hunger, he spread the word that lansones were no longer poisonous, and that the brown spots on it's skin were the fingerprints of the benevolent spirit who pinched the poison away." [312]

#### lason:
Tagalog: n. 1. poison;
2. poison to morals or mind
(origin of word lanzones) [410]

#### lashon:
Hebrew: לשון:
babbler, evil speaker, language, talker, tongue, wedge (of gold)
(one with a poison tongue) [410]

Lanzones fruit grows like bunches of grapes on a tree. Notice how the leaves and branches of the Lanzones tree resemble that of the Carob tree just as Enoch describes.

Sources from The Search For King Solomon's Treasure. pp. 317-18.

# NOAH'S DIRECTIONS TO THE GARDEN OF EDEN FROM THE BOOK OF JUBILEES

## GARDEN OF EDEN
### SHEM'S SOUTHEAST BORDER

## MOUNTAINS OF FIRE
"Gunung Gunung Api" in Javanese
*147 Volcanoes forming a natural geographic border between Shem and Ham in the Far East.* [34]

### GENESIS 3:24 KJV – EAST OF THE GARDEN
So he drove out the man; and he placed at the east of the garden of Eden Cherubims, and a flaming sword which turned every way, to keep the way of the tree of life.



## TESTING THE RESOURCES OF HAVILAH [31][32]

In all of history, the Philippines leads in gold mining since before 1000 B.C. and still remains #2 on earth in untapped gold reserves. There is no other land which competes. It is the ancient land of gold by historical record. [27]

### PEARL

Bdellium is never a Biblical spice and all such spices are recorded in scripture. It is pearl. The Philippines has the largest pearls in all of history with no 2nd. [28]

*Puerto Princessa Pearl. 2006. 34 kg (75 lb.)*

Ancient onyx especially in Egypt was known as alabaster used in ornamental construction. The Philippines has the strongest onyx and marble on earth in Romblon. [29]

Marine life is the true measure for the Land of Creation as it was not wiped out by the Flood. The Epicenter of Marine Biodiversity on ALL of earth is the Philippines in the Sulu Sea. [30]

*Tubbataha Reef in the Sulu Sea.*

### In resources, history, geography, science, language and the Bible, this is Ophir.
See "The Search for King Solomon's Treasure: The Lost Isles of Gold and the Garden of Eden" for Evidences.

### GENESIS 2:11-12 KJV
The name of the first is Pison: that is it which compasseth the whole land of Havilah, where there is gold; And the gold of that land is good: there is bdellium and the onyx stone.

### HAVILAH [31][32]
= GARDEN OF EDEN
= LAND OF CREATION
= OPHIR
= PHILIPPINES

### JUBILEES 3:32
Adam and his wife went forth from the Garden of Eden, and they dwelt in the land of Elda, in the land of their creation.

# ENOCH'S JOURNEY TO THE GARDEN OF EDEN

FLAT EARTH PERSPECTIVE

TREE OF KNOWLEDGE OF GOOD AND EVIL = LANZONES TREE OF THE PHILIPPINES

*Remember, Enoch wrote this for us in the Last Days to understand because technology has afforded us a full perspective of this area from above as he did.*

# WHAT IS NORTHEAST OF THE INDIAN OCEAN? THE GARDEN OF EDEN IN THE PHILIPPINES

AUSTRALIA

GARDEN OF RIGHTEOUSNESS VISAYAS

HAVILAH PHILIPPINES

INDONESIA

NORTHEAST OF INDIAN OCEAN

CHINA

ASIA

EAST

BEYOND THE INDIAN OCEAN

INDIES SPICES
GALBANUM
SARARA
STACTE
PILI

**Enoch Describes These Same 7 Mountains From the Surface:**

**32:1 To the northeast** *(from Erythraean Sea)* **I beheld seven mountains full of choice nard and mastic and cinnamon and pepper.**

MASTIC/ DAMMER

INDIA

GREAT INDIAN DESERT

EAST

FAMOUS FOR CINNAMON SRI LANKA

GREAT INDIAN DESERT [15]

BAY OF BENGAL

EAST

SRI LANKA

VALLEY OF WATER IS LIKELY THE BAY OF BENGAL BEFORE THE FLOOD

EAST

ERYTHRAEAN SEA INDIAN OCEAN

MT. SINAI

**All spices native to Visayas, Philippines. Mastic Resin is akin to Dammer in India and Manila Copal in the Philippines. Though not well known, Cebu Cinnamon is an ancient native plant.**

AFRICA

Enoch Described From the Interior:
*(Ch. 18)*

Seven Mountains of Magnificent Stones:

"**three** towards the **east**..."

"one founded on the other" *(exact match)*

Masbate, Samar & Leyte

coloured stone, pearl, & jacinth

Largest pearls on Earth, Gemstones abound

"**three** towards the **south**..."

"one upon the others"

Negros, Cebu & Bohol

Red stone

Gemstones abound

"middle one reached to heaven like the throne of Elohim, of alabaster..."

Panay (Hebrew: ‏ינפ לע‎ ~ ‏ייִנפ לע‎: al panay: over me, overlooking: ‏םינפ‎: panim: face, surface)

Next to Romblon, strongest marble/onyx on earth.

Ancient onyx stone = ancient alabaster[33]

"I saw a flaming fire..."

Volcanoes prevalent in the Philippines

"there the heavens were completed..."

Land of Creation = Havilah, Philippines *(Cf. Jub. 3:32, Gn. 3:23)*

Epicenter of Marine Biodiversity On All of Earth = Sulu Sea, Philippines

# A QUMRAN FRAGMENT:

# WORDS OF THE ARCHANGEL MICHAEL (4Q529, 6Q23), FR. 1

*"The Complete Dead Sea Scrolls In English." By Geza Vermes. P. 556. [22]*

Though not well preserved and a fragment, this Aramaic writing records the Archangel Michael as he appears to mention the building of evil Shinar at the time of the Tower of Babel. This is clearly a migration of the righteous away from there to the East to the land of Gabriel who is in the Garden of Eden. These 9 mountains, the land of silver (Tarshish) and gold (Ophir) and the Garden of Eden are a match to the modern Philippines. Though Vermes assumes this must be Zion or Sinai, we agree it is a Holy mountain but the Mount of the East in the Garden of Eden far away from Shinar. [See The Search For King Solomon's Treasure for Full Position].

*Volcanoes.*

*Cf. 1 En. 24-25, 32. Same 7 mountains plus 2.*

*Cf. 1 En. 20:7. Gabriel is in charge of the Garden of Eden known as the Angel from the East. Rev. 7:2-3; Who stands in the presence of Yahuah which is the Garden's Holy of Holies. Luke 1:19.*

Words of the book which Michael addressed to the angels... He said: I found there divisions of fire... [and I saw there] **nine mountains**: two to the eas[t, and two to the west, and two to the north and two to the so]uth. **I saw there the angel Gabriel** . . . like a vision. [Then] I showed him the vision. And he said to me:... in the books of my Master, Yahuah of the world, it is written: Behold,... [between] the sons of Ham and the sons of Shem. And behold my Master, Yahuah of the world... when they... the tear from... And behold **a city was built** to the name of my Master, [Yahuah of the world, and there] everything **that is evil** will be done before my Master, Yahuah [of the world]... And my Master, Yahuah of the world, will remember his creation... [and] my Master, Yahuah of the world, [will be] merciful to him and to him... the man will be in the **faraway province**... he, and he will say to him: Behold this... for me **silver and gold**... And he will say:... [and] the **righteous man**...

*Only Shinar and the Tower of Babel fit this unification of the 3 sons of Noah building a city. They have been dispersed since.*

*This is not a place in the Middle East but a faraway province.*

*The land of silver (Tarshish) and gold (Ophir and Sheba).*

*Cf. Gen. 10:26-30. The Bible only records 1 migration at this time for the righteous and that is Ophir/Joktan.*

# NINE ANCIENT MOUNTAINS OF THE EAST

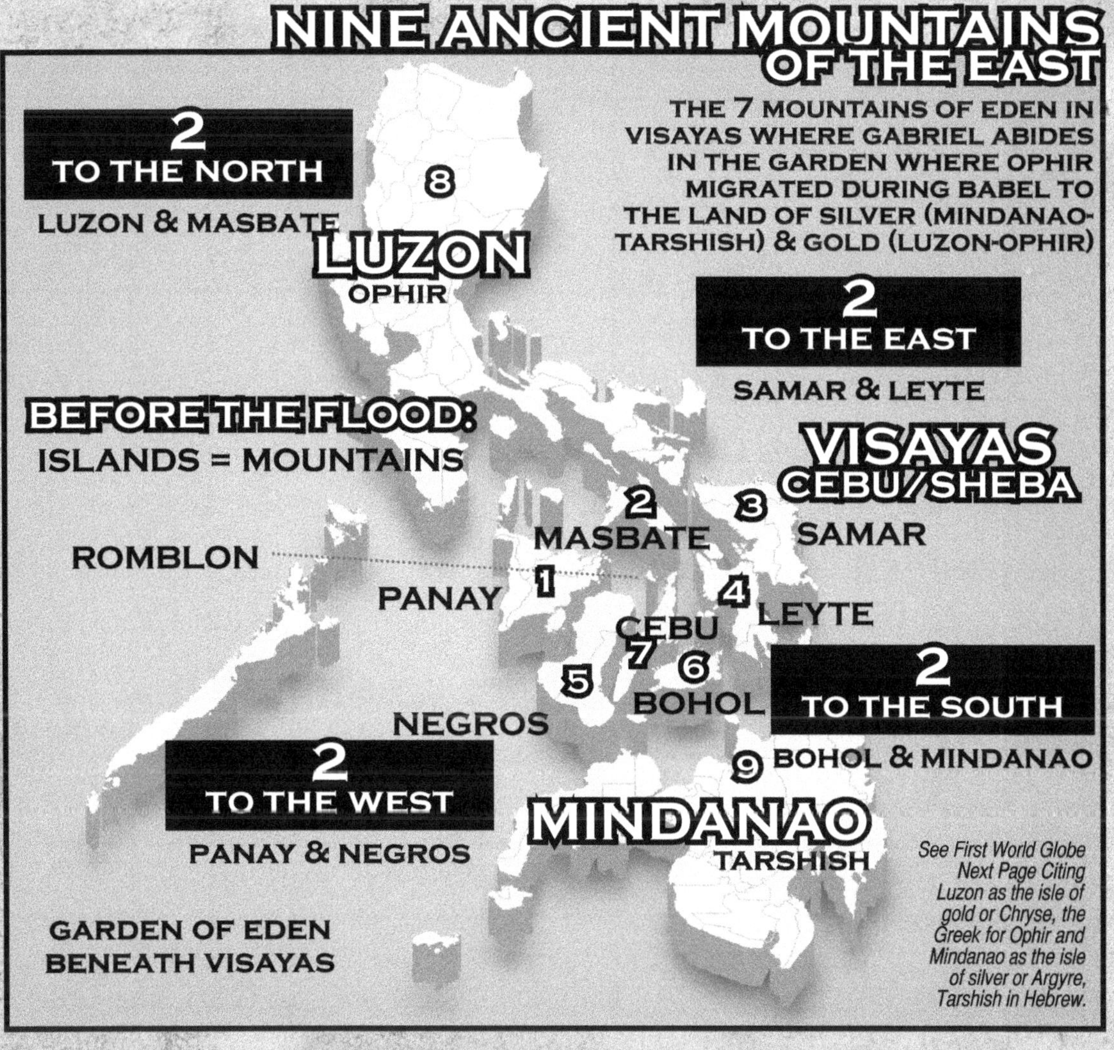


1. MICHAEL LAYS OUT 9 MOUNTAINS WHERE GABRIEL ABIDES IN THE GARDEN OF EDEN. GABRIEL IS IN CHARGE OF THE GARDEN ACCORDING TO ENOCH.

2. HE DEFINES THE LAYOUT JUST AS ENOCH WITH 7 VISAYAS MOUNTAINS OF EDEN PLUS 2 - LUZON AND MINDANAO ADDED. ISLANDS BEFORE THE FLOOD WERE MOUNTAINS.

3. HE MENTIONS SHINAR AND A MIGRATION OF THE RIGHTEOUS TO A FARAWAY LAND OF SILVER AND GOLD.

THIS IS THE MIGRATION OF OPHIR, SHEBA, AND TARSHISH TO THE FAMOUS LAND OF SILVER AND GOLD WHICH WOULD BE NAMED AFTER THESE PATRIARCHS. THIS OCCURRED AT THE TIME OF BABEL AND THEY WENT TO SEPHAR (TREE OF LIFE IN THE GARDEN OF EDEN) AND THE MOUNT OF THE EAST (HOLY MOUNTAIN IN THE GARDEN OF EDEN). GEN. 10:26-30. THIS IS THE MODERN PHILIPPINES.

[See The Search For King Solomon's Treasure for Full Position].

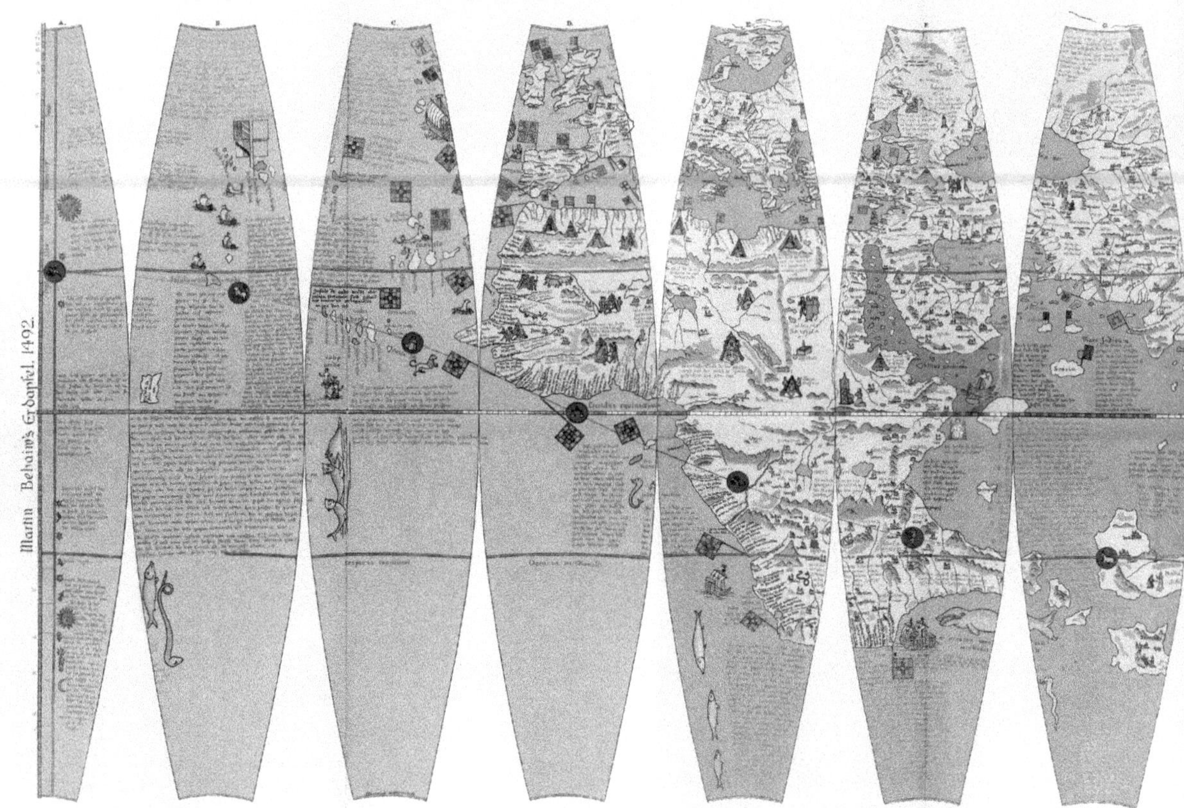

In the First World Globe commissioned by the Portuguese government and released in 1492, the mindset of the age of exploration was firm that Ophir and Tarshish, the land of Solomon's famed gold, were located in Southeast Asia just Northeast of Borneo and Southeast of China as an archipelago we now call the Philippines. This map identifies Luzon Island, Philippines as Chryse, the Greek word for the Hebrew Ophir and Mindanao as Argyre, the Greek word for the Hebrew Tarshish. The British were behind then and remain behind as they make claims only by ignoring this firm history and the Bible as well as Pomponius Mela(43 AD), The Periplus of the Erythraean Sea(70 AD), Dionysius the Tourist(124 AD), etc. which have mapped Chryse(Ophir) South of the Tropic of Cancer in the Philippines all along. Magellan knew this and recorded it.

Columbus believed and noted in journals that this was his destination of Ophir and Tarshish, not America, this same year really using the same data of the most current Portuguese exploration which this mapping identifies. His research also concluded that these same islands housed the Garden of Eden and Arsareth, the land of the Lost Tribes of Northern Israel from 2 Esdras 13. Italian Jewish Scholar, Ferrisol, of the same era, records the very same in specifically identifying the Philippines as the location of the Lost Tribes who migrated according to 2 Esdras. This was soon buried by the British who began paying propagandists in at least 1625 such as Samuel Purchas. Their supposed cases all ignore the existence of the Philippines which is the only land that could even qualify as Ophir, Tarshish, the Garden of Eden and Arsareth. Enoch agrees. See *The Search for King Solomon's Treasure* for details. *www.OphirInstitute.com*

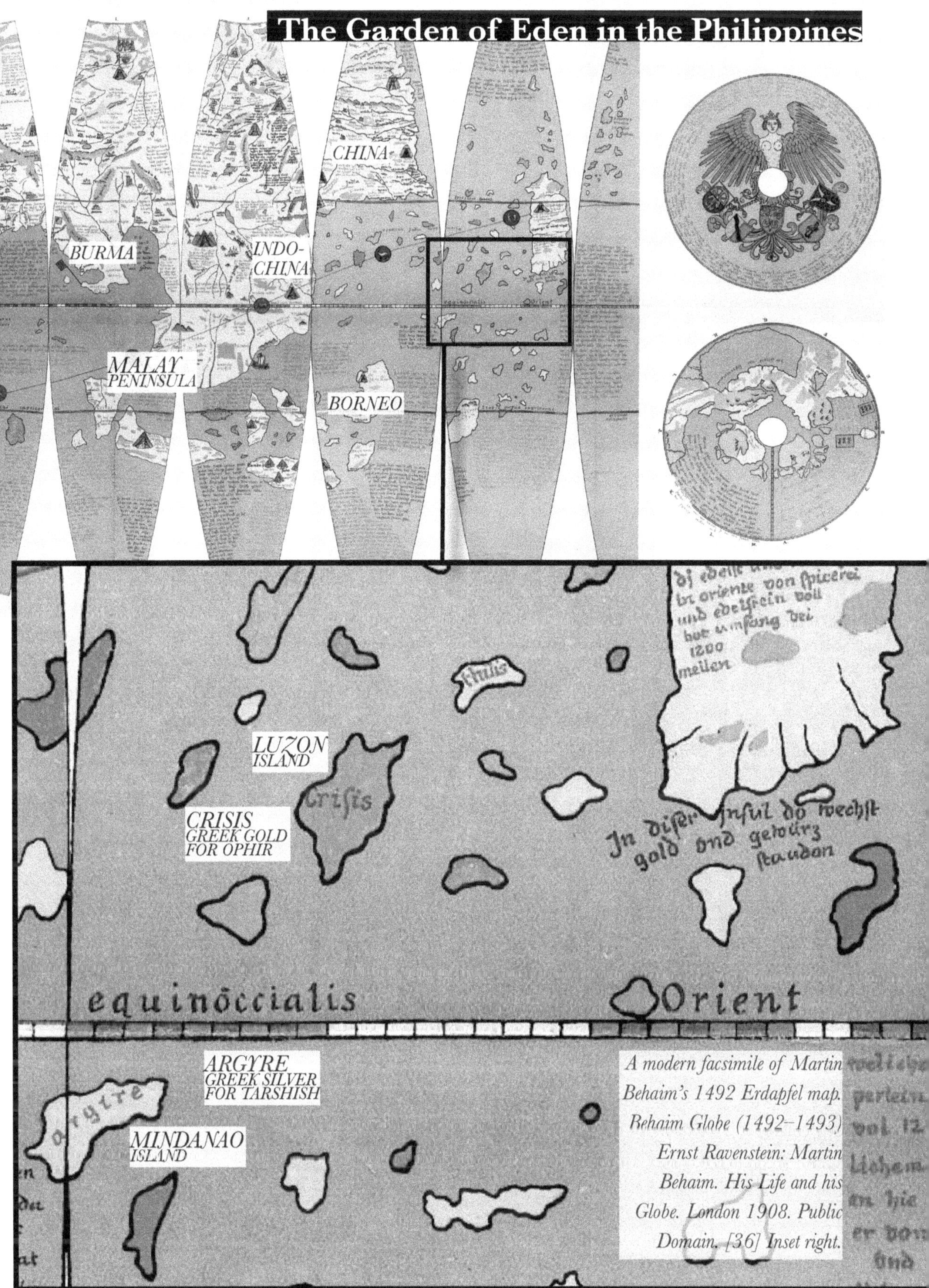



A modern facsimile of Martin Behaim's 1492 Erdapfel map. Behaim Globe (1492–1493) Ernst Ravenstein: Martin Behaim. His Life and his Globe. London 1908. Public Domain. [36] Inset right.

# WHERE DID ENOCH GO?



The Great Prophet Enoch walked so closely with Yahuah that He took Him. Most assume this means He went to Heaven. Yahusha says no man ascended to Heaven.

*Genesis 5:24 KJV And all the days of Enoch were three hundred sixty and five years: And Enoch walked with God: and **he was not; for God took him.***

*John 3:13 KJV And **no man hath ascended up to heaven, but he that came down from heaven, even the Son of man which is in heaven.***

Prior to his translation, Enoch lived in Ancient Havilah near Adam. He was taken from the East portion of Havilah according to Noah. The modern Philippines.

*1 Enoch 60.8 But the male is named Behemoth, who occupied with his breast a waste wilderness named **Duidain, on the east of the garden where the elect and righteous dwell, where my grandfather was taken up, the seventh from Adam...***

Prior to his disappearance, Enoch completed his journey of the Earth, inner Earth and Heaven and was returned to his doorstep. He was given one year to teach his sons before he would be taken.

*1 Enoch 81:5-6 And those **seven holy ones brought me and placed me on the earth before the door of my house,** and said to me: 'Declare everything to thy son Methuselah, and show to all thy children that no flesh is righteous in the sight of Yahuah, for He is their Creator. **One year we will leave thee with thy son,** till thou givest thy (last) commands, that thou mayest **teach thy children and record (it) for them,** and testify to all thy children; and in the **second year they shall take thee from their midst.***

## ENOCH RESIDES IN THE GARDEN OF EDEN INSIDE THE EARTH UNDER THE PHILIPPINES.

Elijah was taken and did not die as well *(2 Ki. 1:1, 11).* Enoch speaks prophetically of Elijah:

*1 Enoch 89:52: "Yahuah of the sheep saved it (the sheep, Elijah the prophet) from the sheep, and brought it up to me and caused it to dwell there."*

Elijah is also in the Garden of Eden with Enoch. This makes sense as they are sustained by the Tree of Life there. Elijah was taken up to Heaven but resides in the Garden not Heaven just as Enoch. Heaven includes the sky and he was clearly then transported to the Garden of Eden not Heaven.

## ELOHIM TOOK HIM WHERE?

## DO YOU KNOW A BETTER EXPERT THAN ENOCH HIMSELF?

Enoch did not ascend to Heaven to reside, he was conducted into the Garden of Eden which is the Holy of Holies of Yahuah within the Earth, where he serves as High Priest.

*Genesis 3:23-24 KJV* *Therefore the Lord God* **sent him forth from the garden of Eden**, *to till the ground from whence he was taken. So he drove out the man; and he placed* **at the east of the garden of Eden** *Cherubims, and a flaming sword which turned every way, to keep the way of the tree of life.*

*Jubilees 4:23-24* *And he(Enoch) was taken from amongst the children of men, and* **we (the angels) conducted him into the Garden of Eden** *in majesty and honour...*
*...that he should recount all the deeds of the generations until the day of condemnation.*

*Jubilees 4:25-26* *And* **he(Enoch) burnt the incense of the sanctuary, (even) sweet spices acceptable before Yahuah on the Mount.** *For Yahuah has four places on the earth,* **the Garden of Eden, and the Mount of the East,** *and this mountain on which thou art this day, Mount Sinai, and Mount Zion...*

*Jubilees 8:18-19* *And he knew that* **the Garden of Eden is the holy of holies, and the dwelling of Yahuah**...

Enoch did not die. His book even records Noah reading his Parable of the Flood in the 500th-year of the life of Enoch over a century after having been taken at 365. They were still counting his days because he was and is still alive. He will remain in the Garden of Eden until the Day of Judgment.

*Hebrews 11:5 KJV* *By faith* **Enoch was translated that he should not see death**; *and was not found, because God had translated him: for before his translation he had this testimony, that he pleased God.*

*1 Enoch 60.1* *In the* **year five hundred**, *in the seventh month, on the fourteenth day of the month* **in the life of Enoch**. *In that Parable I(Noah) saw how a mighty quaking..*

*Genesis 5:23-24 KJV* *And all the days of Enoch were* **three hundred sixty and five years** *: And Enoch walked with God: and he was not; for* **God took him**.

The prophet was visited on Earth after his translation by his son Methuselah and later Noah because the Garden of Eden is below Ancient Havilah where they lived which became Ophir after the Flood known in modern times as the Philippines. They did not enter the incorruptible Garden but Enoch says he came out to see them.

*1 Enoch 106.7-8* *And now, my father (Methuselah), I (Lamech) am here to petition thee and implore thee that thou mayest* **go to Enoch**, *our father, and learn from him the truth, for* **his dwellingplace is amongst the angels.**" *(On Earth, the Garden of Eden with Gabriel and the angels) And when Methuselah heard the words of his son, he came to me(Enoch) to the* **ends of the earth**(Far East); *for he had heard that I was there, and he cried aloud, and* **I heard his voice and I came to him**. *(Cf. Noah also visits 65:1-5)*

*Genesis Apocryphon Col. II. 20: ...he(Methuselah) went to] Enoch his father to learn all things truthfully from him... his will.* **He went at once to Parwain and he found him there...** *[and] he said to Enoch his father, 'O my father, O my lord, to whom I ... And I say to you, lest you be angry with me because I come here... (Cf. 2 Cor. 3:6-7: Parwaim gold used for temple walls.) parwaim:* פרוים *: shortened form of sephar-waim which is Sephar where Ophir migrated (Gen. 10:30) to the Gen. 2 land of Gold, Havilah. Sephar is a Hebrew term for the Tree of Life referring in location to the Garden of Eden in the Orient. –p. 481-482[22]*

# CHAPTER 33:

1 And from thence I went to **the ends of the earth and saw there great beasts**, and each differed from the other; and (I saw) birds also differing in appearance and beauty and voice, the one differing from the other. 2 And **to the east** of those beasts I saw the **ends of the earth** whereon the heaven rests, and the portals of the heaven open. 3 And I saw how the stars of heaven come forth, and I counted the portals out of which they proceed and wrote down all their outlets, of each individual star by itself according to their number and their names, their courses and their positions, and their times and their months, as Uriel the holy angel who was with me showed me. He showed all things to me and wrote them down for me: also their names he wrote for me, and their laws and their companies.

*Enoch suggests he saw beyond Antarctica, essentially the firmament.*

*The stars are not named into constellations which is an occult practice. Yahuah, as expressed by Enoch, knows the individual name of every star. They have companies but those certainly not named for Fallen Angels and their offspring which is astrology.*

*Editors' Note: From Havilah, Philippines, the land of the Garden of Eden, in the ancient perspective, the ends of the earth would be towards Antarctica. Many dinosaur fossils or great beasts have been found in Australia, New Zealand and Antarctica in that direction. These include Titanosaurid, Rhoetosaurus, Allosaurus, Leptocerotops, Stegosaur, Ankylosaurs (the armoured dinosaurs), Mosasaurs, Plesiosaurs (both marine reptilian groups), etc. not to mention those buried on the ocean floor. There were certainly great beasts there for Enoch to observe just as he said.*

*Source: Australia Environmental Education, Australian Museum; Department of Agriculture, Water and the Environment, Australian Antarctic Division; Science Learning Hub, New Zealand Ministry of Business, Innovation and Employment, the Ministry of Education and the Office of the Prime Minister's Chief Science Advisor.*

# 34-35, ENOCH'S JOURNEY NORTH AND WEST TO THE ENDS OF THE EARTH

## CHAPTER 34:



1 And from thence I went **towards the north to the ends of the earth**, and there I saw a **great and glorious device** at the ends of the whole earth. 2 And here I saw **three portals of heaven** open in the heaven: through each of them proceed **north winds**: when they blow there is cold, hail, frost, snow, dew, and rain. 3 And out of one portal they blow for good: but when they blow through the other two portals, it is with violence and affliction on the earth, and they blow with violence.

## CHAPTER 35:

1 And from thence I went **towards the west to the ends of the earth**, and saw there **three portals of the heaven** open such as I had seen in the feasts, the same number of portals, and the same number of outlets.

THE Levite BIBLE

LeviteBible.com

# ENOCH'S COMPLETE JOURNEY OF THE SURFACE OF THE EARTH



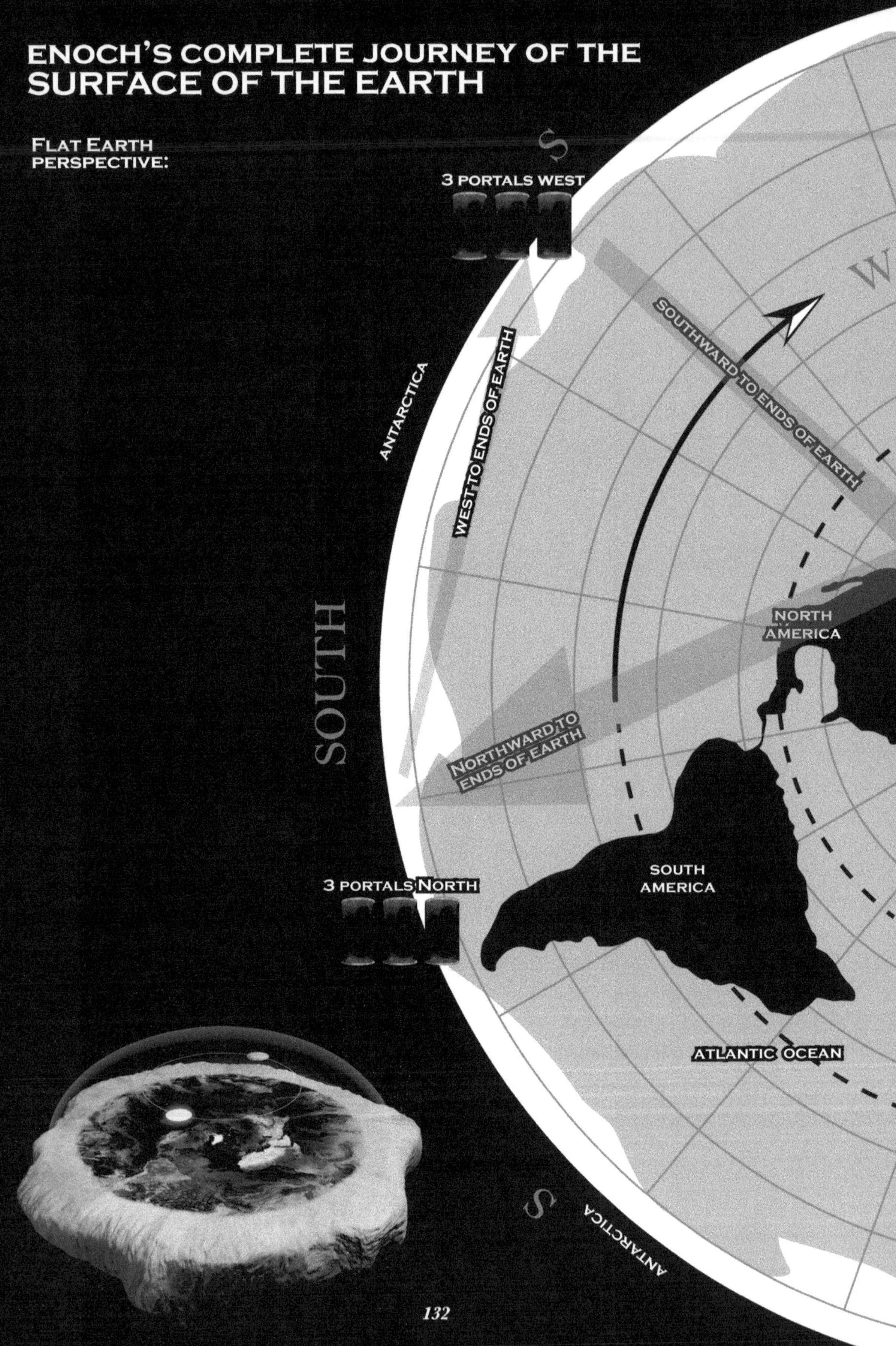

GREAT BEASTS DINOSAUR FOSSILS FOUND IN NEW ZEALAND
PACIFIC OCEAN
AUSTRALIA
GARDEN OF RIGHTEOUSNESS
VISAYAS
HAVILAH
PHILIPPINES
CHINA
ASIA
EXITS INNER EARTH
N
INDIA
EUROPE
MT. SINAI
AFRICA
E
W
3 PORTALS SOUTH
FIRMAMENT RESTS
HEAVEN'S PORTALS
ORIGIN OF STARS
GREAT BEASTS DINOSAUR FOSSILS FOUND IN AUSTRALIA
ENDS OF THE EARTH
ANTARCTICA
GREAT BEASTS DINOSAUR FOSSILS FOUND IN ANTARCTICA
INDONESIA
NORTHEAST OF INDIAN OCEAN
INDIES
BEYOND THE INDIAN OCEAN
EAST
SRI LANKA
EAST
EAST
EAST
EAST
ERYTHRAEAN SEA INDIAN OCEAN
EAST TO ENDS OF EARTH
SOUTH
S
ANTARCTICA
3 PORTALS EAST
S

# 36 ENOCH'S JOURNEY SOUTH AND EAST TO THE ENDS OF THE EARTH

## CHAPTER 36:



1 And from thence I went **to the south to the ends of the earth**, and saw there **three open portals of the heaven**: and thence there come dew, rain, and wind.

2 And from thence I went **to the east to the ends of the heaven** and saw here the **three eastern portals of heaven** open and small portals above them.

3 Through each of these small portals pass the stars of heaven and run their course to the west on the path which is shown to them. 4 And as often as I saw I blessed always Yahuah of Glory, and I continued to bless Yahuah of Glory who has wrought great and glorious wonders, to show the greatness of His work to the angels and to spirits and to men, that they might praise His work and all His creation: that they might see the work of His might and praise the great work of His hands and bless Him for ever.

# SECTION 2:

## 37-71
# THE BOOK OF PARABLES OF ENOCH

## QUOTED BY ENOCH:
1 Enoch 1:2

## QUOTED BY NOAH:
1 Enoch 60:1, 1 Enoch 68:1

## QUOTED BY MOSES:
Jub. 4:16-19, 7:38-39, 10:17-18

*Enoch, Noah, and Moses quote this book thus there is no scholarly position to disinclude this from First Enoch. It has always been included.*

## CHAPTER 37:

*Jub. 4:17. Moses specifies Enoch learnt and wrote wisdom.*

*Cf. Gen. 5:12 "Cainan."*
*Cf. 1 Ch. 1:2.*
*Jub. 4:14. "Kenan," not to be confused with the son of Ham.*

**1** The second vision which he saw, the vision of wisdom—which Enoch the son of Jared, the son of Mahalalel, the son of Cainan, the son of Enos, the son of Seth, the son of Adam, saw. **2** And this is the beginning of the words of wisdom which I lifted up my voice to speak and say to those which dwell on earth: Hear, ye men of old time, and see, ye that come after, the words of the Holy One which I will speak before Yahuah of Spirits. **3** It were better to declare (them only) to the men of old time, but even from those that come after we will not withhold the beginning of wisdom. **4** Till the present day such wisdom has never been given by Yahuah of Spirits as I have received according to my insight, according to the good pleasure of Yahuah of Spirits by whom the lot of eternal life has been given to me. **5** Now three parables were imparted to me, and I lifted up my voice and recounted them to those that dwell on the earth.

*Cf. Heb.11:5.*

*Cf. Rev. 3:10, 6:10, 8:13, 11:10, 13:8, 14, 17:8*

## CHAPTER 38:

The first Parable.

**1** "When the congregation of the righteous shall appear and sinners shall be judged for their sins, And shall be driven from the face of the earth:

**2** And when the Righteous One shall appear before the eyes of the righteous, whose elect works hang upon Yahuah of Spirits, And light shall appear to the righteous and the elect who dwell on the earth. Where then will be the dwelling of the sinners? And where the resting-place of those who have denied Yahuah of Spirits? It had been good for them if they had not been born. **3** When the secrets of the righteous shall be revealed and the sinners judged, And the godless driven from the presence of the righteous and elect, **4** From that time those that possess the earth shall no longer be powerful and exalted: And they shall not be able to behold the face of the holy. For Yahuah of Spirits has caused His light to appear on the face of the holy, righteous, and elect. **5** Then shall the kings and the mighty perish and be given into the hands of the righteous and holy. **6.** And thenceforward none shall seek for themselves mercy from Yahuah of Spirits: For their life is at an end.

*Cf. Matt. 26:24. "It had been good for that man if he had not been born."*

*Cf. 2Cor. 4:6. "To give the light of the knowledge of the glory of God in the face of Jesus Christ."*

# 39
# THE ABODE OF THE RIGHTEOUS AND OF THE ELECT ONE: THE PRAISES OF THE BLESSED

## CHAPTER 39:

[1 And it shall come to pass in those days that elect and holy children will descend from the high heaven, and their seed will become one with the children of men. 2 And in those days Enoch received books of zeal and wrath, and books of disquiet and expulsion.] And mercy shall not be accorded to them, saith Yahuah of Spirits. 3 And in those days a whirlwind carried me off from the earth. And set me down at the end of the heavens. 4 And there I saw another vision, the dwelling-places of the holy. And the resting-places of the righteous. 5 Here mine eyes saw their dwellings with His righteous angels, And their resting-places with the holy. And they petitioned and interceded and prayed for the children of men, And righteousness flowed before them as water, And mercy like dew upon the earth: Thus it is amongst them for ever and ever. 6 And in that place mine eyes saw the **Elect One** of righteousness and of faith, and righteousness shall prevail in his days, And the righteous and elect shall be without number before Him for ever and ever. 7 And I saw his dwelling-place under the wings of Yahuah of Spirits. And all the righteous and elect before Him shall

*Cf. 1 Tim. 5:21. "The elect angels."*

*Cf. John 14:2 "Many mansions."*

*Messiah.*

*Cf. Ps. 17:8.*

be strong as fiery lights, And their mouth shall be full of blessing, and their lips **extol the name of Yahuah of Spirits**, and righteousness before Him shall never fail, [And uprightness shall never fail before Him]. 8 There I wished to dwell, And my spirit longed for that dwelling-place: And there heretofore hath been my portion, For so has it been established concerning me before Yahuah of Spirits.

9 In those days I praised and extolled the name of Yahuah of Spirits with blessings and praises, because He hath destined me for blessing and glory according to the good pleasure of Yahuah of Spirits. 10 For a long time my eyes regarded that place, and I blessed Him and praised Him, saying: 'Blessed is He, and may He be blessed from the beginning and for evermore.'

11 And before Him there is no ceasing. He knows before the world was created what is for ever and what will be from generation unto generation. 12 Those who sleep not bless Thee they stand before Thy glory and bless, praise, and extol, saying: "Holy, holy, holy, is Yahuah of Spirits: He filleth the earth with spirits." 13 And here my eyes saw all those who sleep) not: they stand before Him and bless and say: 'Blessed be Thou, and blessed be the name of Yahuah for ever and ever.' 14 And my face was changed; for I could no longer behold.

*Angels. Cf. Rev. 4:8. "Who rest not... saying."*

# 40-41
# THE FOUR ARCHANGELS

## 41.3-9
## ASTRONOMICAL SECRETS

## CHAPTER 40:

Cf. 14:22, 71:8; Rev. 5:11.

Cf. 18:13. Same stars. See margin note.

1 And after that I saw thousands of thousands and ten thousand times ten thousand I saw a multitude beyond number and reckoning, who stood before Yahuah of Spirits. 2 And on the four sides of Yahuah of Spirits I saw **four presences**, different from those that sleep not, and I learnt their names: for the angel who went with me made known to me their names, and showed me all the hidden things. 3 And I heard the voices of those four presences as they uttered praises before Yahuah of glory. 4 The first voice blesses Yahuah of Spirits for ever and ever. 5 And the second voice I heard blessing the **Elect One** and the elect ones who hang upon Yahuah of Spirits.

Cf. Jub. 1:29; Rev. 4:6. "Round about the throne were four living creatures."

Cf. 45:3-4, 49:2, 4;. Luke 9:35, 23:35. "This is My Son, the Elect One."

6 And the third voice I heard pray and intercede for those who dwell on the earth and supplicate in the name of Yahuah of Spirits. 7 And I heard the fourth voice fending off the Satans and forbidding them to come before Yahuah of Spirits to accuse them who dwell on the earth. 8 After that I asked the angel of peace who went with me, who showed me everything that is hidden: 'Who are these four

Cf. 9:1-3,11,15:2, 47:2, 99:3; Rev. 8:3-4 "Angel with golden censer of incense."

Cf. Rev. 12:10. "The accuser of our brethren is to be cast down."

presences which I have seen and whose words I have heard and written down?

9 And he said to me: 'This first is **Michael**, the merciful and long-suffering; and the second, who is set over all the diseases and all the wounds of the children of men, is **Raphael**: and the third, who is set over all the powers, is **Gabriel**: and the fourth, who is set over the repentance unto hope of those who inherit eternal life, is named **Phanuel**. 10 And these are the four angels of Yahuah of Spirits and the four voices I heard in those days.

Raphael: רפה, רפא: (rapa'), to heal, El אל: "Healing of Elohim." [7] Raphael is told to heal the Earth in 10:7.

Cf. Matt. 19:29. "Inherit eternal life."

פנואל: Phenū'ēl: Paniel, Peniel, Penuel, Fanuel, Orfiel, and Orphiel: "the face of Elohim". Cf. 20. This is the same angel mentioned in the 7 archangels, Remiel, who is "set over those who rise." That is the same as "those who inherit eternal life." Remiel, רעמיאל: "mercy of Elohim" likely referring to his role. Both names are appropriate.

## CHAPTER 41:

1 And after that I saw all the secrets of the heavens, and how the kingdom is divided, and how the actions of men are weighed in the balance. 2 And there I saw the mansions of the elect and the mansions of the holy, and mine eyes saw there all the sinners being driven from thence which deny the name of Yahuah of Spirits, and being dragged off: and they could not abide because of the punishment which proceeds from Yahuah of Spirits.

Cf. John 14:2 "Many mansions." New Jerusalem. The context is the Day of Judgment.

3 And there mine eyes saw the secrets of the lightning and of the thunder, and the secrets of the winds, how they are divided to blow over the earth, and the secrets of the clouds and dew, and there I saw from whence they proceed in that place and from whence they saturate the dusty earth. 4 And there I saw closed chambers out of which the winds are divided, the chamber of the hail and winds, the chamber of the mist, and of the clouds, and the cloud thereof hovers over the earth from the beginning of the world. 5 And I saw the chambers of the sun and moon, whence they proceed and whither they come again, and their glorious return, and how one is superior to the other, and their stately orbit, and how they do not leave their orbit, and they add nothing to their orbit and they take nothing from it, and they keep faith with each other, in accordance with the oath by which they are bound together. 6 And **first the sun goes forth and traverses his path** according to the commandment of Yahuah of Spirits, and mighty is His name for ever and ever. 7 And after that I saw the hidden and the visible path of the moon, and she accomplishes the course of her path in that place by day and by night—the one holding a position opposite to the other before Yahuah of Spirits. And they give thanks and praise and rest not, for unto them is their thanksgiving rest. 8 For the sun changes oft for a blessing or a curse. And the course of the path of the moon is light to the righteous. And darkness to the sinners in the name of Yahuah, "Who made a separation between the light and the darkness, and divided the spirits of men, and strengthened the spirits of the righteous, in the name of His righteousness. 9 For no angel hinders and no power is able to hinder; for He appoints a judge for them all and he judges them all before Him.

*Cf. 72. The sun is the start of the day, week, month, year, seasons, etc. throughout scripture.*

*Cf. 73.*

*Cf. Acts 17:31. "He will judge the world in by the man whom He hath ordained."*

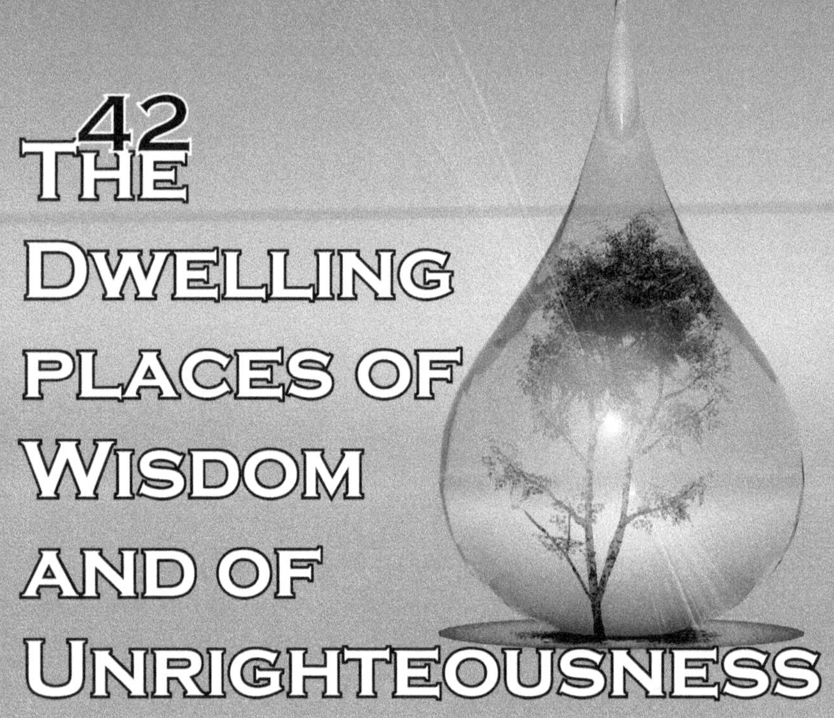


## CHAPTER 42:

1 Wisdom found no place where she might dwell; Then a dwelling-place was assigned her in the heavens. 2 Wisdom went forth to make her dwelling among the children of men and found no dwelling-place: Wisdom returned to her place and took her seat among the angels. 3 And unrighteousness went forth from her chambers: Whom she sought not she found and dwelt with them as rain in a desert and dew on a thirsty land.

## CHAPTER 43:

1 And I saw other lightnings and the stars of heaven, and I saw how **He called them all by their names** and they hearkened unto Him. 2 And I saw how they are weighed in a righteous balance according to their proportions of light: (I saw) the width of their spaces and the day of their appearing, and how their revolution produces lightning: and (I saw) their revolution according to the number of the angels, and (how) they keep faith with each other. 3 And I asked the angel who went with me who showed me what was hidden: 'What are these?' 4 And he said to me: 'Yahuah of Spirits hath showed thee their parabolic meaning (lit. 'their parable'): these are the names of the holy who dwell on the earth and believe in the name of Yahuah of Spirits for ever and ever.'

## CHAPTER 44:

1 Also another phenomenon I saw in regard to the lightnings; how some of the stars arise and become lightnings and cannot part with their new form.

# 45-57 THE SECOND PARABLE

## 45
### THE LOT OF THE APOSTATES: THE NEW HEAVEN AND THE NEW EARTH

## CHAPTER 45:

1 And this is the Second Parable concerning those who deny the name of the dwelling of the holy ones and Yahuah of Spirits. 2 And into the heaven they shall not ascend, And on the earth they shall not come: Such shall be the lot of the sinners Who have denied the name of Yahuah of Spirits Who are thus preserved for the day of suffering and tribulation.

3 On that day **Mine Elect One** shall sit on the throne of glory And shall try their works, and their places of rest shall be innumerable. And their souls shall grow strong within them when they see Mine elect ones, And those who have called upon My glorious name:

4 Then will I cause **Mine Elect One** to dwell among them. And I will **transform the heaven** and make it an eternal blessing and light, 5 And I will **transform the earth** and make it a blessing: And I will cause Mine elect ones to dwell upon it: But the sinners and evil-doers shall not set foot thereon. 6 For I have provided and satisfied with peace My righteous ones and have caused them to dwell before Me: But for the sinners there is judgment impending with Me, So that I shall destroy them from the face of the earth.

*Cf. 40:5, 49:2, 4;. Luke 9:35. "This is My Son, the Elect One."*

*Cf. Rev. 7:15. "He that sitteth on the throne shall dwell among them."*

*Cf. 72:1, 91:16; 2 Pet. 3:13. "New Heavens, new Earth."*

# THE
# HEAD OF DAYS
## AND THE
# SON OF MAN

# CHAPTER 46:

*Cf. "Head of Days." Dan. 7:9, 13, and 22 "Ancient of Days." Head or first is the same. Messiah.*

1 And there I saw One who had a **Head of Days**, And His head was white like wool, And with Him was another being whose countenance had the appearance of a man, And his face was full of graciousness, like one of the holy angels. 2 And I asked the angel who went with me and showed me all the hidden things,

*Cf. Dan. 7:13. "Son of Man." Messiah used this 82 times in the Gospels as His title. It originates in 1 Enoch.*

concerning that **Son of Man**, who he was, and whence he was (and) why he went with the **Head of Days**? 3 And he answered and said unto me: This is the **Son of Man** who

*Cf. Col. 2:3. "In whom are hid all the treasures of wisdom and knowledge."*

hath righteousness with whom dwelleth righteousness, And who revealeth all the treasures of that which is hidden. Because Yahuah of Spirits hath chosen him, And whose lot hath the pre-eminence before Yahuah of Spirits in uprightness for ever. 4 And this **Son of Man** whom thou hast

*Cf. Luke 1:52. "He hath put down princes from their thrones."*

seen Shall raise up the kings and the mighty from their seats, [And the strong from their thrones] And shall loosen the reins of the strong. And break the teeth of the sinners; 5 [And he shall put down the kings from their thrones and kingdoms] Because they do not extol and praise Him, Nor humbly acknowledge whence the kingdom was bestowed upon them. 6 And he shall put down the countenance of the strong, And shall fill them with shame. And darkness shall be their dwellings and worms shall be their bed, And they shall have no hope of rising from their beds. Because they do not extol the name of Yahuah of Spirits.

7 And these are they who judge the stars of heaven, [And raise their hands against the Most High], And tread upon the earth and dwell upon it. And all their deeds manifest unrighteousness, And their power rests upon their riches And their faith is in the gods which they have made with their hands. And they deny the name of Yahuah of Spirits,

8 And they persecute the houses of His congregations, And the faithful who hang upon the name of Yahuah of Spirits.

*These evil ones misjudge or mislead in teaching of the stars of Heaven. Modern Scientism fits this rebuke. 2 Pet. 3 refers to them as scoffers who pursue their own lusts offering willing ignorance. The delusion of "The God Delusion" sorcerers. They attempt to disprove Elohim yet they have to create a complete new paradigm which fails.*

## CHAPTER 47:

*Cf. Luke 18:7. "Shall not God avenge His elect which cry to Him day and night, and they may not have to suffer for ever."*

*Cf. 97:3-5, 99:3, 16, 104:3, 22:5-7; Rev. 6:10 "Righteous souls cry out for vengeance."*

*Cf. 9:1-3,11,15:2, 40:7, 99:3; Rev. 8:3-4 "Angel with golden censer of incense."*

1 And in those days shall have ascended the prayer of the righteous. And the blood of the righteous from the earth before Yahuah of Spirits. 2 In those days the holy ones who dwell above in the heavens shall unite with one voice and supplicate and pray [and praise, and give thanks and bless the name of Yahuah of Spirits] on behalf of the blood of the righteous which has been shed and that the prayer of the righteous may not be in vain before Yahuah of Spirits,

That judgment may be done unto them, And that they may not have to suffer for ever. 3 In those days I saw the **Head of Days** when He seated himself upon the throne of His glory, And the **books of the living** were opened before Him And all His host which is in heaven above and His counsellors stood before Him, 4 And the hearts of the holy were filled with joy; Because the number of the righteous had been offered. And the prayer of the righteous had been heard, And the blood of the righteous been required before Yahuah of Spirits.

*Cf. "Head of Days." Dan. 7:9, 13, and 22 "Ancient of Days."*

*Cf. 30:22, 36:10; Rev. 20:12. "The book of life."*

# 48
# The Fount of Righteousness:

## The Son of Man – The Stay of the Righteous: Judgment of the Kings and the Mighty

# CHAPTER 48:

Cf. Rev. 7:17, 21:6. "Shall guide them unto fountains of waters of life."

Cf. Prov. 13:14. "The law of the wise is a fountain of life."

1 And in that place I saw the fountain of righteousness which was inexhaustible: And around it were many fountains of wisdom; And all the thirsty drank of them, and were filled with wisdom. And their dwellings were with the righteous and holy and elect.

Cf. Dan. 7:13. "Son of Man." Messiah used this 82 times in the Gospels as His title. It originates in 1 Enoch

Cf. "Head of Days." Dan. 7:9, 13, and 22 "Ancient of Days."

Cf. Jn. 1:1-4, 8:12. Yahusha was in the beginning before the angels.

Cf. Jub. 2:2. Angels created Day 1 of Creation.

Cf. Jn. 8:12. "Light of the world... light of life."

Cf Phil 2:10 "At the name of Jesus every knee should bow."

2 And at that hour that **Son of Man** was named in the presence of Yahuah of Spirits, And his name before the **Head of Days**. 3 **Yea, before the sun and the signs were created. Before the stars of the heaven were made. His name was named before Yahuah of Spirits.** 4 He shall be a staff to the righteous whereon to stay themselves and not fall. And he shall be the light of the Gentiles, And the hope of those who are troubled of heart. 5 All who dwell on earth shall fall down and worship before him, And will praise and bless and celebrate with song Yahuah of Spirits. 6. And for this reason **hath he been chosen and hidden before Him, before the creation of the world** and for evermore.

7 And the wisdom of Yahuah of Spirits hath revealed him to the holy and righteous; For he hath preserved the lot of the righteous; Because they have hated and despised this world of unrighteousness, And have hated all its works and ways in the name of Yahuah of Spirits: **For in his name they are saved**, And according to his good pleasure hath it been in regard to their life, 8 In these days downcast in countenance shall the kings of the earth have become, And the strong who possess the land because of the works of their hands; For on the day of their anguish and affliction they shall not (be able to) save themselves, 9 And I will give them over into the hands of Mine elect **as straw in the fire so shall they burn** before the face of the holy; As lead in the water shall they sink before the face of the righteous, And **no trace of them shall any more be found**. 10 And on the day of their affliction there shall be rest on the earth, And before them they shall fall and not rise again: And there shall be no one to take them with his hands and raise them: For they have **denied Yahuah of Spirits and His Anointed**. The name of Yahuah of Spirits be blessed.

Cf. 108:8; 1 Jn. 2:15.

Cf. Gal. 1:4; Heb. 4:12. "This present evil world."

Cf. 1 Cor. 6:11. "Justified in the name of the Lord Jesus."

Cf. 2 Esd. 15:23. "Fire is gone forth from his wrath... sinners like the straw."

Cf. Rev. 14:9-10. "The worshippers of the beast are tormented with fire and brimstone in presence angels... and the lamb."

Cf. Jude 1:4.

There has never been salvation without Yahusha period. No religion can replace that including Judaism which is not the relationship of the Bible.

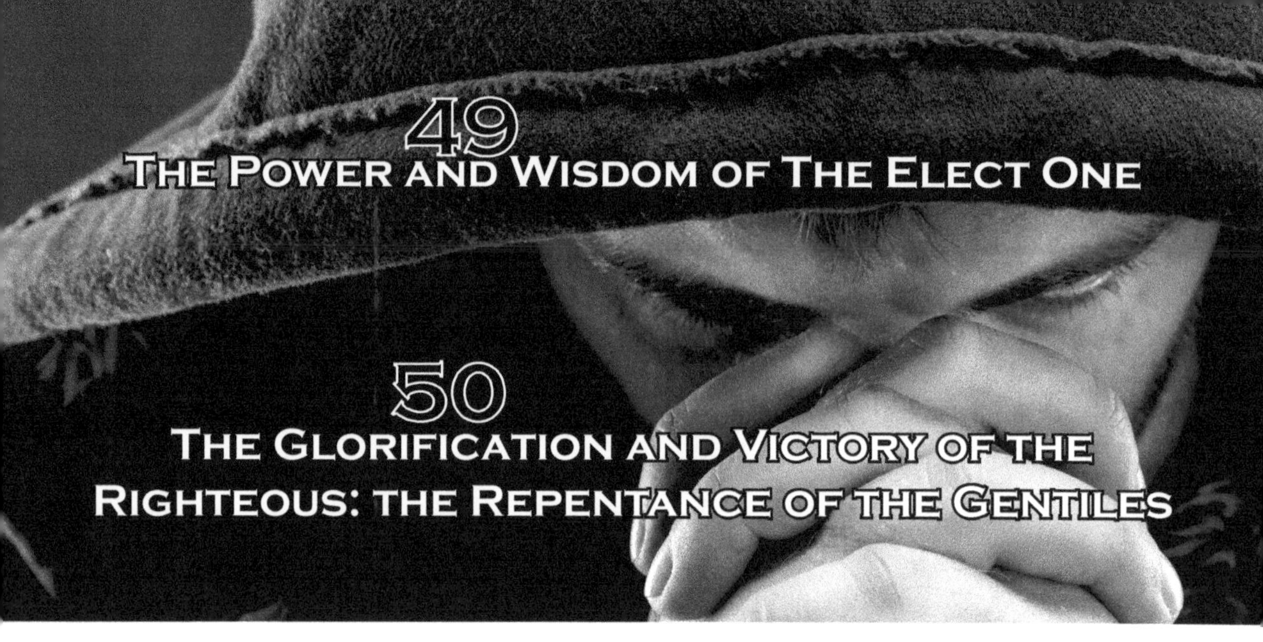


# CHAPTER 49:

1 For wisdom is poured out like water. And glory faileth not before him for evermore. 2 For he is mighty in all the secrets of righteousness, and unrighteousness shall disappear as a shadow. And have no continuance; Because the Elect One standeth before Yahuah of Spirits, And his glory is for ever and ever, And his might unto all generations. 3 And in him dwells the spirit of wisdom, And the spirit which gives insight, And the spirit of understanding and of might. And **the spirit of those who have fallen asleep in righteousness**. 4 And he shall judge the secret things, And none shall be able to utter a lying word before him; For he is the Elect One before Yahuah of Spirits according to His good pleasure.

*Cf. Eph. 1:9. "According to His good pleasure."*

# CHAPTER 50:

1 And in those days a change shall take place for the holy and elect, And the light of days shall abide upon them, And glory and honor shall turn to the holy, 2 On the day of affliction on which evil shall have been treasured up against the sinners. And the righteous shall be victorious in the name of Yahuah of Spirits: And He will cause the others to witness (this) that they may repent And forgo the works of their hands. 3 They shall have no honor through the name of Yahuah of Spirits,

Yet through His name shall they be saved, And Yahuah of Spirits will have compassion on them, For His compassion is great. 4 And He is righteous also in His judgment. And in the presence of His glory unrighteousness also shall not maintain itself: At His judgment the unrepentant shall perish before Him.

5 And from henceforth I will have no mercy on them, saith Yahuah of Spirits.

## CHAPTER 51:

*Cf. 2 Esd. 7:32-33.*

*Cf. 61:5; Rev. 20:13. "Tho sea... Hades gave up the dead."*

1 And **in those days shall the earth also give back that which has been entrusted to it**. And Sheol also shall give back that which it has received, And hell shall give back that which it owes. For **in those days the Elect One shall arise**, 2 And he shall choose the righteous and holy from among them: For the day has drawn nigh that they should be saved. 3 And the Elect One shall in those days sit on My throne, And his mouth shall pour forth all the secrets of wisdom and counsel: For Yahuah of Spirits hath given (them) to him and hath glorified him. 4 And in those days shall the mountains leap like rams, And the hills also shall skip like lambs satisfied with milk, And the faces of [all] the angels in heaven shall be lighted up with joy. 5 And the earth shall rejoice, And the righteous shall dwell upon it, And the elect shall walk thereon.

*Charles moved 5 a here. We do not label.*

*Cf. Luke 21:23. "Your redemption draweth nigh."*

*Cf. 2 Esd. 7:32-33.*

## CHAPTER 52:

1 And after those days in that place where I had seen all the visions of that which is hidden—for I had been carried off in a whirlwind and they had borne me towards the west. 2 There mine eyes saw all the secret things of heaven that shall be a mountain of iron and a mountain of copper, and a mountain of silver, and a mountain of gold, and a mountain of soft metal, and a mountain of lead. 3 And I asked the angel who went with me, saying, 'What things are these which I have seen in secret?' 4 And he said unto me: 'All these things which thou hast seen shall serve the dominion of **His Anointed** that he may be potent and mighty on the earth." 5 And that angel of peace answered, saying unto me: 'Wait a little and there shall be revealed unto thee all the secret things, which surround Yahuah of Spirits. 6 And these mountains which thine eyes have seen, The mountain of iron, and the mountain of copper, and the mountain of silver, And the mountain of gold, and the mountain of soft metal, and the mountain of lead, All these shall be in the presence of the Elect One, As wax before the fire, And like the water which streams down from above [upon those mountains], And they shall become powerless before his feet. 7 And it shall come to pass in those days that none shall be saved, Either by gold or by silver, And none be able to escape. 8 And there shall be no iron for war. Nor shall one clothe oneself with a breastplate. Bronze shall be of no service. And tin [shall be of no service and] shall not be esteemed. And lead shall not be desired. 9 And all these things shall be [denied and] destroyed from the surface of the earth, When the Elect One shall appear before the face of Yahuah of Spirits.'

1 There mine eyes saw a deep

## CHAPTER 53:

valley with open mouths, and all who dwell on the earth and sea and islands shall bring to him gifts and presents and tokens of homage, but that deep valley shall not become full. 2 And their hands commit lawless deeds, And the sinners devour all whom they lawlessly oppress: Yet the sinners shall be destroyed before the face of Yahuah of Spirits, And they shall be banished from off the face of His earth. And they shall **perish for ever and ever**. 3 For I saw all the angels of punishment abiding (there) and preparing all the instruments of Satan. 4 And

I asked the angel of peace who went with me: 'For whom are they preparing these instruments? '5 And he said unto me: 'They prepare these for the kings and the mighty of this earth, that they may thereby be destroyed. 6 And after this **the Righteous and Elect One shall cause the house of his congregation to appear**: henceforth they shall be no more hindered in the name of Yahuah of Spirits. 7 And these mountains shall not stand as the earth before his righteousness But the hills shall be as a fountain of water. And the righteous shall have rest from the oppression of sinners.

*Cf. Acts 3:14, 7:52, 22:14. "The Righteous One, i.e.Christ."*

# CHAPTER 54:

1 And I looked and turned to another part of the earth, and saw there a deep valley with burning fire. 2 And they brought the kings and the mighty, and began to cast them into this deep valley. 3 And there mine eyes saw how they made these their instruments, iron chains of immeasurable weight. 4 And I asked the angel of peace who went with me, saying 'For whom are these chains being prepared?' 5 And he said unto me: 'These are being prepared for the hosts of Azazel; so that they may take them and cast them into the abyss of complete condemnation and they shall cover their jaws with rough stones as Yahuah of Spirits commanded.

*Cf. Matt. 25:41. "Prepared for the devil and his angels."*

6 And Michael, and Gabriel, and Raphael and Phanuel shall take hold of them on that great day, and cast them on that day into the burning furnace that Yahuah of Spirits may take vengeance on them for their unrighteousness in becoming **subject to Satan** and leading astray those who dwell on the earth.'

*Cf. 67:7; Rev. 13:14. "Deceiveth them that dwell on the earth."*

7 And in those days shall

## 54.7 NOACHIC FRAGMENT ON THE FIRST WORLD JUDGMENT

*Cf. Gen. 7:11.* punishment come from Yahuah of Spirits, and He will open all the chambers of waters which are above the heavens, and of the fountains which are beneath the earth. 8 And all the waters shall be joined with the waters: that which is above the heavens is the masculine, and the water which is beneath the earth is the feminine. 9 And they shall destroy all who dwell on the earth and those who dwell under the ends of the heaven.

*Cf. Gen. 7:21-22.*

10 And when they have recognized their unrighteousness which they have wrought on the earth, then by these shall they perish.'

## CHAPTER 55:

*Cf. "Head of Days." Dan. 7:9, 13, and 22 "Ancient of Days."*

1 And after that the **Head of Days** repented and said: 'In vain have I destroyed all who dwell on the earth.'

2 And He swore by His great name: 'Henceforth I will not do so to all who dwell on the earth, and I will set a sign in the heaven: and this shall be a *Cf. Gen. 9:12-15.* pledge of good faith between Me and them for ever, so long as heaven is above the earth. And this is in accordance with My command. 3 When I have desired to take hold of them by the hand of the angels on the day of tribulation and pain because of this, I will cause My chastisement and My wrath to abide upon them, saith Elohim, Yahuah of Spirits. 4 Ye mighty kings who dwell on the earth, ye shall have to behold Mine Elect One, how he sits on the throne of glory and judges Azazel, and all his associates, and all his hosts in the name of Yahuah of Spirits.''

*Cf. Matt. 25:31. "When the Son of man shall come in his glory, and all the holy angels with him, then shall he sit upon the throne of his glory:"*

# CHAPTER 56:

1 And I saw there the hosts of the angels of punishment going, and they held scourges and chains of iron and bronze. 2 And I asked the angel of peace who went with me, saying: 'To whom are these who hold the scourges going? 3 And he said unto me: 'To their elect and beloved ones that they may be cast into the chasm of the abyss of the valley. 4 And then that valley shall be filled with their elect and beloved, And the days of their lives shall be at an end, And the days of their leading astray shall not thenceforward be reckoned. 5 And in those days the angels shall return And hurl themselves to the east upon the Parthians and Medes: They shall stir up the kings; so that a spirit of unrest shall come upon them, And they shall rouse them from their thrones that they may break forth as lions from their lairs. And as hungry wolves among their flocks. 6 And they shall go up and tread under foot the land of His elect ones, [And the land of His elect ones shall be before them a threshing-floor and a highway]: 7 But the city of my righteous shall be a hindrance to their horses. And they shall begin to fight among themselves. And their right hand shall be strong against themselves, And a man shall not know his brother, Nor a son his father or his mother, Till there be no number of the corpses through their slaughter. And their punishment be not in vain, 8 In those days **Sheol shall open its jaws**. And they shall be swallowed up therein, And their destruction shall be at an end; Sheol shall devour the sinners in the presence of the elect.'

*Lake of Fire on the Day of Judgment.*

*The Nephilim.*

*In the end, Sheol opens and the wicked are then thrown into the Lake of Fire. No man is in a burning Hell prior to that day. Cf. Rev. 1:18. This is why Yahusha said He has the keys to Hades and the death. In other words, the entire underworld and only He can open it.*

# CHAPTER 57:

1 And it came to pass after this that I saw another host of wagons, and men riding thereon, and coming on "the winds from the east, and from the west to the south. 2 And the noise of their wagons was heard, and when this turmoil took place the holy ones from heaven remarked it, and the **pillars of the earth were moved from their place**, and the sound thereof was heard from the one end of heaven to the other, in one day. 3 And they shall all fall down and worship Yahuah of Spirits. And this is the end of the second Parable.

*Cf. 2 Esd. 13:5. "...a multitude of men out of number, from the four winds of the heaven, to subdue the man that came out of the sea (Messiah)."*

# 58-71 The Third Parable

## 58 The Blessedness of the Saints

## 59 The Lights and the Thunder

# CHAPTER 58:

# CHAPTER 59:

1 And I began to speak the third Parable concerning the righteous and elect. 2 Blessed are ye, ye righteous and elect. For glorious shall be your lot. 3 And the righteous shall be in the light of the sun. And the elect in the light of eternal life, the days of their life shall be unending. And the days of the holy without number. 4 And they shall seek the light and find righteousness with Yahuah of Spirits: There shall be peace to the righteous in the name of the Eternal Yahuah. 5 And after this it shall be said to the holy in heaven that they should seek out the secrets of righteousness, the heritage of faith: For it has become bright as the sun upon earth, And the darkness is past.

6 And there shall be a light that never endeth, And to a limit (lit. 'number') of days they shall not come, for the darkness shall first have been destroyed, [And the light established before Yahuah of Spirits] And the light of uprightness established for ever before Yahuah of Spirits.

*Cf. Jn. 8:12. "Light of the world... light of life."*

*Cf. Dan. 12:2; Matt. 19:29; Luke 18:30; Jn. 3:16, 36, 4:14, 5:24, 6:27, 40, 12:50; Rom. 6:22; Gal. 6:8; 1 Tim. 1:16.*

*Cf. 1 Jn. 2:8.*

*Cf. Is. 60:19-20. "The sun shall be no more thy light by day; neither for brightness shall the moon give light unto thee: but the LORD shall be unto thee an everlasting light."*

1 In those days mine eyes saw the secrets of the lightnings, and of the lights, and the judgments they execute (lit. 'their judgment'): and they lighten for a blessing or a curse as Yahuah of Spirits willeth.
2 And there I saw the secrets of the thunder and how when it resounds above in the heaven the sound thereof is heard and he caused me to see the judgments executed on the earth, whether they be for well-being and blessing, or for a curse according to the word of Yahuah of Spirits. 3 And after that all the secrets of the lights and lightnings were shown to me, and they lighten for blessing and for satisfying.]

## CHAPTER 60:

*Enoch did not die. Noah still counted his years proving such.*

*Cf. 54.*

**1** In the year five hundred, in the seventh month, on the fourteenth day of the month in the life of Enoch. In that Parable I saw how a mighty quaking made the heaven of heavens to quake, and the host of the Most High, and the angels, a thousand thousands and ten thousand times ten thousand, were disquieted with a great disquiet.

*Cf. "Head of Days." Dan. 7:9, 13, and 22 "Ancient of Days."*

*Cf. 14:18-23, 90:20; Dan. 7; 1 Ki. 22:19; Is. 6; Ez. 1, 3:22-24, 10:1. Biblical throne visions that match.*

**2** And the **Head of Days** sat on the throne of His glory, and the angels and the righteous stood around Him. **3** And a great trembling seized me 'And fear took hold of me, And my loins gave way, And dissolved were my reins, And I fell upon my face. **4** And Michael sent another angel from among the holy ones and he raised me up, and when he had raised me up my spirit returned; for I had not been able to endure the look of this host, and the commotion and the quaking of the heaven. **5** And Michael said unto me: 'Why art thou disquieted with such a vision? Until this day lasted the day of His mercy; and He hath been merciful and long-suffering towards those who dwell on the earth. **6** And when the day, and the power, and the punishment, and the judgment come, which Yahuah of Spirits hath prepared for those who worship not the righteous law, and for those who deny the righteous judgment, and for those who take His name in vain—that day is prepared, for the elect a covenant, but for sinners an inquisition.

*Cf. 62:1; 2Esd. 7:37.*

**25** When the punishment of Yahuah of Spirits shall rest upon them, it shall rest in order that the punishment of Yahuah of Spirits may not come in vain, and it shall slay the children with their mothers and the children with their fathers. Afterwards the judgment shall take place according to His mercy and His patience. **7** And on that day were two monsters parted, a female monster named Leviathan, to dwell in the

*Cf. 2Esd. 6:49-52.*

## QUAKING OF THE HEAVEN: BEHEMOTH AND LEVIATHAN: THE ELEMENTS

abysses of the ocean over the fountains of the waters. **8** But the male is named Behemoth, who occupied with his breast a waste wilderness named **Duidain, on the east of the garden where the elect and righteous dwell, where my grandfather was taken up, the seventh from Adam**, the first man whom Yahuah of Spirits created. **9** And I besought the other angel that he should show me the might of those monsters, how they were parted on one day and cast, the one into the abysses of the sea, and the other unto the dry land of the wilderness. **10** And he said to me: 'Thou son of man, herein thou dost seek to know what is hidden.' **11** And the other angel who went with me and showed me what was hidden told me, what is first and last in the heaven in the height, and beneath the earth in the depth, and at the ends of the heaven, and on the foundation of the heaven. **12** And the chambers of the winds, and how the winds are divided, and how they are weighed, and (how) the portals of the winds are reckoned, each according to the power of the wind, and the power of the lights of the moon, and according to the power that is fitting: and the divisions of the stars according to their names, and how all the divisions are divided. **13** And the thunders according to the places where they fall, and all the divisions that are made among the lightnings that it may lighten, and their host that they may at once obey. **14** For the thunder has places of rest (which) are assigned (to it) while it is waiting for its peal; and the thunder and lightning are inseparable, and although not one and undivided, they both go together through the spirit and separate not. **15** For when the lightning lightens, the thunder utters its voice, and the spirit enforces a pause during the peal, and divides equally between them; for the treasury of their peals is like

Cf. 10:4 Dudael, where the earth was opened and Raphael cast into the abyss, is likely Duidain. [6]

This is the land of Havilah, where Adam's generations lived up unto the Flood. The Philippines. The largest caldera on Earth is to the East of the Philippines. [23]

Cf. Jub. 4:23. "conducted him (Enoch) into the Garden of Eden."

Cf. Jub. 7:39, Jude 1:14. "the seventh from Adam."

Cf. 2 Esd. 6:49-52; Job 41:1; Is. 27:1.

Cf. Dan. 7:13. "Son of Man." Messiah used this 82 times in the Gospels as His title. It originates in 1 Enoch.

Cf. Jub. 2:2, 4.

the sand, and each one of them as it peals is held in with a bridle, and turned back by the power of the spirit, and pushed forward according to the many quarters of the earth. **16** And the spirit of the Cf. Rev. 16:6 "Angel of the waters." sea is masculine and strong, and according to the might of his strength he draws it back with a rein, and in like manner it is driven forward and disperses amid all the mountains of the earth.

Cf. Jub. 2:2, 4. **17** And the spirit of the hoar-frost is his own angel, and the spirit of the hail is a good angel. **18** And the spirit of the snow has forsaken (his chamber) on account of his strength—there is a special spirit therein, and that which ascends from it is like smoke, and its name is frost. **19** And the spirit of the mist is not united with them in their chambers, but it has a special chamber; for its course is glorious both in light and in darkness, and in winter and in summer, and in its chamber is an angel. **20** And the spirit of the dew has its dwelling at the ends of the heaven, and is connected with the chambers of the rain, and its course is in winter and summer: and its clouds and the clouds of the mist are connected, and the one gives to the other. **21** And when the spirit of the rain goes forth from its chamber, the angels come and open the chamber and lead it out, and when it is diffused over the whole earth it unites with the water on the earth. And whensoever it unites with the water on the earth... **22** For the waters are for those who dwell on the earth; for they are nourishment for the earth from the Most High who is in heaven: therefore there is a measure for the rain, and the angels take it in charge. **23** And these things I saw towards the **Garden of the Righteous**. **24** And the angel of peace who was with me said to me : 'These two monsters, prepared conformably to the greatness of Elohim, shall feed. . . .

It seems to be is describing condensation and evaporation.

Cf. 60:8. Duidain/ Dudael. East of the Garden is the persepctive of Noah in this fragment. He lived there in the modern Philippines.

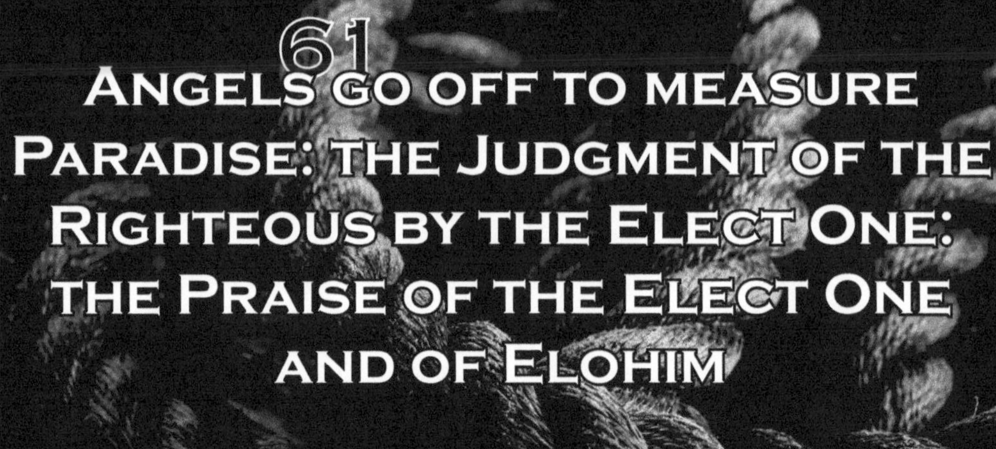


## CHAPTER 61:

1 And I saw in those days how long cords were given to those angels, and they took to themselves wings and flew, and they went towards the north. 2 And I asked the angel, saying unto him: 'Why have those (angels) taken these cords and gone off? And he said unto me: 'They have gone to measure.' 3 And the angel who went with me said unto me; 'These shall bring the measures of the righteous, And the ropes of the righteous to the righteous. That they may stay themselves on the name of Yahuah of Spirits for ever and ever.

*Some angels do have wings.*

*They went to the North to enter the Inner Earth.*

4 The elect shall begin to dwell with the elect. And those are the measures which shall be given to faith and which shall strengthen righteousness. 5 And these measures shall reveal all the secrets of the depths of the earth, and those who have been destroyed by the desert, and those who have been devoured by the beasts. And those who have been devoured by the fish of the sea. That they may return and stay themselves on the day of the **Elect One**; For none shall

*Inner Earth or Sheol, Hades.*

*Cf. 51:1; Rev. 20:13. "The sea... Hades gave up the dead."*

be destroyed before Yahuah of Spirits, and none can be destroyed. 6 And all who dwell above in the heaven received a command and power and one voice and one light like unto fire. 7 And that One (with) their first words they blessed, and extolled and lauded with wisdom, and they were wise in utterance and in the spirit of life. 8 And **Yahuah of Spirits placed the Elect One on the throne of glory**. And he shall judge all the works of the holy above in the heaven. And in the balance shall their deeds be weighed. 9 And when he shall lift up his countenance to judge their secret ways according to the word of the name of Yahuah of Spirits, And their path according to the way of the righteous judgment of Yahuah of Spirits, Then shall they all with one voice speak and bless, And glorify and extol and sanctify the name of Yahuah of Spirits. 10 And He will summon all the host of the heavens, and all the holy ones above, and the host of Elohim, the Cherubim, Seraphim, and

*Cf. Matt. 19:28, 25:31. "When the Son of man shall come in his glory, and all the holy angels with him, then shall he sit upon the throne of his glory:"*

Ophannim, and all the angels of power, and all the angels of principalities, and the Elect One, and the other powers on the earth (and) over the water. 11 On that day shall raise one voice, and bless and glorify and exalt in the spirit of faith, and in the spirit of wisdom, and in the spirit of patience, and in the spirit of mercy, and in the spirit of judgment and of peace, and in the spirit of goodness, and shall all say with one voice: "Blessed is He, and may the name of Yahuah of Spirits be blessed for ever and ever." 12 **All who sleep not above in heaven** shall bless Him: All the holy ones who are in heaven shall bless him. And all the elect who **dwell in the garden of life**: And every spirit of light who is able to bless, and glorify, and extol, and hallow Thy blessed name. And all flesh shall beyond measure glorify and bless Thy name for ever and ever. 13 For great is the mercy of Yahuah of Spirits, and He is long-suffering. And all His works and all that He has created He has revealed to the righteous and elect in the name of Yahuah of Spirits.'

*Cf. Rom. 8:34; Eph. 1:21; Col. 1:16; 2Th.1:7. "Neither angels, nor principalities, nor powers."*

*Angels.*

# 62 Judgment of the Kings and the Mighty: Blessedness of the Righteous

# 63 The unavailing Repentance of the Kings and the Mighty

# 64 Vision of the fallen Angels in the Place of Punishment

# CHAPTER 62:

*Cf. 60:6; 2Esd. 7:37.*

1 And thus Yahuah commanded the kings and the mighty and the exalted, and those who dwell on the earth, and said: 'Open your eyes and lift up your horns if ye are able to recognize the Elect One.'

*Cf. Matt. 19:28, 25:31. "When the Son of man shall come in his glory, and all the holy angels with him, then shall he sit upon the throne of his glory:"*

2 And Yahuah of Spirits seated him on the throne of His glory. And the spirit of righteousness was poured out upon him, And the word of his mouth slays all the sinners, And all the unrighteous are destroyed from before his face.

*Cf. 2 Esd. 13:10, 38. "he shall destroy them without labor, by the law which is like unto fire."*

*Cf. Rev. 1:16, 2:15, 19:15, 21. "...sword proceeded out of his mouth."*

3 And there shall stand up in that day all the kings and the mighty, And the exalted and those who hold the earth, And they shall see and recognize How he sits on the throne of his glory, And righteousness is judged before him. And no lying word is spoken before him.

*Cf. Rev. 6:15-16.*

*Cf. 1 Th. 5:3. "Then sudden destruction Cometh upon them as upon a woman with child."*

4 Then shall pain come upon them as on a woman in travail, [And she has pain in bringing forth] When her child enters the mouth of the womb, And she has pain in bringing forth. 5 And one portion of them shall look on the other. And they shall be terrified. And they shall be downcast of countenance, And pain shall seize them, When they see that **Son of Man** sitting on the throne of his glory. 6 And the kings and the mighty and all who possess the earth shall bless and glorify and extol him who rules over all, who was hidden. 7 For from the beginning the **Son of Man was hidden. And the Most High preserved him in the presence of His might**. And revealed him to the elect. 8 And the congregation of the elect and holy shall be sown. And all the elect shall stand before him on that day. 9 And all the kings and the mighty and the exalted and those who rule the earth shall fall down before him on their faces. And worship and set their hope upon that **Son of Man**, and petition him and supplicate for mercy at his hands. 10 Nevertheless Yahuah of Spirits will so press them that they shall hastily go forth from His presence, and their faces shall be filled with shame. And the darkness shall grow deeper on their faces.

11 And He will deliver them to the angels for punishment to execute vengeance on them because they have oppressed His children and His elect.

12 And they shall be a spectacle for the righteous and for His elect: They shall rejoice over them, Because the wrath of Yahuah of Spirits

*Cf. Dan. 7:13. "Son of Man." Messiah used this 82 times in the Gospels as His title. It originates in 1 Enoch.*

*Cf. Matt. 28:18. "All authority hath been given to Me in heaven and on earth."*

resteth upon them, And His sword is drunk with their blood. 13 And the righteous and elect shall be saved on that day, And they shall never thenceforward see the face of the sinners and unrighteous. 14 And Yahuah of Spirits will abide over them. **And with that Son of Man shall they eat and lie down and rise up for ever and ever.**

Cf. Rev. 3:20 "I will come unto him and sup with him."

15 And the righteous and elect shall have risen from the earth, and ceased to be of downcast countenance.

Cf. 2 Cor. 5:2-4.

16 And they shall have been clothed with garments of glory. And these shall be the garments of life from Yahuah of Spirits: And your garments shall not grow old. Nor your glory pass away before Yahuah of Spirits.

# CHAPTER 63:

1 In those days shall the mighty and the kings who possess the earth implore (Him) to grant them a little respite from His angels of punishment to whom they were delivered, that they might fall down and worship before Yahuah of Spirits and confess their sins before Him. 2 And they shall bless and glorify Yahuah of Spirits, and say: 'Blessed is Yahuah of Spirits and the Yahuah of Kings, and Yahuah of the Mighty and Yahuah of the Rich and Yahuah of glory and Yahuah of wisdom, 3 And splendid in every secret thing is Thy power from generation to generation. And Thy glory for ever and ever: Deep are all Thy secrets and innumerable. And Thy righteousness is beyond reckoning. 4 We have now learnt that we should glorify And bless Yahuah of Kings and Him who is king over all kings. 5 And they shall say: 'Would that we had rest to glorify and give thanks And confess our faith before His glory! 6 And now we long for a little rest but find it not: We follow hard upon and obtain (it) not: And light has vanished from before us, And darkness is our dwelling-place for ever and ever: 7 For we have not believed before Him nor glorified the name of Yahuah of Spirits, [nor glorified our Yahuah] But our hope was in the sceptre of our kingdom, and in our glory. 8 And in the day of our suffering and tribulation He saves us not. And we find no respite for confession that our Yahuah is true in all His works, and in His judgements and His justice, And His

*Cf. Rom. 2:11; Col. 3:25. "For there is no respect of persons with God." Origin: 1 Enoch. Meaning there is no prejudice in status.*

*Cf. Luke 16:9. "Mammon of unrighteousness."*

*Cf. Dan. 7:13. "Son of Man." Messiah used this 82 times in the Gospels as His title. It originates in 1 Enoch.*

judgments have **no respect of persons**. 9 And we pass away from before His face on account of our works, and all our sins are reckoned up in righteousness.' 10 Now they will say unto themselves: 'Our souls are full of unrighteous gain, but it does not prevent us from descending from the midst thereof into the burden of Sheol.' 11 And after that their faces shall be filled with darkness and shame before that **Son of Man**, And they shall be driven from his presence. And the sword shall abide before his face in their midst. 12 Thus spake Yahuah of Spirits: 'This is the ordinance and judgment with respect to the mighty and the kings and the exalted and those who possess the earth before Yahuah of Spirits.'

## CHAPTER 64:

1 And other forms I saw hidden in that place. 2 I heard the voice of the angel saying: 'These are the angels who descended to the earth, and revealed what was hidden to the children of men and seduced the children of men into committing sin.'

*Cf. Gen. 6:1-4; Jub. 5:1-2; Jude 1:6; 2 Pet. 2:4.*

167

# 65 Enoch Foretells to Noah the Deluge and his own Preservation

# 66 The Angels of the Waters Bidden to Hold them in Check

# 67 Elohim's Promise to Noah: Places of Punishment of the Angels and of the Kings

# CHAPTER 65:

*Noah visits Enoch at the Garden of Eden entrance. This is not new as Methuselah also visited. Cf. 106.7-8. "...his dwelling-place is amongst the angels." Garden of Eden. Cf. Gen. Ap., Col. II. 20: "He went at once to Parwain and he found him there." Parwaim is Sepharwaim where Ophir migrated to the land of the Garden.*

1 And in those days **Noah** saw the earth that it had sunk down and its destruction was nigh. 2 And he arose from thence and went to the **ends of the earth**, and **cried aloud to his grandfather Enoch**: and Noah said three times with an embittered voice: 'Hear me hear me, hear me.' 3 And I said unto him: 'Tell me what it is that is falling out on the earth that the earth is in such evil plight and shaken, lest perchance I shall perish with it.' 4 And thereupon there was a great commotion on the earth, and a voice was heard from heaven,

*Cf. 106.7-8. Same with Methuselah, Enoch exits the Garden. No man enters otherwise.*

and I fell on my face. 5 And **Enoch my grandfather came and stood by me**, and said unto me: 'Why hast thou cried unto me with a bitter cry and weeping? 6 And a command has gone forth from the presence of Yahuah concerning those who dwell on the earth that their ruin is accomplished because they have learnt all the secrets of the angels, and all the violence of the Satans, and all their powers—the most secret ones and all the power of those who practice sorcery,

*Satan is not a name but a title of "adversary." Today, wo have 1 satan. Before the Flood there were 200.*

and the power of witchcraft, and the power of those who make molten images for the whole earth:

7 And how silver is produced from the dust of the earth, and how soft metal originates in the earth. 8 For lead and tin are not produced from the earth like the first: it is a fountain that produces them, and an angel stands therein, and that angel is pre-eminent.' 9 And after that my grandfather Enoch took hold of me by my hand and raised me up, and said unto me: 'Go, for I have asked Yahuah of Spirits as touching this commotion on the earth. 10 And He said unto me: "Because of their unrighteousness their judgment has been determined upon and shall not be withheld by Me for ever. Because of the sorceries which they have searched out and learnt, the earth and those who dwell upon it shall be destroyed." 11 And these—they have no place of repentance for ever, because they have shown them what was hidden, and they are the damned: but as for thee, my son, Yahuah of Spirits knows that thou art pure, and guiltless of this reproach concerning the secrets.

*Cf. Rev. 18:23; Matt. 24:12; 2 Esd. 5:2. These are the same signs of the End Times. "As it was in the days of Noah, so it will be at the coming of the Son of Man."*

*Modern science does not know the true origin of these metals. They guess.*

*Cf. Rev. 18:23; Matt. 24:12; 2 Esd. 5:2. These are the same signs of the End Times. These days of Noah return in the end. "...by thy sorceries were all nations deceived."*

**12** And He has destined thy name to be among the holy, And will preserve thee amongst those who dwell on the earth, And has destined thy righteous seed both for kingship and for great honors. And from thy seed shall proceed a fountain of the righteous and holy without number for ever.'

## CHAPTER 66:

**1** And after that he showed me the angels of punishment who are prepared to come and let loose all the powers of the waters which are beneath in the earth in order to bring judgment and destruction on all who [abide and] dwell on the earth, **2** And Yahuah of Spirits gave commandment to the angels who were going forth, that they should not cause the waters to rise but should hold them in check; for those angels were over the powers of the waters. **3** And I went away from the presence of Enoch.

## CHAPTER 67:

**1** And in those days the word of Elohim came unto me, and He said unto me: 'Noah, thy lot has come up before Me, a lot without blame, a lot of love and uprightness. **2** And now the angels are making a wooden (building), and when they have completed that task I will place My hand upon it and preserve it, and there shall come forth from it the seed of life, and a change shall set in so that the earth will not remain without inhabitant. **3** And I will make fast thy seed before me for ever and ever, and I will spread abroad those who dwell with thee: it shall not be unfruitful on the face of the earth, but it shall be blessed and multiply on the earth in the name of Yahuah. **4** And He will imprison those angels, who have shown unrighteousness, in that burning valley which my grandfather Enoch had formerly shown to me in the west among the mountains of gold and silver and iron and soft metal and tin. **5** And I saw that valley in which there was a great convulsion and a convulsion of the waters.

**6** And when all this took place, from that fiery molten metal and from the convulsion thereof in that place, there was produced a smell of sulphur, and it was connected with those waters, and that valley of the angels who had led astray

*Cf. Rev. 9:14-15.*

*Cf. Gen. 7:16, Jub. 5:24.*

*The ark. Cf. Gen. 6:14, Jub. 5:22. Noah had the assistance of the angels. Perhaps they built the frame but we know Noah and his sons built the ark as well. Such a project would require a massive undertaking which man has never truly reproduced the ark with such supplies. These specs are similar to a supertanker in wood without nails or metal. Noah had help.*

*Tartarus, Gehenna, The Lake of Fire. They are not thrown into it yet but in its valley in the "Lowest Hell."*

Cf. 54:6;
Rev. 13:14.
"Deceiveth
them that
dwell on the
earth."

(mankind) burned beneath that land. 7 And through its valleys proceed streams of fire, where these angels are punished who had led astray those who dwell upon the earth. 8 But those waters shall in those days serve for the kings and the mighty and the exalted, and those who dwell on the earth, for the healing of the body, but for the punishment of the spirit; now their spirit is full of lust, that they may be punished in their body, for they have denied Yahuah of Spirits and see their punishment daily, and yet believe not in His name. 9 And in proportion as the burning of their bodies becomes severe, a corresponding change shall take place in their spirit for ever and ever; for before Yahuah of Spirits none shall utter an idle word. 10 For the judgment shall come upon them, because they believe in the lust of their body and deny the Spirit of Yahuah.

11 And those same waters shall undergo a change in those days; for when those angels are punished in these waters, these water-springs shall change their temperature, and when the angels ascend, this water of the springs shall change and become cold, 12 And I heard Michael answering and saying: 'This judgment wherewith the angels are judged is a testimony for the kings and the mighty who possess the earth. 13 Because these waters of judgment minister to the healing of the body of the kings and the lust of their body; therefore they will not see and will not believe that those waters will change and become a fire which burns for ever.

# 68
# Michael and Raphael astonished at the Severity of the Judgment

# 69
# The Names and Functions of the (fallen Angels and) Satans: the secret Oath

## 69.26-29
## Close of the Third Parable

# CHAPTER 68:



1 **And after that my grandfather Enoch gave me the teaching of all the secrets in the book and in the Parables which had been given to him, and he put them together for me in the words of the book of the Parables.**
2 And on that day Michael answered Raphael and said: 'The power of the spirit transports and makes me to tremble because of the severity of the judgment of the secrets, the judgment of the angels: who can endure the severe judgment which has been executed and before which they melt away? 3 And Michael answered again and said to Raphael: 'Who is he



whose heart is not softened concerning it, and whose reins are not troubled by this word of judgment (that) has gone forth upon them because of those who have thus led them out? 4 And it came to pass when he stood before Yahuah of Spirits, Michael said thus to Raphael: 'I will not take their part under the



eye of Yahuah; for Yahuah of Spirits has been angry with them because they do as if they were Yahuah.
5 Therefore all that is hidden shall come upon them for ever and ever; for neither angel nor man shall have his portion (in it), but alone they have received their judgment for ever and ever.

# CHAPTER 69:

1 And after this judgment they shall terrify and make them to tremble because they have shown this to those who dwell on the earth. 2 And behold the names of those angels [and these are their names: the first of them is Samyaza, the second Artaqifa, and the third Armen, the fourth Kokabel, the fifth Turael, the sixth Rumyal, the seventh Danyal, the eighth Neqael, the ninth Baraqel, the tenth Azazel the eleventh Armaros, the twelfth Bataryal, the thirteenth Busaseyal, the fourteenth Hananel, the fifteenth Turel, and the sixteenth Simapesiel, the seventeenth Jetrel, the eighteenth Tumael, the nineteenth Turel, the twentieth Rumael, the twenty-first Azazel. 3 And these are the **chiefs of their angels** and their names, and their chief ones over hundreds and over fifties and over tens.] 4 The name of the first **Jeqon**: that is, the one who led astray [all] the sons of Elohim, and brought them down to the earth, and led them astray

through the daughters of men. 5 And the second was named **Asbeel**: he imparted to the holy sons of Elohim evil counsel, and led them astray so that they defiled their bodies with the daughters of men. 6 And the third was named **Gadreel**: he it is who showed the children of men all the blows of death, and **he led astray Eve**, and showed [the weapons of death to the sons of men] the shield and the coat of mail, and the sword for battle, and all the weapons of death to the children of men. 7 And from his hand they have proceeded against those who dwell on the earth **from that day and for evermore.** 8 And the fourth was named **Penemue**: he taught the children of men the bitter and the sweet, and he taught them all the secrets of their wisdom. 9 And **he instructed mankind in writing with ink and paper**, and thereby many sinned from eternity to eternity and until this day. 10 For men were not created for such a purpose, to give confirmation to their good faith with pen and ink. 11 For men were created exactly like the angels, to the intent that they should continue pure and righteous, and death, which destroys everything,

could not have taken hold of them, but through this their knowledge they are perishing, and through this power fit is consuming men. 12 And the fifth was named **Kasdeya**: this is he who showed the children of men all the wicked smitings of spirits and demons, and the **smitings of the embryo in the womb, that it may pass away**, and [the smitings of the soul] the bites of the serpent, and the smitings which befall through the noontide heat, the son of the serpent named Taba'et. 13 And this is the task of **Kasbeel**, the chief of the oath which he showed to the holy ones when he dwelt high above in glory, and its name is **Biqa**. 14 This (angel) requested Michael to show him the hidden name, that he might enunciate it in the oath, so that those might quake before that name and oath who revealed all that was in secret to the children of men. 15 And this is the power of this oath, for it is powerful and strong, and he placed this oath Akae in the hand of Michael. 16 And these are the secrets of this oath... And they are strong through his oath: And the heaven was suspended before the world was created, And for ever. 17 And through it the earth was founded upon the water. And from the secret recesses of the mountains come beautiful waters. From the creation of the world and unto eternity. 18 And through that oath the sea was created. And as its foundation He set for it the sand against the time of (its) anger, And it dare not pass beyond it from the creation of the world unto eternity. 19 And through that oath are the depths made fast, And abide and stir not from their place from eternity to eternity. 20 And through that oath the sun and moon complete their course, And deviate not from their ordinance from eternity to eternity. 21 And through that oath the stars complete their course And He calls them by their names, And they answer Him from eternity to eternity. [22 And in like manner the spirits of the water, and of the winds, and of all zephyrs, and (their) paths from all the quarters of the winds.

*Cf. 2 Esd. 4:13. The Forest and the Sea.*

*Cf. Rev. 7:1 "The four angels of the winds."*

23 And there are preserved the voices of the thunder and the light of the lightnings: and there are preserved the chambers of the hail and the chambers of the hoar-frost, and the chambers of the mist, and the chambers of the rain and the dew. 24 And all these believe and give thanks before Yahuah of Spirits, and glorify (Him) with all their power,

and their food is in every act of thanksgiving: they thank and glorify and extol the name of Yahuah of Spirits for ever and ever.] 25 And this oath is mighty over them. And through it [they are preserved and] their paths are preserved, And their course is not destroyed. 26 And there was great joy amongst them. And they blessed and glorified and extolled because **the name of that Son of Man had been revealed unto them.** 27 And he sat on the throne of his glory. And the sum of judgment was given unto the **Son of Man**, And he caused the sinners to pass away and be destroyed from off the face of the earth, And those who have led the world astray. 28 With chains shall they be bound, And in their assemblage-place of destruction shall they be imprisoned. And all their works vanish from the face of the earth. 29 And from henceforth there shall be nothing corruptible, For that **Son of Man** has appeared. And has seated himself on the throne of his glory, and all evil shall pass away before his face, And the word of that **Son of Man** shall go forth and be strong before Yahuah of Spirits. This is the third Parable of Enoch.

*Cf. Dan. 7:13. "Son of Man." Messiah used this 82 times in the Gospels as His title. It originates in 1 Enoch.*

*Cf. John 5:22,27. "He hath committed all judgment unto the Son."*

*Cf. Matt. 25:31. "When the Son of man shall come in his glory, and all the holy angels with him, then shall he sit upon the throne of his glory:"*

# 70 The final Translation of Enoch

# 71 Two earlier Visions of Enoch

# CHAPTER 70:



1 And it came to pass after this that his name during his lifetime was raised aloft to that **Son of Man** and to Yahuah of Spirits from amongst those who dwell on the earth.



2 And he was raised aloft on the chariots of the spirit and his name vanished among them. 3 And from that day I was no longer numbered amongst them; and he set me between the two winds, between the north and the west, where the angels took the cords to measure for me the place for the elect and righteous. 4 And there I saw the first fathers and the righteous who from the beginning dwell in that place.



# CHAPTER 71:



1 And it came to pass after this that **my spirit was translated And it ascended into the heavens**: And I saw the holy sons of Elohim. They were stepping on flames of fire: Their garments were white [and their raiment], And their faces shone like snow.

2 And I saw two streams of fire and the light of that fire shone like hyacinth, And I fell on my face before Yahuah of Spirits. 3 And the angel Michael [one of the archangels] seized me by my right hand. And lifted me up and led me forth into all the secrets, And he showed me all the secrets of righteousness. 4 And he showed me all the secrets of the ends of the heaven, And all the chambers of all the stars, and all the luminaries. Whence they proceed before the face of the holy ones. 5 And he translated my spirit into the heaven of heavens. And I saw there as it were a structure built of crystals. And between those crystals, tongues of living fire. 6 And my spirit saw the girdle which girt that house of fire. And on its four sides were streams full of living fire, And they girt that house. 7 And round about were Seraphim, Cherubim, and Ophannim: And these are they who sleep not and guard the throne of His glory. 8 And I saw angels who could not be counted, A thousand thousands, and ten thousand times ten thousand, Encircling that house, And Michael, and Raphael, and

Gabriel, and Phanuel, And the holy angels who are above the heavens, Go in and out of that house. 9 And they came forth from that house. And Michael and Gabriel, Raphael and Phanuel, and many holy angels without number. 10 And with them the **Head of Days**, His head white and pure as wool, and His raiment indescribable. 11 And I fell on my face, And my whole body became relaxed, And my spirit was transfigured; And I cried with a loud voice,... with the spirit of power. And blessed and glorified and extolled. 12 And these blessings which went forth out of my mouth were well pleasing before that **Head of Days**. 13 And that **Head of Days** came with Michael and Gabriel, Raphael and Phanuel, thousands and ten thousands of angels without number. [Lost passage wherein the Son of Man was described as accompanying the **Head of Days**, and Enoch asked one of the angels (as in 46.3) concerning the **Son of Man** as to who he was.]

14 And he (i.e. the angel) came to me and greeted me with His voice, and said unto me: 'This is the **Son of Man** who is born unto righteousness. And righteousness abides over him, And the righteousness of the **Head of Days** forsakes him not.' 15 And he said unto me: 'He proclaims unto thee peace in the name of the world to come; For from hence has proceeded peace since the creation of the world, And so shall it be unto thee for ever and for ever and ever. 16 And all shall walk in his ways since righteousness never forsaketh him: With him will be their dwelling-places, and with him their heritage, And they shall not be separated from him for ever and ever and ever.

17 And so there shall be length of days with that **Son of Man**, And the righteous shall have peace and an upright way In the name of Yahuah of Spirits for ever and ever.'

*Cf. 40.*

*Cf. "Head of Days." Dan. 7:9, 13, and 22 "Ancient of Days."*

*Cf. Dan. 7:13. "Son of Man." Messiah used this 82 times in the Gospels as His title. It originates in 1 Enoch.*

# SECTION 3:
## THE ASTRONOMICAL BOOK

72-82

# THE BOOK OF THE COURSES OF THE HEAVENLY LUMINARIES

**1** The Book of the courses of the luminaries of the heaven, the relations of each, according to their classes, their dominion and their seasons, according to their names and places of origin, and according to their months, which Uriel, the holy angel, who was with me, who is their guide, showed men and he showed me all their laws exactly as they are, and how it is with regard to all the years of the world and unto eternity, till the new creation is accomplished which dureth till eternity. **2** And this is the **first law of the luminaries: the luminary the Sun has its rising** in the eastern portals of the heaven, and its setting in the western portals of the heaven. **3** And I saw **six portals** in which the **sun rises**, and **six portals** in which the **sun sets**: and the **moon rises and sets in these portals**, and the leaders of the stars and those whom they lead: **six in the east and six in the west**, and all following each other in accurately corresponding order: also many windows to the right and left of these portals. **4 And first there goes forth the great luminary, named the Sun**, and his circumference is like the circumference of the heaven, and he is quite filled with illuminating and heating fire.

*Cf. 45:4-5, 91:16; 2 Pet. 3:13. "New Heavens, new Earth."*

*Cf. 41:6-7; Jub. 1:8-9, 6:36-38. Sun is the start of the day in Enoch and Jubilees. Not the moon.*

*The sun is first and starts the day not the moon.*

*Cf. 41:6-7; Jub. 1:8-9, 6:36-38. Enoch scientifically observed the sun moving in a course from it's initial position. Modern Scientism is a religion not science.*

By scientific observation, Enoch enlightens all ages regarding the movement of the sun, moon and stars. No scientist has ever observed this process, they never will and none of them is remotely as smart nor qualified as Enoch, the first among men to write and teach even science. They only see the luminaries in a massive paradigm of deception that cannot be accurate. This is part of the strong delusion of our age which began essentially thousands of years ago with a religious cult who today we call scientists, yet they focus on their occult religion in incredibly extreme faith unproven, not academics. They do not practice science, but a religion of Scientism easily disproven, full of failed theories built upon failed guesses in a vacuum.

# LUMINARY LAW #1:
## THE SUNRISE STARTS THE DAY.
## A DAY IS 24-HOURS.
## THE SUN MOVES AND HAS A COURSE.

# THE SUN STOOD STILL... MOON STAYED...

Joshua 10:12-13
Habakkuk 3:11

# ANGELS SHOWED ENOCH THE RULE OF THE SUN...

Jubilees 4:21

*All Qumran quotes from The Complete Dead Sea Scrolls In English" by Geza Vermes. [22]

**Old Testament Examples:**

Gen. 1-2, 19:34
Ex. 10:4, 13, 12:6-8, 10-12, 29-31, 16:4-25, 32:5-6
Lev. 7:15-16, 22:30
Deut. 16:4, 16
Num. 33:3
Jos. 5:10-12, 7:13-14
Judges 9:42, 45, 19:5-9
1 Sam. 19:10-24
Daniel 8:14, 26

**New Testament Examples:**

Matt. 28:1
Mark 14:1-2, 12, 17-18 16:1-2, 15:1, 25, 33, 42-43, 20:1-12
John 20:1, 19, 26
Luke 23:44-46, 54-56
Acts 2:15, 4:3-5, 9, 10:3, 9, 23, 30, 3:1, 20:7, 23:12, 15, 23, 31-32

**QUMRAN SCOLLS:**
Jub. 2:8-9, 2:2-3, 6:33-38, 17:15-16, 18:3;
1 Enoch 41:6-7, 72;
Prayer or Hymn Celebrating the Morning and the Evening *(4Q408, p. 386)*;
The Temple Scroll *(p. 193)*;
Hymn 23, XX, The Thanksgiving Hymns *(p. 296-7)*;
The Community Rule *(p. 112)*;
Community Rule Manuscript from Cave 4 *(p. 122)*;
The Damascus Document *(p. 141) the sun's orb becomes distant or leaves from the gate at sunrise, not sunset. "(wherein it sinks)" was added in fraud and is illiterate, misunderstanding the operation.*

Legitimate, Exiled Temple Priests at Qumran/Bethabara used Jubilees for Torah's calendar as the "exact determination of their times." This is in concert with Enoch and the whole of scripture. Pharisees did not as "Israel turns a blind eye" referring to their Babylonian Lunar Calendar by the first century which fails scripture already profaning the Sabbath and Feasts even in Genesis 1 and the Gospels. "...behold it is strictly defined in the Book of the Divisions of the Times into their Jubilees and Weeks." — *The Damascus Document, 4Q266, fr. 8 i, 6-9, p. 139.*

# THE CREATION DAY

*day: יום : yôm, yôwm, yome, Strong's H3117*
*The KJV translates in the following manner: day (2,008x), time (64x), chronicles (with*
*H1697) (37x), daily (44x), ever (18x), year (14x), continually (10x), when (10x), as (10x),*
*while (8x), full (8x), always (4x), whole (4x), alway (4x), miscellaneous (44x)*

*night: ליל: layil, lah'-yil: Strong's H3915*
*properly, a twist (away of the light), i.e. night; figuratively, adversity:—(mid-)night (season).*

*evening: ערב: 'ereb, eh'-reb; from H6150; dusk:— day, even(-ing,*
*tide), night.*

*morning: בקר: bôqer, bo'-ker; properly, dawn (as the break of day);*
*generally, morning:—(+) day, early, morning, morrow*

*EVENING (6 HOURS) + MORNING (6 HOURS) = NIGHT (12 HOURS)*

## FOLLOWING THE MOON OR SUNSET AS THE BEGINNING OF THE DAY IS ERROR!

### Jubilees 6:33-38

*But if they do neglect and do not observe them according to His commandment, then they will disturb all their seasons, and the years will be dislodged from this (order), [and they will disturb the seasons and the years will be dislodged] and they will neglect their ordinances. And all the children of Israel will forget, and will not find the path of the years, and will forget the new moons, and seasons, and sabbaths, and they will go wrong as to all the order of the years. For I know and from henceforth shall I declare it unto thee, and it is not of my own devising; for the book (lieth) written before me, and on the heavenly tables the division of days is ordained, lest they forget the feasts of the covenant and walk according to the feasts of the Gentiles after their error and after their ignorance. For there will be those who will assuredly make observations of the moon-- now (it) disturbeth the seasons and cometh in from year to year ten days too soon. For this reason the years will come upon them when they will disturb (the order), and make an abominable (day) the day of testimony, and an unclean day a feast day, and they will confound all the days, the holy with the unclean, and the unclean day with the holy; for they will go wrong as to the months and sabbaths and feasts and jubilees. For this reason I command and testify to thee that thou mayest testify to them; for after thy death thy children will disturb (them), so that they will not make the year three hundred and sixtyfour days only, and for this reason they will go wrong as to the new moons and seasons and sabbaths and festivals, and they will eat all kinds of blood with all kinds of flesh.*

## Genesis 1:3-5 KJV

And God said, Let there be light: and there was light. [Light was His 1st Creation]
And God saw the light, that it was good: and God divided the light from the darkness.

## And God called the light Day [Day comes 1st],

and the darkness he called Night. [Night comes 2nd After Creating All Daylight]

### And the *evening* and the *morning* were the *first day*.

[Yom = 24 hr Day or Daylight - Never Just Night]

DAY (12 hrs. Daylight) +
Evening (6 hours: 6 pm-midnight) + Morning (6 hours: midnight-sunrise)
(Evening and morning do not equal 24 hours)

## = 24 hours

(The Sabbath Day, Day 7 affirms this must be 24 hours)

### Genesis 1 KJV

(Daytime = Create + Evening and Morning = 24-hour Day)
6a: And God said, Let there be a firmament in the midst of the waters…
8b: And the evening and the morning were the second day.
9a: And God said, Let the waters under the heaven be gathered…
13: And the evening and the morning were the third day.
20:a And God said, Let the waters bring forth abundantly…
23: And the evening and the morning were the fifth day.
24 a: And God said, Let the earth bring forth the living creature…
31b: And the evening and the morning were the sixth day.

### Genesis 1:14-19 KJV

And God said, Let there be lights in the firmament of the heaven to divide the day [1st] from the night
[2nd]; and let them be for signs, and for seasons, and for days, and years: And let them be for lights
in the firmament of the heaven to give light upon the earth: and it was so. And God made two great
lights; the greater light to rule the day [1st], and the lesser light [which has precedence?] to rule the
night [2nd]: he made the stars also.
And God set them in the firmament of the heaven to give light upon the earth, And to rule over the day
[1st] and over the night [2nd], and to divide the light [1st] from the darkness [2nd]:
and God saw that it was good. [Creation during Day]
And the evening and the morning were the fourth day.

The Creation Day has always set forth a calendar based on the sun or sunrise not the moon or sunset
as the start. Day 1 establishes this pattern even before the sun was created. The sun is then created
during that same timeline as the measure for the day, Sabbath(week), month, year, Sabbath of years,
Jubilee(49 years), etc. The moon is the Babylonian measure in an occult religion. This is why they
include Tammuz, their god, on that supposed Hebrew Calendar which is NOT Hebrew.

**5 The chariot on which he ascends, the wind drives, and the sun goes down from the heaven and returns through the north in order to reach the east,** and is so **guided** that he comes to the **appropriate** (lit. 'that') **portal** and shines in the face of the heaven. **6** In this way he **rises in the first month in the great portal**, which is the **fourth** [those six portals in the east]. **7** And in that fourth portal from which the sun rises in the first month are **twelve window-openings**, from which proceed a flame when they are opened in their season. **8** When the sun rises in the heaven, he comes forth through that **fourth portal thirty mornings in succession**, and **sets accurately in the fourth portal in the west** of the heaven. **9** And **during this period the day becomes daily longer and the night nightly shorter to the thirtieth morning. 10** On that day the **day is longer than the night by a ninth part**, and the **day amounts exactly to ten parts and the night to eight parts. 11** And the **sun rises from** that fourth portal, and sets **in the fourth and returns to the fifth portal of the east thirty mornings**, and rises from it and **sets in the fifth portal. 12** And then the **day becomes longer by two parts** and amounts to **eleven parts**, and the **night** becomes shorter and amounts to **seven parts**.

**13** And it returns to the **east** and enters into the **sixth portal**, and **rises and sets in the sixth portal one and thirty mornings** on account of its sign. **14** On that day the **day becomes longer than the night**, and the **day becomes double the night**, and the day becomes **twelve parts**, and the **night** is shortened and becomes **six parts. 15** And the sun mounts up to make the day shorter and the night longer, and the sun returns to the **east** and enters into the **sixth portal**, and **rises from it and sets thirty mornings. 16** And when **thirty mornings** are accomplished, the **day decreases** by exactly one part, and **becomes eleven parts, and the night seven. 17** And the **sun goes forth from that sixth portal in the west**, and goes to the east and rises in the fifth portal for thirty mornings, and **sets in the west again in the fifth western portal.** **18** On that day the **day** decreases by two parts, and amounts to **ten parts,** and the **night** to **eight parts.** **19** And the **sun goes forth from that fifth portal and sets in the fifth portal of the west**, and **rises in the fourth portal for one and thirty mornings** on account of its sign, and sets in the west. **20** On that day the **day is equalized with the night**, [and becomes of equal length], and the **night amounts to nine parts and the day to nine parts.** **21** And the sun rises from that portal and sets in the west, and returns to the east and rises **thirty mornings in the third portal and sets in the west in the third portal. 22** And on that day the **night becomes longer than the day**, and **night becomes longer than night**, and **day shorter than day** till the **thirtieth morning**, and the **night** amounts exactly to **ten parts** and the **day to eight parts.** **23** And the **sun rises from that third portal and sets in the third portal in the west** and returns to the east, and for **thirty mornings rises in the second portal in the east**, and in like manner **sets in the second portal** in the **west** of the heaven. **24** And on that day the **night** amounts to **eleven parts** and the **day** to **seven parts. 25** And the **sun rises** on that day from that **second portal** and **sets** in the west in the **second portal**, and returns to the **east** into the **first portal** for **one and thirty mornings**, and **sets in the first portal** in the west of the heaven. **26** And on that day the **night becomes longer** and amounts to the **double of the day**: and the **night amounts exactly to twelve parts and the day to six. 27** And the sun has (therewith) traversed the divisions of his orbit and turns again on those divisions of his orbit, and enters that portal **thirty mornings** and sets also in the west opposite to it. **28** And on that night has the night decreased in length by a ninth part, and the **night** has become **eleven parts** and the **day seven parts. 29** And the **sun** has returned and **entered into the second portal in the east**, and returns on those his divisions of his orbit for **thirty mornings**, rising and setting. **30** And on that day the night decreases in length, and the **night** amounts to **ten parts** and the **day to eight**. **31** And on that day the **sun rises** from that portal, and sets in the west, and returns to the east, and rises in the **third portal** for **one and thirty mornings**, and sets in the west of the heaven. **32** On that day the **night** decreases and amounts to **nine parts**, and the **day to nine parts**, and the night is equal to the day and the year is exactly as to its **days three hundred and sixty-four**. **33** And the length of the day and of the night, and the shortness of the day and of the night arise— **through the course of the sun these distinctions are made** (lit. 'they are separated'). **34** So it comes that its course becomes daily longer and its course nightly shorter. **35** And this is the **law and the course of the sun**, and his return as often as he returns sixty times and rises, i. e. the great luminary which is named the Sun, for ever and ever. **36** And that which (thus) rises is the great luminary, and is so named according to its appearance, according as Yahuah commanded.

**37** As he rises, so he sets and decreases not, and rests not, **but runs day and night**, and his **light is sevenfold brighter than that of the moon**; but as regards **size they are both equal**.

*Enoch is not talking about your timezone but the full pattern of the sun around the Earth.*

*The sun and moon are equal in size.*

*On a cloudy day, one can observe the sun's peering through the clouds. If we were to follow the angle of those rays, they would reveal the position of the sun which must be far, far closer than 93 million miles (150 million km) away which Scientism claims yet never proves. We must require them to prove thier positions rather than espouse their religious occult doctrines of sun worship. Also, notice the hotspots which occur even when it is not cloudy. This seems impossible under the supposed academic position which appears poorly thought through.*

# THE SUN'S COURSE:

Enoch's day and night counts 18 hours total from the East to West Gates only. This would be missing part of the day and night for the return of the sun and moon from the West gate to the East gate. There must be a transition, many miss, of 3 hours each between the West and East Gates for the sun and the moon culminating in 24 hours in total. Enoch is actually defining that distance essentially. Enoch's calculations for months and the year require a 24-hour day in context. This is where the Chariot of Wind drives the sun and at the end of most months even changes course requiring such added force. However, many do not account for this time differential each day and assume Enoch only propagates an 18-hour day which is inaccurate.

As this is the area which does change between most months, it is separated much akin to Genesis 1's separation of בקר: boqer – the 6 hours of the morning before sunrise, and ערב: ereb – the 6 hours of evening differentiated from the 12 hours of daylight. This is the area of the newly perceived International Date Line in the middle of the Pacific which appears to split this time as well. This is a worldwide perspective of the sun's course. However, Enoch lived in ancient Havilah, the modern Philippines, and was taken into the Garden of Eden just beneath it within the Earth. He is not offering calculations for all time zones nor hemispheres which are a matter of perspective. This requires an extreme amount of testing this publishing will not embark. In these days of increasing knowledge, however, this will come into focus.

# RULES:

## YEAR: 364 DAYS  (Cf. Jub. 6:32, 38: Observing the moon will cause error.)

## MONTHS: 12 (12 - 30 DAYS + 4 INTERCALARY DAYS)

1 day is added at the end of each quarter. Jubilees also qualifies 52 weeks separated as four 13-week periods of 91 days each (Jub. 6:29-32).

## SEASONS: 4

## NAMES OF THE SUN: ORYARES AND TOMAS

## LAST DAY OF THE YEAR: SPRING EQUINOX
## NEXT DAY IS ABIB 1: HEAD OF THE YEAR

The Spring Equinox is the day of the year when the sun and the moon have equal time as 12 hours each. For the Northern Hemisphere, it is said to occur on March 20th roughly each year. However, this is not accurate to the amount of sunlight especially in Enoch's zone.

Note: The following charts are an attempt at visualizing Enoch's observations of the sun from his data provided. We are not scientists and this is not intended to provide scientifc conlusions. Enoch was qualified to do so and he was the one who saw these workings. We hope those with larger science minds and backgrounds will find these useful in comparing and fully testing patterns beyond our capabilities without retracting in illiterate ridicule as Enoch knew better than all of us. For those of us layman, however, this serves to enhance understanding of what the Prophet Enoch wrote.

# THE SUN'S COURSE:



## MONTH 1 (ABIB): 30 DAYS

*Ex. 13:4, 23:15, 34:18; Deut. 16:1: **Abib**.*

*Nisan is Babylonian Nisanu which is why it only appears in the Bible in the reign of Artaxerxes in Neh. 2:1 and Esther 3:7 also in 1st Esd. 5:6 regarding the reign of Darius. It is appropriate to identify that Persian reign by a Babylonian month. That does not change the Bible which calls the First Month Abib and no "Hebrew" calendar would use the Babylonian name especially not the false god Tammuz rebuked in scripture, for a month. Ezra records Torah including its calendar were restored when the Southern Kingdom returned from Babylon. They did not institute the Babylonian calendar nor the Babylonian synagogues. That was the Pharisees in 165 B.C. Only 4 months of the year have names which follow the pattern of the Feast month and the next month only for Spring and Fall. All others are referred to by number only.*

## LAST DAY: 10 HOURS + RETURN

## LAST NIGHT: 8 HOURS + RETURN

*Enoch's calculation does not include the return from the west to the east gate which must be 3 hours sun and 3 hours moon or perhaps proportionately applied to total 24 hours. Note the International Date Line today is also found between.*

**Portals:** *Propel sun with wind.*

**Windows of Fire:** *Regulate and fuel sun's heat.*

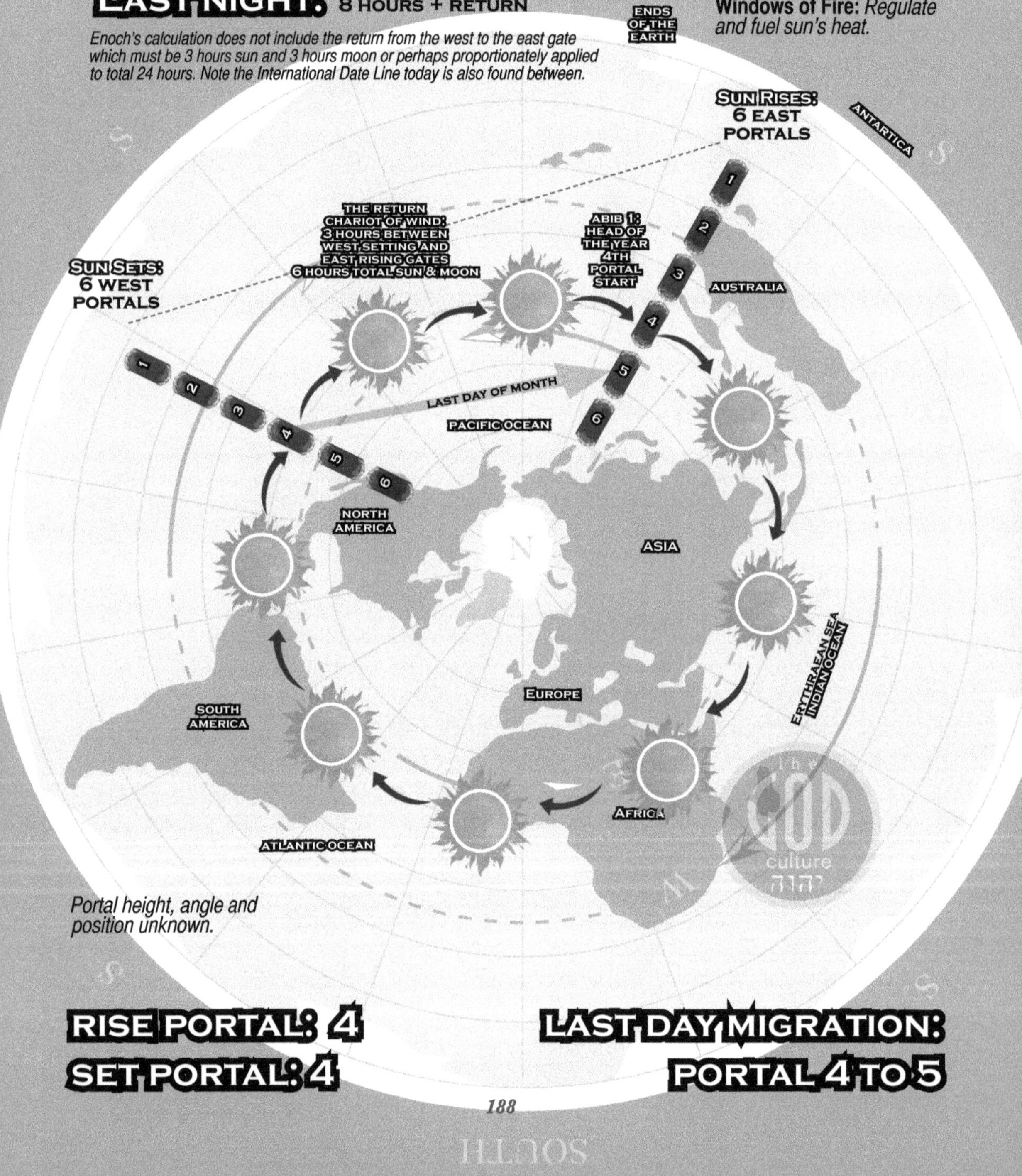

*Portal height, angle and position unknown.*

## RISE PORTAL: 4

## SET PORTAL: 4

## LAST DAY MIGRATION:

## PORTAL 4 TO 5

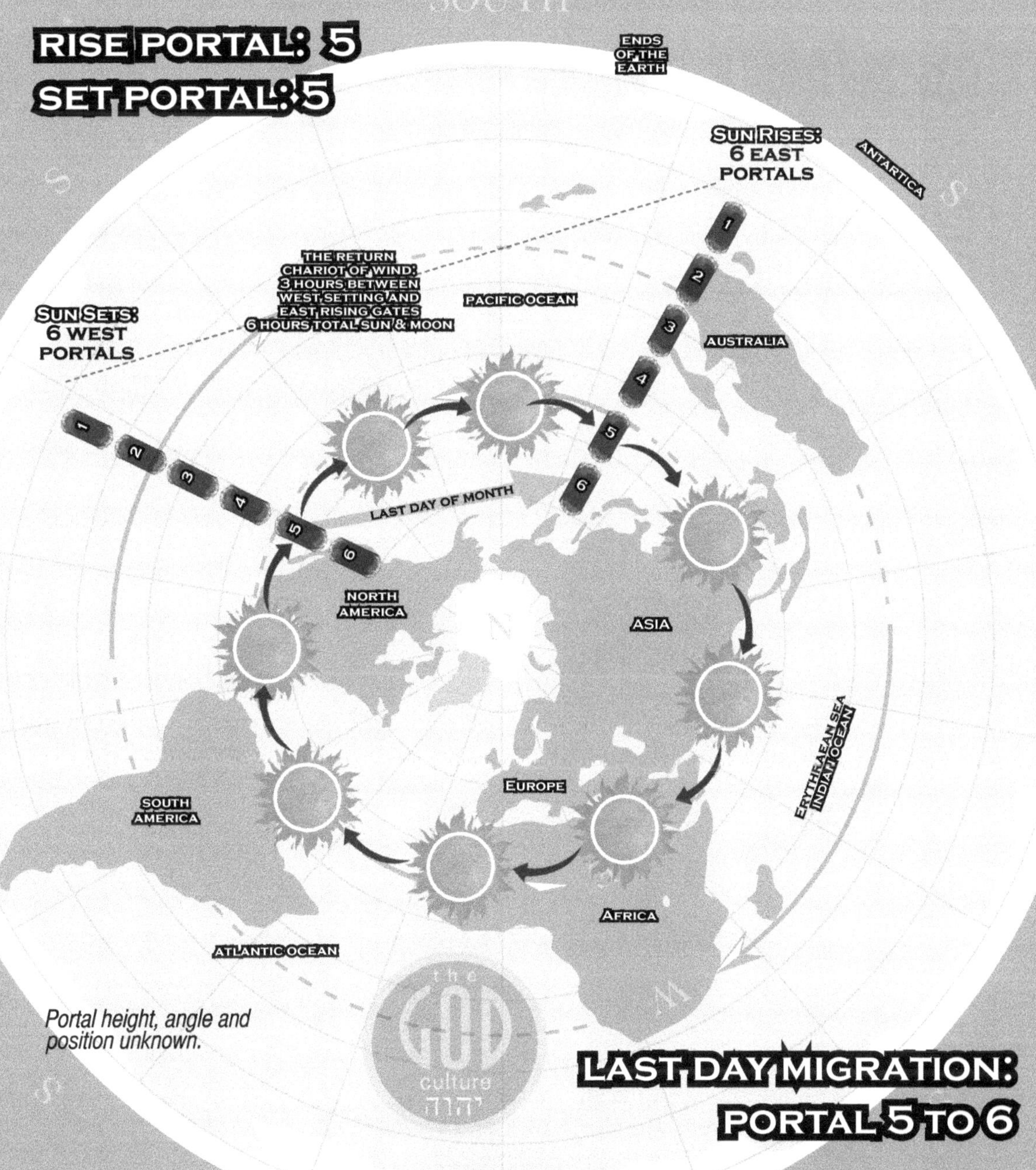

SOUTH

RISE PORTAL: 5
SET PORTAL: 5

ENDS OF THE EARTH

SUN RISES:
6 EAST
PORTALS

ANTARTICA

THE RETURN
CHARIOT OF WIND:
3 HOURS BETWEEN
WEST SETTING AND
EAST RISING GATES
6 HOURS TOTAL SUN & MOON

PACIFIC OCEAN

AUSTRALIA

SUN SETS:
6 WEST
PORTALS

1
2
3
4
5
6

LAST DAY OF MONTH

NORTH
AMERICA

ASIA

EUROPE

ERYTHRAEAN SEA
INDIAN OCEAN

SOUTH
AMERICA

AFRICA

ATLANTIC OCEAN

Portal height, angle and
position unknown.

the
GOD
culture
יהוה

LAST DAY MIGRATION:
PORTAL 5 TO 6

MONTH 2 (ZIF): 30 DAYS

1 Ki. 6:1, 37: Zif
Modern Hebrew Fraud Calendar: Iyar is a Babylonian month of Ayaru never
in the Bible.

LAST DAY: 11 HOURS + RETURN
LAST NIGHT: 7 HOURS + RETURN

Enoch's calculation does not include the return from the west to the
east gate which must be 3 hours sun and 3 hours moon or perhaps
proportionately applied to total 24 hours. Note the International Date
Line today is also found between.

# MONTH 3: 31 DAYS

*Ex. 19:1; 1Chr. 27:5; 2Chr. 15:10, 31:7; Ez. 31:1: **3rd Month**.*

*Occult Month Inserted Erroneously: Est. 8:9: Sivan in Persia accoding to Persian scribes in the passage. Simanu in Babylon. Esther is not scripture and she never served YHWH nor gives Him credit for any of her political story of her genocide against scripture.*

## LAST DAY: 12 HOURS + RETURN

## LAST NIGHT: 6 HOURS + RETURN

*Enoch's calculation does not include the return from the west to the east gate which must be 3 hours sun and 3 hours moon or perhaps proportionately applied to total 24 hours. Note the International Date Line today is also found between.*

**Portals:** *Propel sun with wind.*

**Windows of Fire:** *Regulate and fuel sun's heat.*

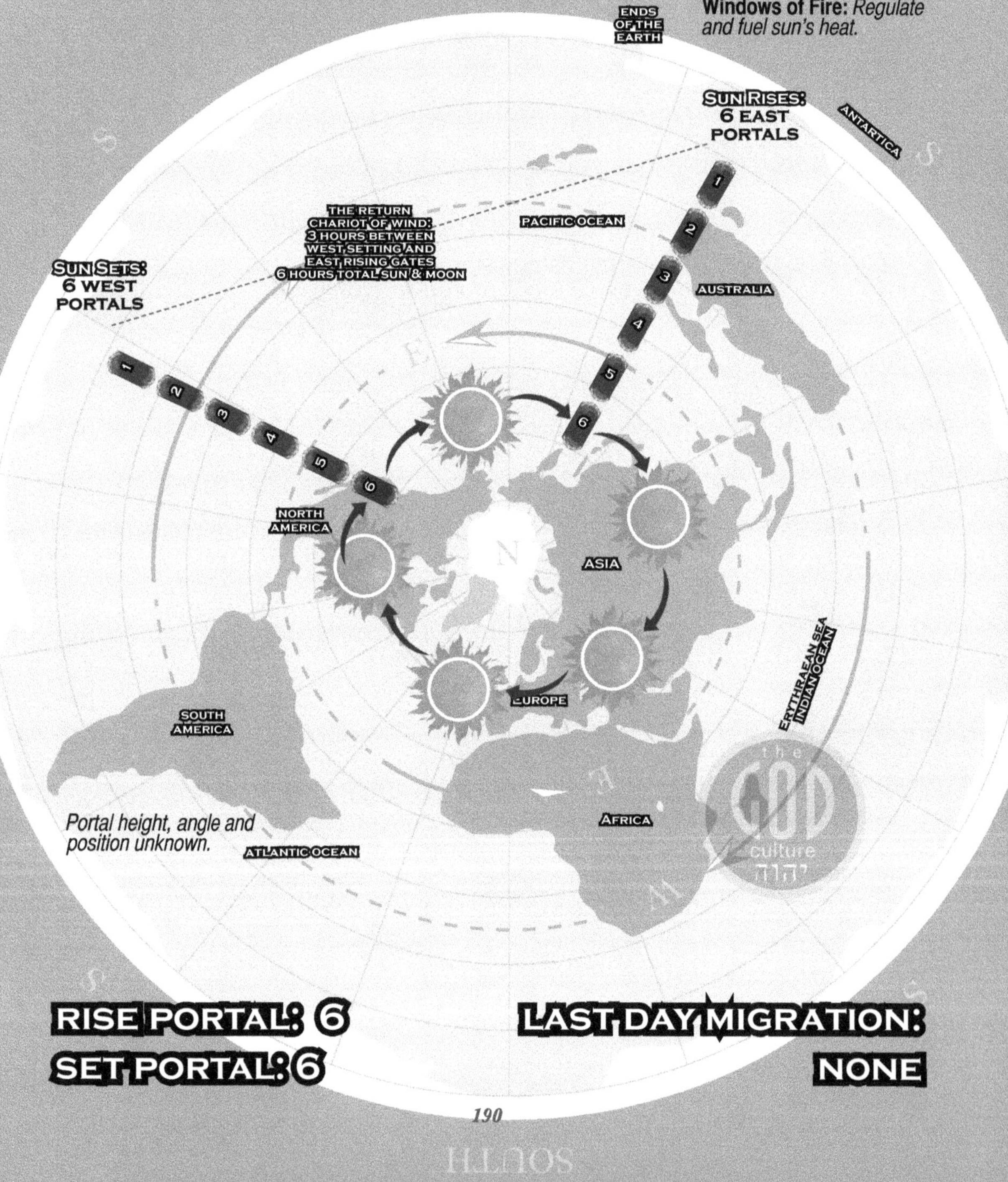

## RISE PORTAL: 6

## SET PORTAL: 6

## LAST DAY MIGRATION:

## NONE

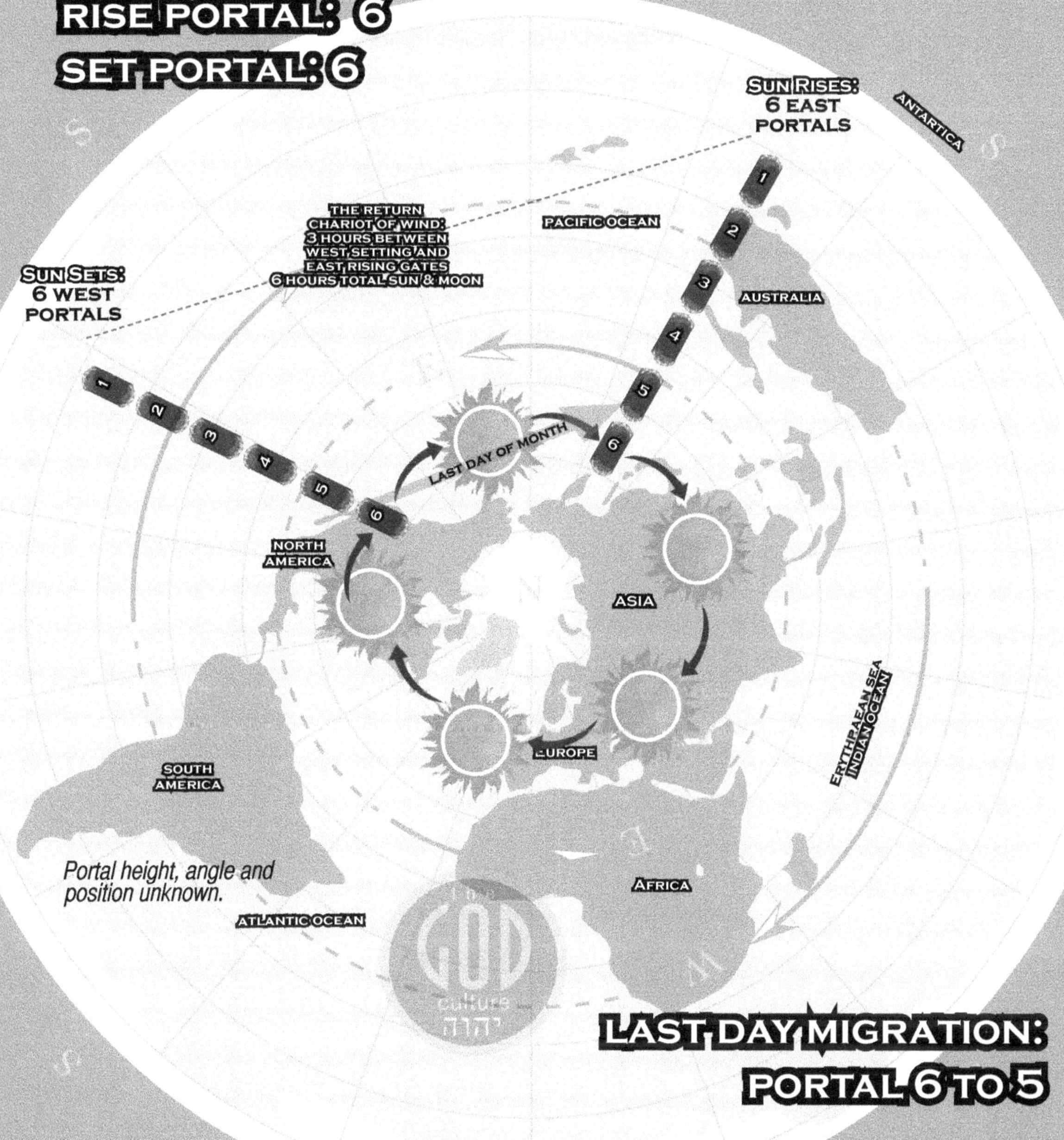


# MONTH 4: 30 DAYS

*2Ki. 25:3; Jer. 39:2, 52:6; Ez. 1:1; Zec. 8:19:* **4th month.**
*In one of the most illiterate frauds in modern times, Tammuz is the supposed Hebrew
month on the false Jewish calendar. Tammuz is a false god rebuked in Ez. 8:14 not a
Hebrew month. It is not just a month but a Babylonian god: Du`uzu = Tammuz.*

## LAST DAY: 11 HOURS + RETURN
## LAST NIGHT: 7 HOURS + RETURN

*Enoch's calculation does not include the return from the west to the
east gate which must be 3 hours sun and 3 hours moon or perhaps
proportionately applied to total 24 hours. Note the International Date
Line today is also found between.*

# MONTH 5: 30 DAYS

*Num. 33:38; 2Ki. 25:8; Ezr. 7:8-9; Jer. 1:3:* **5th month.**
*Ab or Av is Babylonian which is Abu in origin. The Modern Hebrew Calendar is a Babylonian fraud.*

## LAST DAY: 10 HOURS + RETURN
## LAST NIGHT: 8 HOURS + RETURN

*Enoch's calculation does not include the return from the west to the east gate which must be 3 hours sun and 3 hours moon or perhaps proportionately applied to total 24 hours. Note the International Date Line today is also found between.*

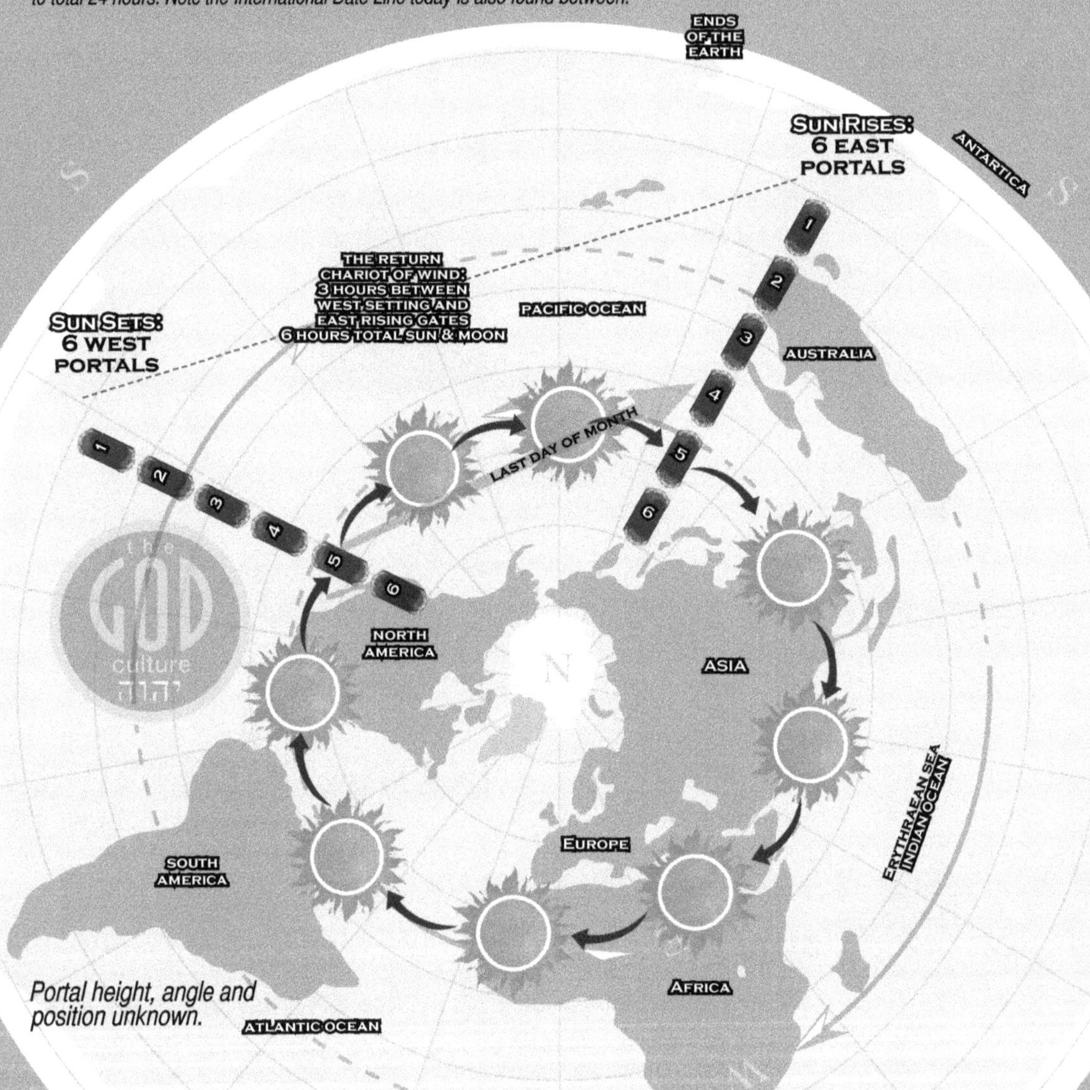


## RISE PORTAL: 5
## SET PORTAL: 5

## LAST DAY MIGRATION:
## PORTAL 5 TO 4

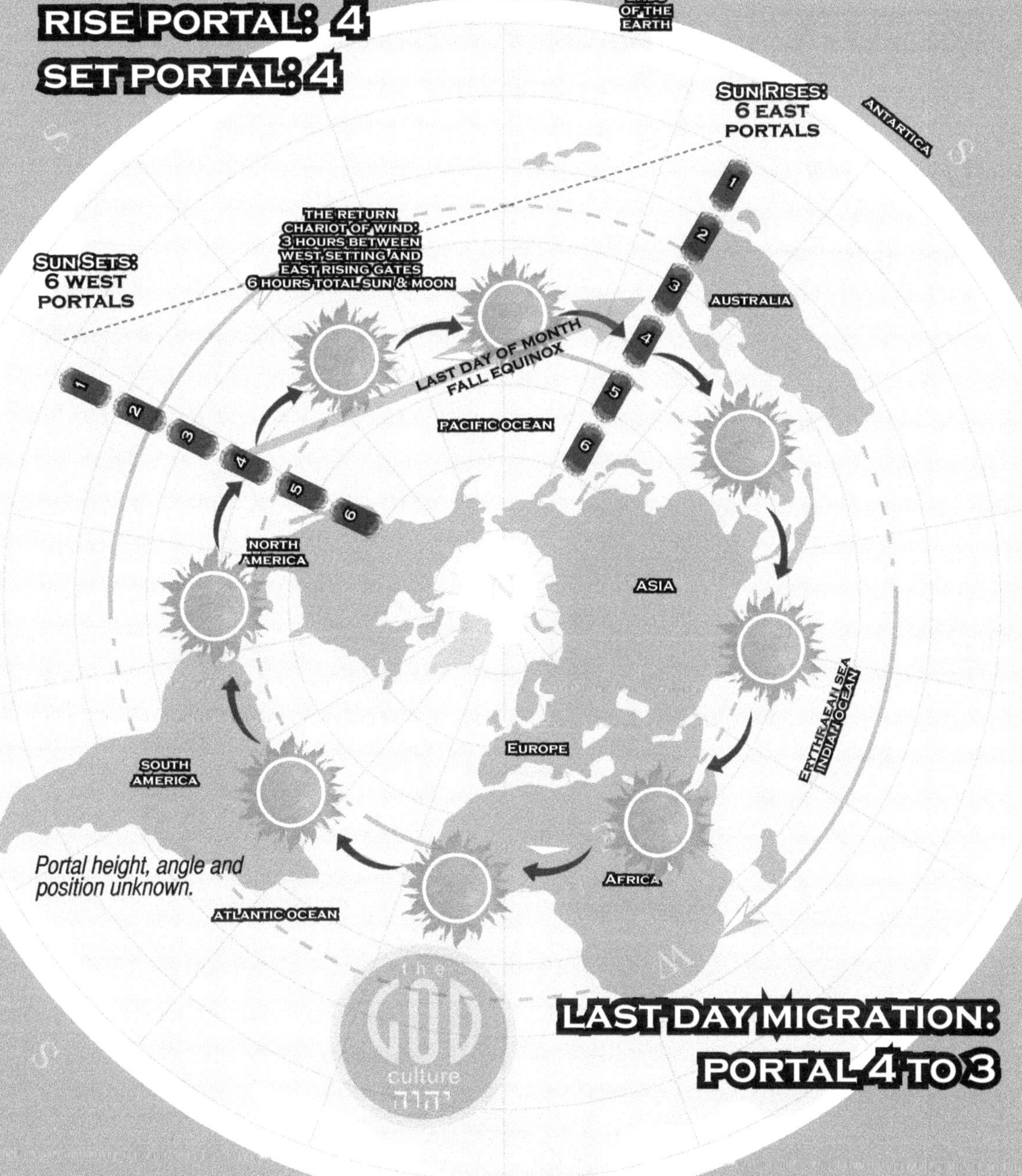


# MONTH 6: 31 DAYS

*1Chr. 27:9; Ez. 8:1; Hag 1:1, 15; Luke 1:26, 36: 6th Month.*
*Neh. 6:15: Elul: Babylonian: Ululu. Ezra just returned from Babylonian captivity.*
*He doesn't change the Bible calendar which is renewed in those days.*

## LAST DAY: 9 HOURS + RETURN
## LAST NIGHT: 9 HOURS + RETURN

*Enoch's calculation does not include the return from the west to the east gate which must be 3 hours sun and 3 hours moon or perhaps proportionately applied to total 24 hours. Note the International Date Line today is also found between.*

# FALL EQUINOX ON THE 31ST. NEXT DAY: ETHANIM 1

# MONTH 7 (ETHANIM): 30 DAYS

*1 Ki. 8:2: **Ethanim**.*
*The Babylonian Hebrew Calendar of today, uses Tishrei erroneously. Tashritu is the Babylonian month, not Bible.*

## LAST DAY: 8 HOURS + RETURN

## LAST NIGHT: 10 HOURS + RETURN

*Enoch's calculation does not include the return from the west to the east gate which must be 3 hours sun and 3 hours moon or perhaps proportionately applied to total 24 hours. Note the International Date Line today is also found between.*

**Portals:** *Propel sun with wind.*

**Windows of Fire:** *Regulate and fuel sun's heat.*



## RISE PORTAL: 3

## SET PORTAL: 3

## LAST DAY MIGRATION:

## PORTAL 3 TO 2

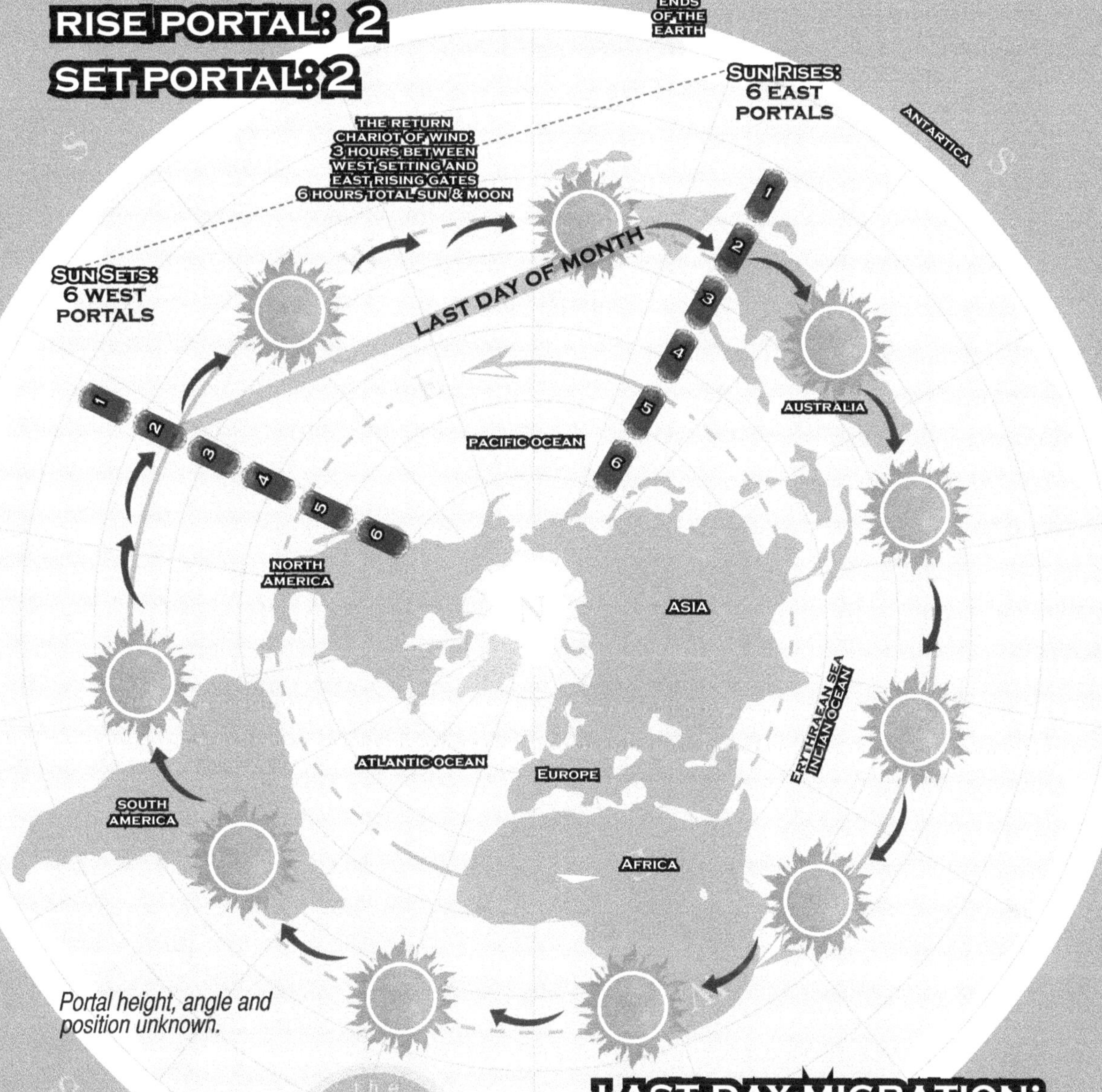


# LAST DAY: 7 HOURS + RETURN

# LAST NIGHT: 11 HOURS + RETURN

*Enoch's calculation does not include the return from the west to the east gate which must be 3 hours sun and 3 hours moon or perhaps proportionately applied to total 24 hours. Note the International Date Line today is also found between.*

# MONTH 9: 31 DAYS

*1Chr. 27:12; Ezr. 10:9; Jer. 36:9, 22; Hag. 2:10, 18:* **9th Month**
*Babylonian: Kislimu*
*Neh. 1:1 in Persian palace; Zec 7:1 in 4th year of King Darius: Chisleu (There is no "V" in Ancient Hebrew.)*
*These were not changing the Bible month however which is unnamed.*

## LAST DAY: 6 HOURS + RETURN

## LAST NIGHT: 12 HOURS + RETURN

*Enoch's calculation does not include the return from the west to the east gate which must be 3 hours sun and 3 hours moon or perhaps proportionately applied to total 24 hours. Note the International Date Line today is also found between.*

**Portals:** *Propel sun with wind.*

**Windows of Fire:** *Regulate and fuel sun's heat.*

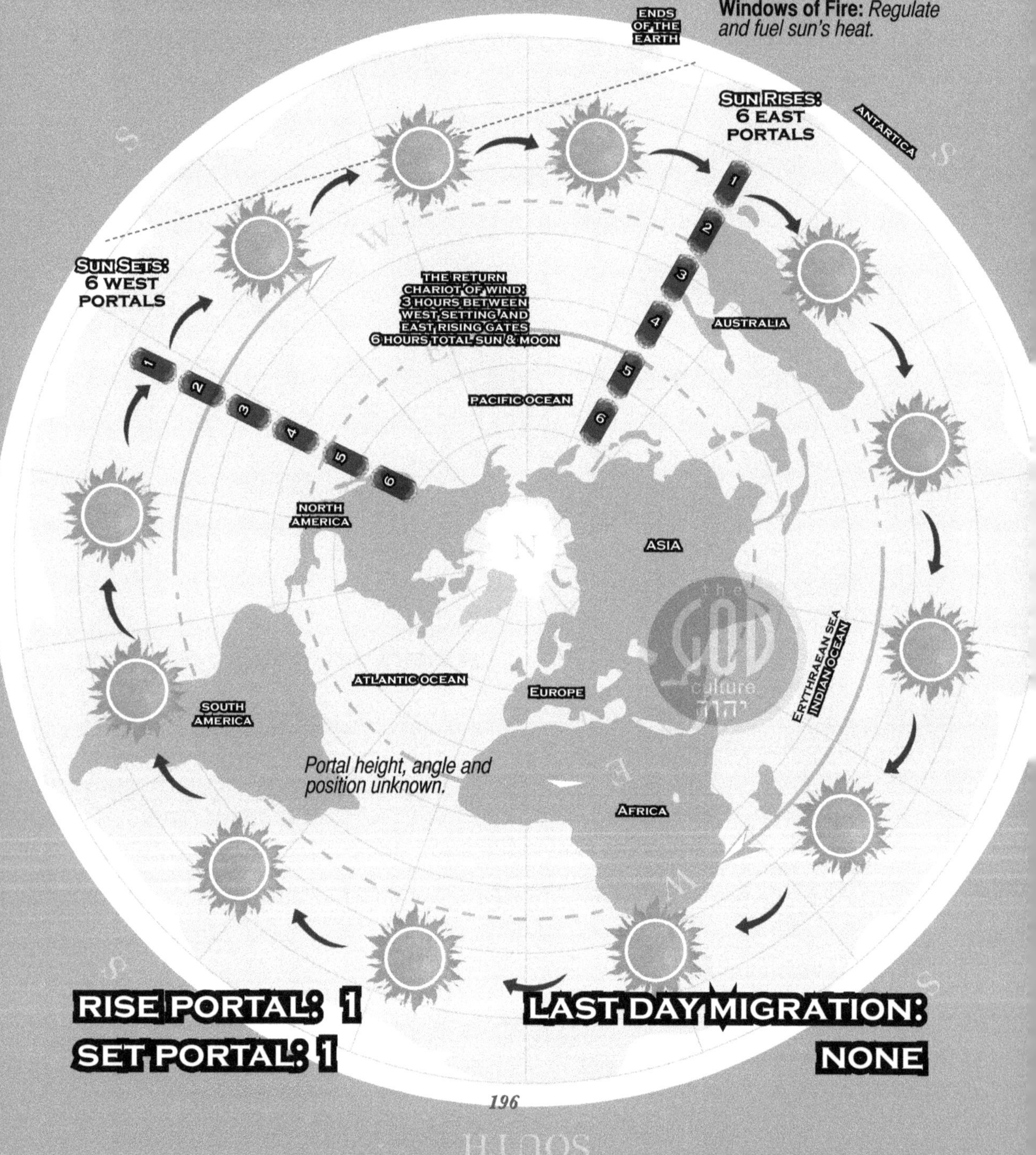

## RISE PORTAL: 1

## SET PORTAL: 1

## LAST DAY MIGRATION:

## NONE

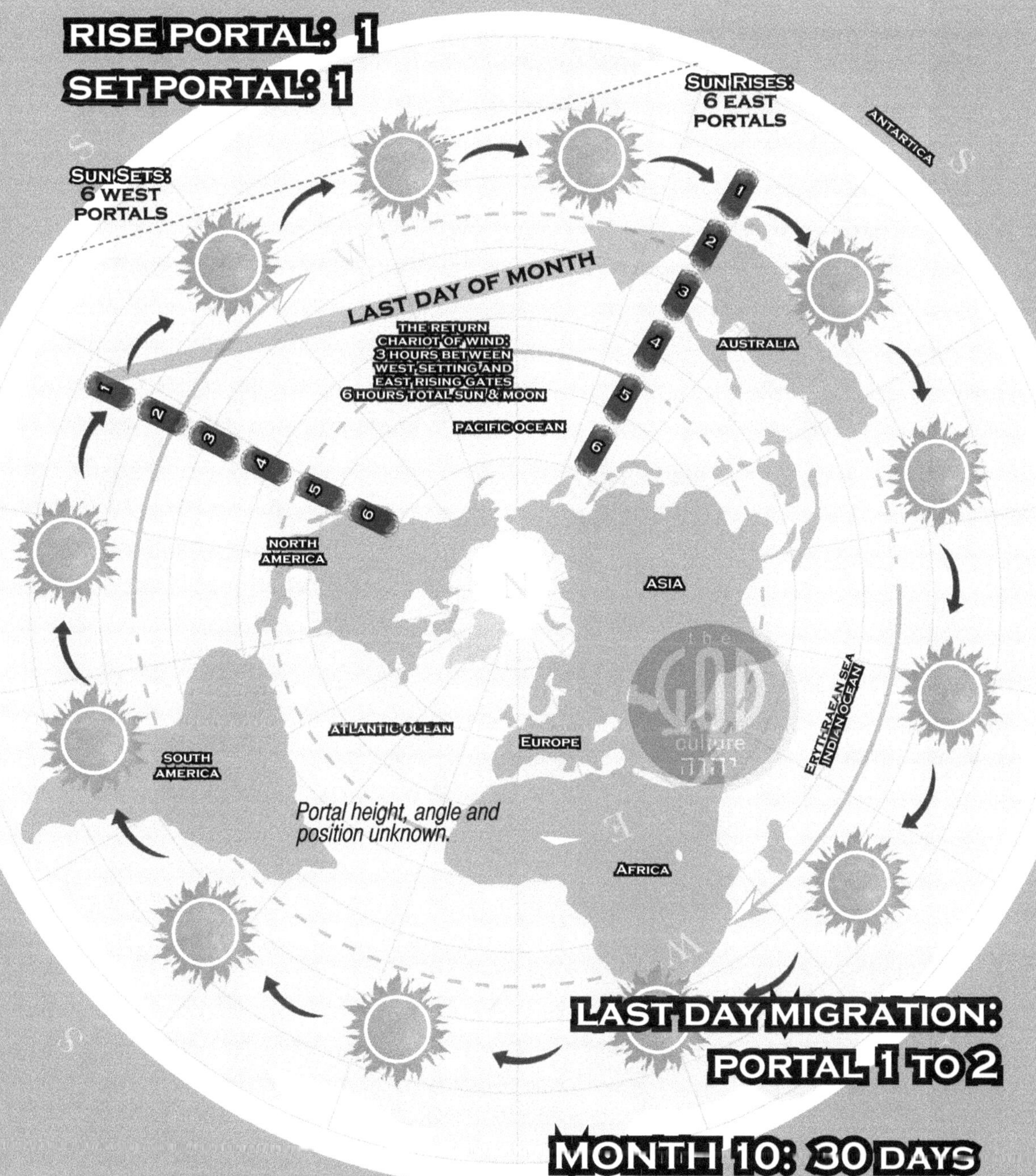


Gen 8:5; 2Ki 25:1; 1Ch 27:13; Ezr 10:16; Jer 39:1, 52:4, Eze 24:1, 29:1, 33:21: **10th Month**
Est 2:16: Tebeth: Babylonian: Tebetu: Again, Esther is not scripture.

## LAST DAY: 7 HOURS + RETURN
## LAST NIGHT: 11 HOURS + RETURN

Enoch's calculation does not include the return from the west to the east gate which must be 3 hours sun and 3 hours moon or perhaps proportionately applied to total 24 hours. Note the International Date Line today is also found between.

# MONTH 11: 30 DAYS

*Deut. 1:3; 1Chr. 27:14:* **11th Month**
*Zec. 1:7: Sebat, in the second year of Darius. A Babylonian measure, not a Bible month. This is Babylonian in origin: Shabatu.*

# LAST DAY: 8 HOURS + RETURN
# LAST NIGHT: 10 HOURS + RETURN

*Enoch's calculation does not include the return from the west to the east gate which must be 3 hours sun and 3 hours moon or perhaps proportionately applied to total 24 hours. Note the International Date Line today is also found between.*

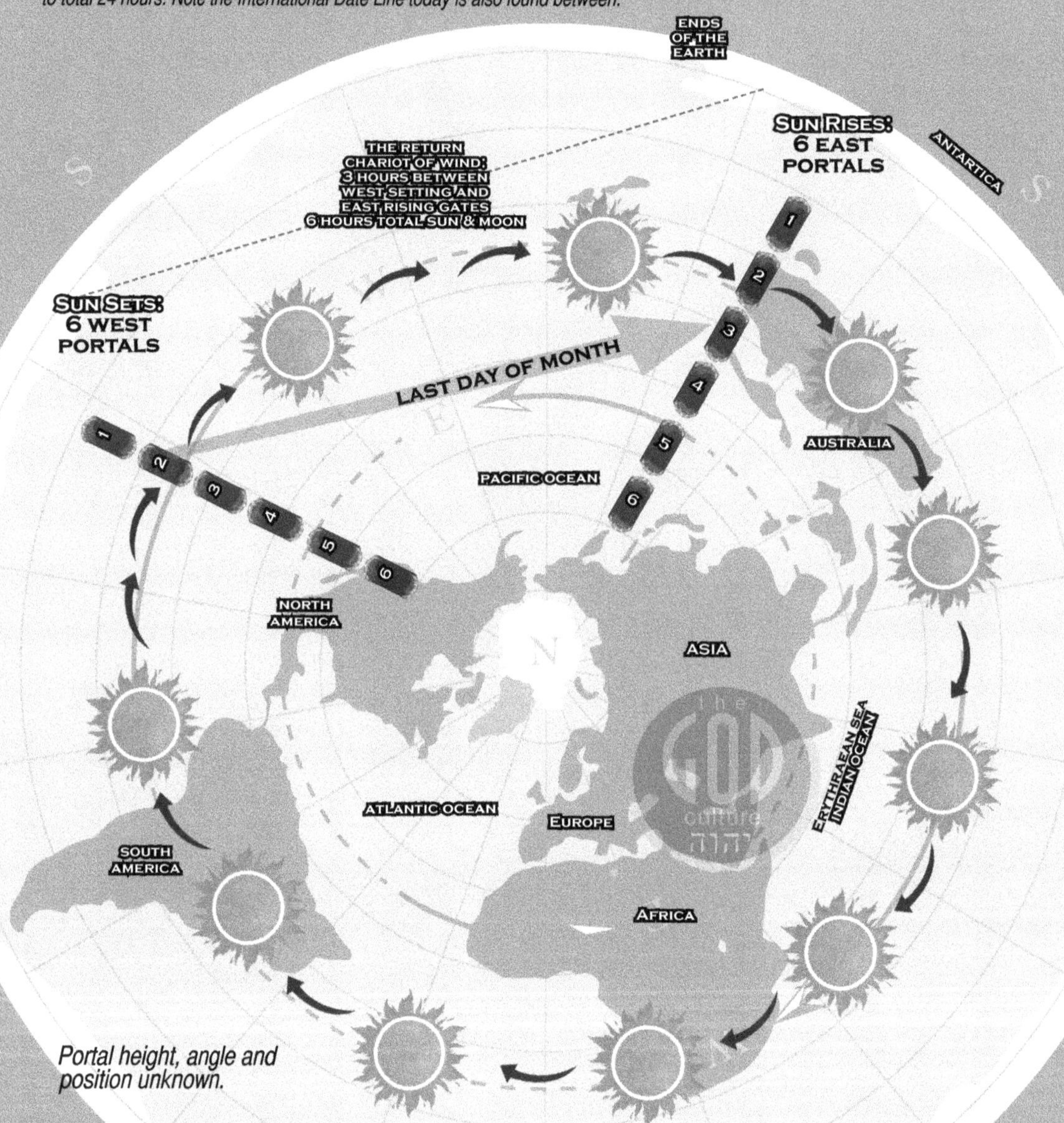


# RISE PORTAL: 2
# SET PORTAL: 2

# LAST DAY MIGRATION:
# PORTAL 2 TO 3

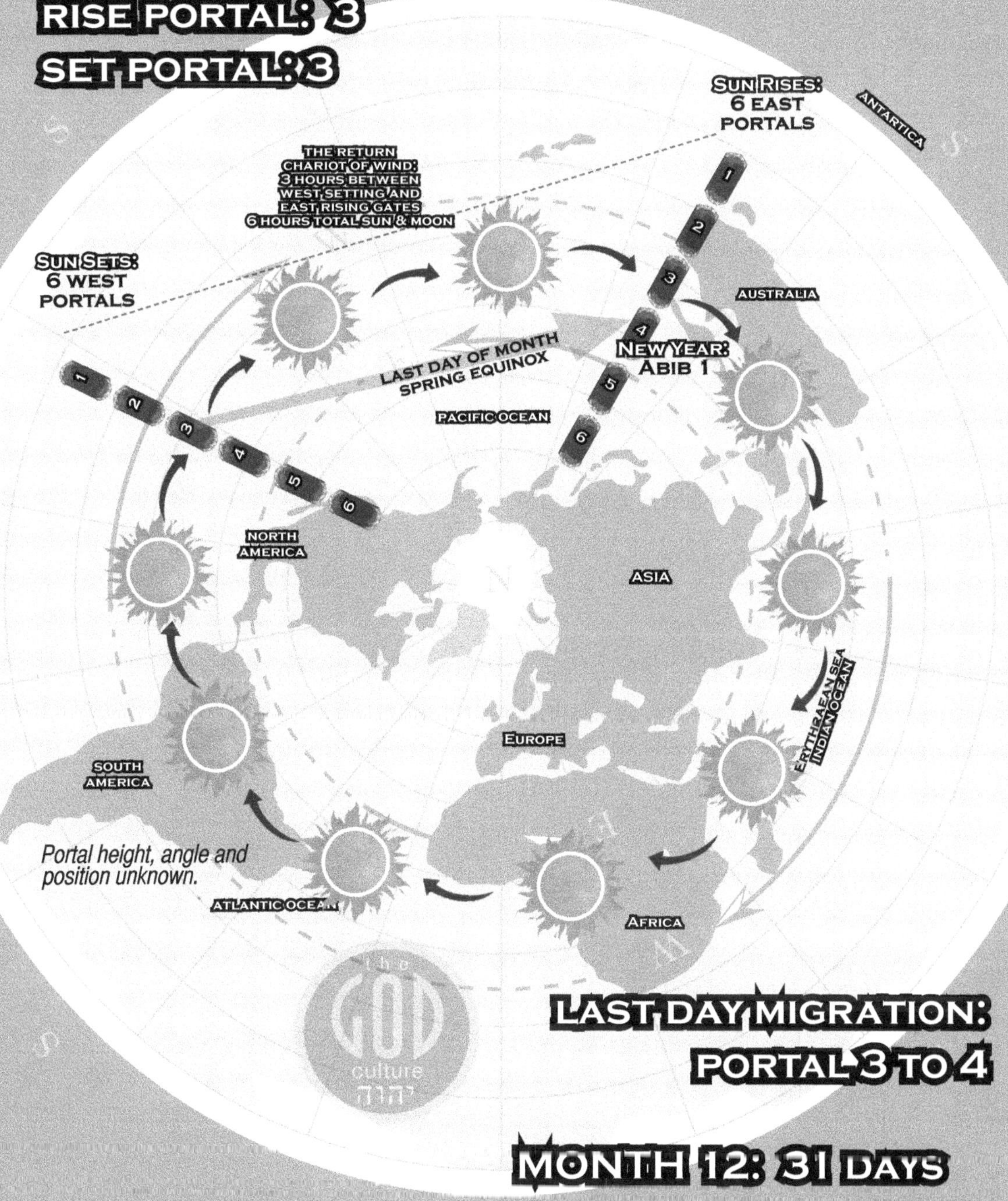


# LAST DAY MIGRATION: PORTAL 3 TO 4

# MONTH 12: 31 DAYS

2Ki. 25:27; 1Chr. 27:15; Jer. 52:31; Ez. 32:1: **12th Month**
Adar is Babylonian not Bible: Adaru. Enoch and Jubilees nor the Bible ever have a 13th month.
Ezr 6:15: Adar, in the sixth year of the reign of Darius: a Babylonian month.
Est. 3:7, 8:12; 9:1, 15, 17, 19, 21. Esther is not scripture.

# LAST DAY: 9 HOURS + RETURN
# LAST NIGHT: 9 HOURS + RETURN

Enoch's calculation does not include the return from the west to the east gate which must be 3 hours sun and 3 hours moon or perhaps proportionately applied to total 24 hours. Note the International Date Line today is also found between.

# SPRING EQUINOX ON THE 31ST. LAST DAY OF YEAR. NEXT DAY: ABIB 1

# WHO CHANGED THE CALENDAR IN ISRAEL AND WHEN?

**THE BIBLE CALENDAR: JUBILEES 2:9** *(Cf. 1 Enoch 72, 4Q320, 4Q394, 4Q266)*
*And Elohim appointed the sun to be a great sign on the earth for days and for sabbaths and for months and for feasts and for years and for sabbaths of years and for jubilees and for all seasons of the years. (Jub. 6:33-36: Moon leads to error in these measures coming in 10 days too soon on the year. It is also off 22 of 52 Sabbaths on the week each year and every day on the day. Enoch defines the sun as this measure as well and that the moon "alters her settings" for "her own pecular course" certain months. That is not the Bible calendar.)*

**52 WEEKS** *(Jub. 6:30)*; **12 - 30-DAY MONTHS + 4 INTERCALARY DAYS** *(1 Enoch 72)*
**364 DAYS** *(Jub. 6:32, 1 Enoch 72:32)*
**DAY BEGINNING: SUNRISE** *(1 Enoch 72, Jub. 2:9, Jub. 6:33-36)*

# CALENDAR TIMELINE:

**1700 B.C. - ISRAEL'S CALENDAR SET ON THE SUN NEVER THE MOON:**
*(Gen. 1, Jub. 2:8-9, 6:30-36,  1 Enoch 72)* **Same since Creation.**

**400 B.C. - ISRAEL RESTORED YAHUAH'S CALENDAR (1st Esdras 5:51):**
After the return from Babylon.

**200 B.C.-100 A.D. - TEMPLE PRIESTS CONTINUED THE SUN CALENDAR OF ENOCH AND MOSES (4Q320, 4Q394, 4Q266)**

**165 B.C. TEMPLE DEFILED BY HASMONEANS AND PHARISEES WHO CHANGED THE CALENDAR: (Dam. Doc. 4Q266)** The exiled Temple Priests in Qumran record the Pharisees turned a blind eye to Torah's calendar in Jubilees which they rejected as scripture even then. They were usurpers not authorities and their changes represent fraud and they are cursed. These are modern Rabbis and Judaism.

**100 B.C. - EXILED TEMPLE PRIESTS CONTINUED THE SOLAR BIBLE CALENDAR IN QUMRAN (4Q320, 4Q394, Dam. Doc. 4Q266)**

**NEW TESTAMENT CONTINUED THE SUN CALENDAR OF ENOCH AND MOSES:** Mark 15:42-47 *(Also, Luke 23:54-56 KJV)* exposes two calendars at work in Israel. Mary and the women were keeping the Sabbath during the day on the 15th of Abib during and after the crucifixion when they refused to buy spices nor work. Joseph of Arimathea was not as he purchased linens on what Mary kept as Sabbath but his Pharisee Sabbath began at sundown erroneously. The Pharisees who were on the Babylonian Lunar Calendar exploiting a false half day for Unleavened Bread's Sabbath due to their inept calendar which never matches the Bible *(Mark 14:1-2)*. They were not killing Yahusha on a Feast Day on their calendar because they have a gap not found on the Biblical calendar and ultimately, they did crucify him on the Biblical Feast Sabbath. This is also the reason it could be both the preparation day before the Sabbath *(Pharisee calendar)* and the Sabbath drew on *(Bible calendar)* at the same time *(Luke 23:54-56 KJV)*. There are no discrepancies in the Gospel just misunderstandings by men.

# The Moon and its Phases



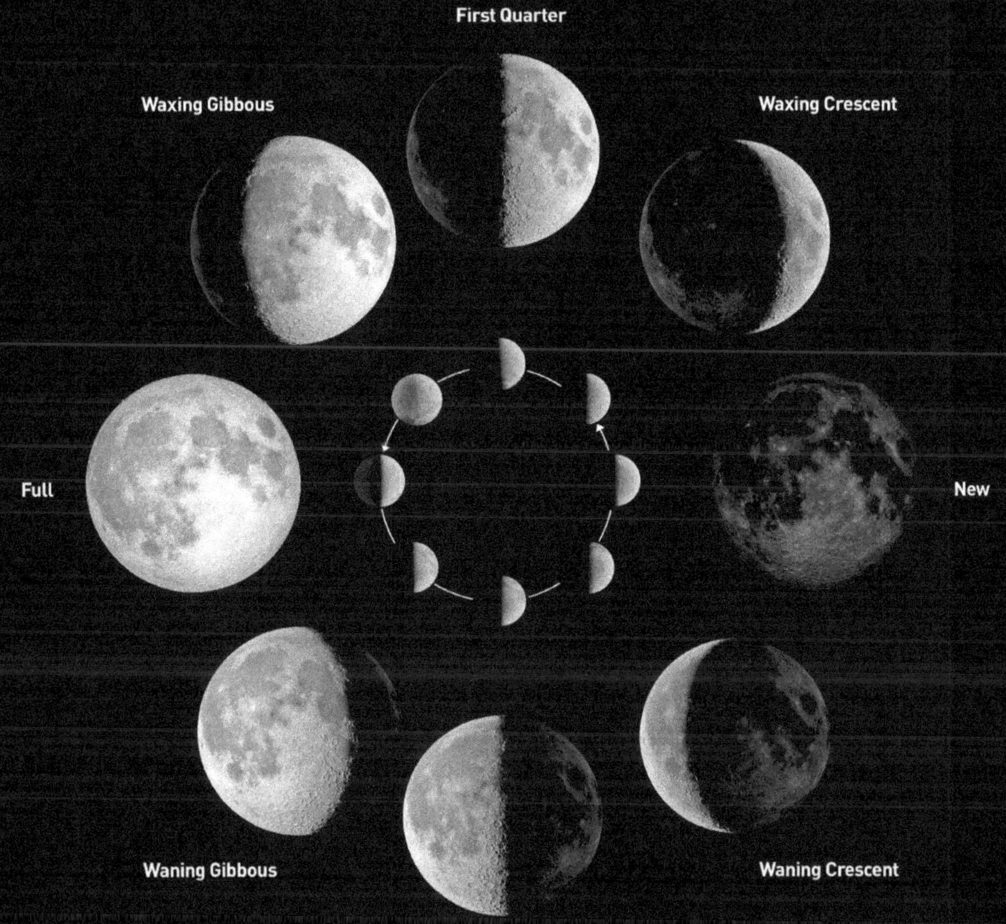



# 74-75
# The Lunar Year

## CHAPTER 73:

1. And after this law I saw another law dealing with the smaller luminary, which is named the **Moon**. 2. And her circumference is like the circumference of the heaven, and **her chariot in which she rides is driven by the wind**, and light is given to her in (definite) measure.

3. And her rising and setting **changes every month**: and her days are like the days of the sun, and **when her light is uniform (i. e. full) it amounts to the seventh part of the light of the sun**. 4. And thus she rises. And her **first phase** in the east comes forth on the **thirtieth morning**: and on that day she becomes visible; and constitutes for you the **first phase of the moon on the thirtieth day** together with the sun in the portal where the sun rises. 5. And the one half of her goes forth by a seventh part, and her whole circumference is **empty, without light**, with the exception of **one-seventh part of it**, (and) the fourteenth part of her light. 6. And when she receives one-seventh part of the half of her light, her light amounts to **one-seventh part and the half** thereof. 7. And she sets with the sun and when the sun rises the moon rises with him and receives the half of one part of light, and in that night in the beginning of her morning the moon sets with the sun, and is invisible that night with the fourteen parts and the half of one of them. 8. And she rises on that day with exactly a seventh part, and comes forth and recedes from the rising of the sun, and in her remaining days she becomes bright in the (remaining) thirteen parts.

*Enoch's First Phase: Waxing Crescent. 1/7th part. light. Begins on the 30th not the 1st.*

## CHAPTER 74:

1. And I saw another course, a law for her, (and) how according to that law she performs her monthly revolution. 2. And all these Uriel, the holy angel who is the leader of them all, showed to me, and their positions, and I wrote down their positions as he showed them to me, and I wrote down their months as they were, and the appearance of their lights till fifteen days were accomplished.

3. In single seventh parts she accomplishes all her light in the east, and in single seventh

parts accomplishes all her darkness in the west. 4. And in **certain months she alters her settings**, and in certain months she pursues **her own pecular course**. 5. In **two months the moon sets with the sun** in those **two middle portals the third and the fourth**. 6. She goes forth for **seven days**, and turns about and returns again through the portal where the sun rises, and accomplishes all her light: and she recedes from the sun, and in **eight days** enters the **sixth portal** from which the sun goes forth. 7. And when the sun goes forth from the fourth portal she goes forth seven days, until she goes forth from the fifth and turns back again in seven days into the fourth portal and accomplishes all her light: and she recedes and enters into the first portal in eight days. 8. And she returns again in seven days into the fourth portal from which the sun goes forth. 9. Thus I saw their position—how the moons rose and the sun set in those days. 10. And if **five years** are added together the **sun has an overplus of thirty days**, and all the days which accrue to it for one of those five years, when they are full, amount to **364 days**. 11.

*The moon has a far more complex and pecular course than the sun.*

And the overplus of the sun and of the stars amounts to six days: in 5 years 6 days every year come to 30 days: and **the moon falls behind the sun and stars to the number of 30 days**. 12. And **the sun and the stars bring in all the years exactly**, so that they do not advance or delay their position by a single day unto eternity; but **complete the years with perfect justice in 364 days**. 13. In **3 years** there are **1092 days**, and in **5 years 1820 days**, so that in **8 years** there are **2912 days**. 14. For the moon alone the days amount in **3 years** to **1062 days**, and in **5 years** she **falls 50 days behind**: [i. e. to the sum (of 1770) there is to be added (1000 and) 62 days]. 15. And in **5 years** there are **1770 days**, so that for the moon the days in **8 years** amount to **2832 days**, 16. [For in **8 years** she **falls behind to the amount of 80 days**], all the days she falls behind in 8 years are 80. 17. And **the year is accurately completed in conformity with their world-stations and the stations of the sun**, which rise from the portals through which it (**the sun) rises and sets 30 days**.

*The sun is the measure for the year, not the moon.*

*The sun is the measure for years never the moon. These calculations all equal 364 days per year.*

*The moon is 10 days too short each year. It cannot be used to determine the year. 364 days is the Bible calendar. 354 is Babylonian, not Bible. This is why the modern Hebrew Calendar is not Hebrew but Babylonian.*

*Only the sun is the accurate measure for the year and the month.*

## CHAPTER 75:

Cf. Jub. 6:23, 29-32. 364-day year, 4 intercalary days.

1 And the leaders of the heads of the thousands, who are placed over the whole creation and over all the stars, have also to do with the **four intercalary days**, being inseparable from their office, according to the reckoning of the year, and these render service on the **four days which are not reckoned in the reckoning of the year**. 2 And owing to them men go wrong therein, for those luminaries truly render service on the world-stations, one in the first portal, one in the third portal of the heaven, one in the fourth portal, and one in the sixth portal, and the exactness of the year is accomplished through its separate **three hundred and sixty-four stations**. 3 For the signs and the times and the years and the days the angel Uriel showed to me, whom Yahuah of glory hath set for ever over all the luminaries of the heaven, in the heaven and in the world, that they should rule on the face of the heaven and be seen on the earth, and be leaders for the day and the night, i. e. the sun, moon, and stars, and all the ministering creatures which make their revolution in all the chariots of the heaven.

4 In like manner **twelve doors** Uriel showed me, open in the circumference of the sun's chariot in the heaven, through which the rays of the sun break forth: and from them is warmth diffused over the earth, when they are opened at their appointed seasons. 5 [And for the winds and the spirit of the dew when they are opened, standing open in the heavens at the ends. 6 As for the **twelve portals in the heaven, at the ends of the earth**, out of which go forth the sun, moon, and stars, and all the works of heaven in the east and in the west, 7 There are many windows open to the left and right of them, and one window at its (appointed) season produces warmth corresponding (as these do) to those doors from which the stars come forth according as He has commanded them, and wherein they set corresponding to their number. 8 And I saw **chariots in the heaven**, running in the world, **above those portals** in which revolve the **stars that never set**. 9 And one is larger than all the rest, and it is that that makes its course through the entire world.

## CHAPTER 76:

1 And at the **ends of the earth** I saw **twelve portals** open to all the quarters (of the heaven), from which the **winds** go forth and blow over the earth. 2 **Three** of them are open on the face (i. e. the **east**) of the heavens, and **three** in the **west**, and **three** on the right (i. e. the **south**) of the heaven, and **three** on the left (i. e. the **north**). 3 And the three first are those of the east,

and three are of the north, and three [after those on the left] of the south, and three of the west. 4 Through four of these come winds of blessing and prosperity, and from those eight come hurtful winds: when they are sent, they bring destruction on all the earth and on the water upon it, and on all who dwell thereon, and on everything which is in the water and on the land. 5 And the **first wind** from those portals, called the **east wind**, comes forth through the first portal which is in the east, inclining towards the south: **from it come forth desolation, drought, heat, and destruction**. 6 And through the second portal in the middle comes what is fitting, and from it there come rain and fruitfulness and prosperity and dew; and through the third portal which lies toward the north come cold and drought.

7 And after these come forth the south winds through three portals: through the first portal of them inclining to the east comes forth a hot wind. 8 And through the middle portal next to it there come forth fragrant smells, and dew and rain, and prosperity and health. 9 And through the third portal lying to the west come forth dew and rain, locusts and desolation. 10 And after these the north winds: from the seventh portal in the east come dew and rain, locusts and desolation. 11 And from the middle portal come in a direct direction health and rain and dew and prosperity; and through the third portal in the west come cloud and hoar-frost, and snow and rain, and dew and locusts. 12 And after these [four] are the west winds: through the first portal adjoining the north come forth dew and hoar-frost, and cold and snow and frost.

13 And from the middle portal come forth dew and rain, and prosperity and blessing; and through the last portal which adjoins the south come forth drought and desolation, and burning and destruction.

14 And the twelve portals of the four quarters of the heaven are therewith completed, and all their laws and all their plagues and all their benefactions have I shown to thee, my son Methuselah.

*East wind brings destruction: Famine: Cf. Gen. 41:6, 23, 27; Brought locusts: Ex. 10:13; Parted the Red Sea: Ex. 14:21; Ships of Tarshish broken up: Ps. 48:7.*

*Cf. 79:1, 81:5; Jub. 7:38.*

*Land of Creation, the first land is in the Far East.*

*Cf. Rom. 9:5; 2Cor.11:31. "God is blessed for ever."*

*Portals where the sun sets.*

**1** And the **first quarter** is called the **east**, because it is the first: and the **second**, the **south**, because the Most High will descend there, yea, there in quite a special sense will He who is blessed for ever descend. **2** And the **west quarter** is named the **diminished**, because there all the luminaries of the heaven wane and go down. **3** And the **fourth quarter, named the north**, is divided into three parts: the first of them is for the dwelling of **men**: and the **second** contains **seas of water**, and the **abysses** and **forests** and **rivers**, and **darkness** and **clouds**; and the **third part** contains the **garden of righteousness**. **4** I saw **seven high mountains**, higher than all the mountains which are on the earth: and thence comes forth hoar-frost, and days, seasons, and years pass away.

*North quarter is the middle or navel of the Earth at the North pole. It includes the Garden of Eden which sets it's South border.*

*This is a worldwide perspective. 7 high mountains = 7 continents today.*

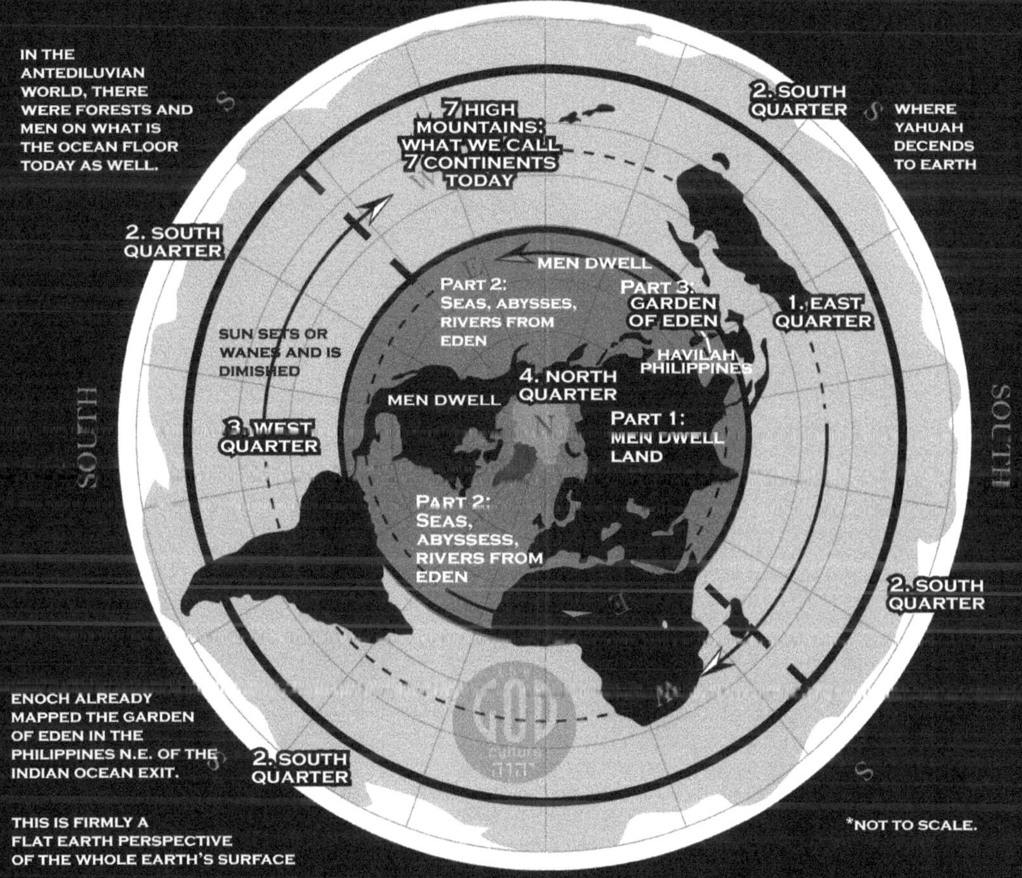

# THE SEVEN WORLD RIVERS AND THE RIVERS FROM EDEN



**5** I saw **seven rivers on the earth larger than all the rivers**: one of them coming **from the west** pours its waters into the **Great Sea**. **6** And these **two come from the north** to the sea and pour their waters **into the Erythraean Sea in the east**. **7** And the remaining four come forth on the side of the north to their own sea, (two of them to) the **Erythraean Sea**, and two into the Great Sea and discharge themselves there [and some say: into the desert]. **8 Seven great islands** I saw in the sea and in the mainland: two in the mainland and five in the Great Sea.



## PRIOR TO THE FLOOD, THESE WOULD BE THE GENESIS 2 RIVERS FROM EDEN.

Though Genesis catalogues these as five rivers which we have located in our strong theory, Enoch wrote what he saw as seven. With these rivers are large lakes of sort which is the same Hebrew word for "seas" (yam). That word in Hebrew is a broad term for large bodies of water including the Dead Sea, or lake really, the Nile River, etc. It is not specific to oceans. We find these ancient rivers on the bottom of the ocean floor today but prior to the flood, the earth was only 15% (1/7) water according to 2nd Esdras 6:42, 47 and 49-52. This leaves the great deep Mid-Ocean Ridge and Trenches which just so happen to be the location of the fountains of the great deep called "hydrothermal vents."

**1. Pison River:** *Comes from the west coast of North America fitting Enoch. There would be a great lake in the Sulu Sea of the Philippines or it could refer to what will be the world ocean after the flood.*

**TWO RIVERS FROM NORTH INTO INDIAN OCEAN:**

**2. Origin River From Eden:** *Just a portion comes North into the Indian Ocean.*

**3. Gihon River:** *Flows North around Africa until it flows into the Indian Ocean.*

**TWO MORE RIVERS INTO GREAT SEA:**

**4. Parat River:** *Flows North into what is the Pacific.*

**5. Origin River From Eden:** *Last portion flows from Indian Ocean into the Pacific.*

**TWO MORE RIVERS INTO INDIAN OCEAN:**

**6. Hiddekel River:** *Flows in the Indian Ocean from North.*

**7. Origin River From Eden:** *There is a portion in the middle of this worldwide river near Madagascar which travels North in the Indian Ocean.*

**We have no current track on the seven isles in the Great Sea.*

# 78
# THE SUN AND MOON: THE WAXING AND WANING OF THE MOON

## CHAPTER 78:

1 And the **names of the sun** are the following: the first **Oryares**, and the second **Tomas**. 2 And the **moon has four names**: the first name is **Asonya**, the second **Ebla** the third **Benase**, and the fourth **Erae**. 3 These are the two great luminaries: their circumference is like the circumference of the heaven, and the **size of the circumference of both is alike**. 4 In the circumference of the sun there are seven portions of light which are added to it more than to the moon, and in definite measures it is transferred till the seventh portion of the sun is exhausted. 5 And they set and enter the portals of the west, and make their revolution by the north, and come forth through the eastern portals on the face of the heaven. 6 And when the moon rises one-fourteenth part appears in the heaven: [the light becomes full in her]: on the fourteenth day she accomplishes her light. 7 And fifteen parts of light are transferred to her till the fifteenth day (when) her light is accomplished, according to the sign of the year, and she becomes fifteen parts, and the moon grows by (the addition of) fourteenth parts. 8 And in her waning (the moon) decreases on the first day to fourteen parts of her light, on the second to thirteen parts of light, on the third to twelve, on the fourth to eleven, on the fifth to ten, on the sixth to nine, on the seventh to eight, on the eighth to seven, on the ninth to six, on the tenth to five, on the eleventh to four, on the twelfth to three, on the thirteenth to two, on the fourteenth to the half of a seventh, and all her remaining light disappears wholly on the fifteenth. 9 **And in certain months the month has twenty-nine days and once twenty-eight**. 10 And Uriel showed me another law: **when light is transferred to the moon, and on which side it is transferred to her by the sun**. 11 During all the period during which the moon is growing in her light, she is transferring it to herself when opposite to the

sun during fourteen days [her light is accomplished in the heaven], and when she is illumined throughout, her light is accomplished in the heaven. 12 And on the first day she is called the new moon, for on that day the light rises upon her. 13 She becomes full moon exactly on the day when the sun sets in the west, and from the east she rises at night, and the moon shines the whole night through till the sun rises over against her and the moon is seen over against the sun.

14 On the side whence the light of the moon comes forth, there again she wanes till all the light vanishes and all the days of the month are at an end and her circumference is empty, void of light. 15 And **three months she makes of thirty days**, and at her time she makes **three months of twenty-nine days each**, in which she accomplishes her waning in the first period of time, and in the first portal for one **hundred and seventy-seven days**.

16 And in the time of her going out she appears for **three months (of) thirty days each**, and for **three months she appears (of) twenty-nine each**. 17 At night she appears like a man for twenty days each time, and by day she appears like the heaven, and there is nothing else in her save her light,

1 And now, my son, I have

## CHAPTER 79:

*Cf. 76:14, 81:5; Jub. 7:38.*

shown thee everything, and the law of all the stars of the heaven is completed. 2 And he showed me all the laws of these for every day, and for every season of bearing rule, and for every year, and for its going forth, and for the order prescribed to it every month and every week: 3 And the waning of the moon which takes place in the sixth portal: for in this sixth portal her light is accomplished, and after that there is the beginning of the waning: 4 (And the waning) which takes place in the first portal in its season, **till one hundred and seventy-seven days are accomplished: reckoned according to weeks, twenty-five (weeks) and two days**. 5 She falls behind the sun and the order of the stars exactly five days in the course of one period, and when this place which thou seest has been traversed. 6 Such is the picture and sketch of every luminary which Uriel the archangel, who is their leader, showed unto me.

*Affirmation a week is 7 days. 177 days is 25 weeks + 2 days which makes these 7-day weeks.*

# 80
# Perversion of Nature and the heavenly Bodies owing to the sin of Men

# 81
# The Heavenly Tablets and the mission of Enoch

# 82
# Charge given to Enoch: the four intercalary days: the Stars which lead the Seasons and the Months

# CHAPTER 80:

1 And in those days the angel Uriel answered and said to me: 'Behold, I have shown thee everything, Enoch, and I have revealed everything to thee that thou shouldest see this sun and this moon, and the leaders of the stars of the heaven and all those who turn them, their tasks and times and departures. 2 And **in the days of the sinners the years shall be shortened**, And their **seed shall be tardy on their lands** and fields, and **all things on the earth shall alter**, And shall not appear in their time: And the rain shall be kept back And the heaven shall withhold (it). 3 And in those times the **fruits of the earth shall be backward**. And shall not grow in their time And the fruits of the trees shall be withheld in their time. 4 And **the moon shall alter her order**. And not appear at her time. 5 [And in those days the sun shall be seen and he shall journey in the evening on the extremity of the great chariot in the west] And shall **shine more brightly than accords with the order of light**. 6 And many chiefs of the stars shall transgress the order (prescribed). And these shall alter their orbits and tasks, And not appear at the seasons prescribed to them. 7 And **the whole order of the stars shall be concealed from the sinners**, And the thoughts of those on the earth **shall err concerning them**, [And they shall be altered from all their ways]. Yea, **they shall err and take them to be gods**. 8 And evil shall be multiplied upon them, And punishment shall come upon them so as to destroy all.'

*Cf. Matt. 24:22; Mark 13:20.*

*Reconciling time in our day is difficult. However, one must consider whether these courses are in this stage now.*

*Modern Scientism is stacked with sinners and occultists. Are they erring?*

*The sun, moon and stars are included in pagan worship and even some so-called "Christian" worship.*

# CHAPTER 81:

1 And he said unto me: 'Observe, Enoch, these **heavenly tablets**. And read what is written thereon, And **mark every individual fact**.' 2 And I observed the heavenly tablets, and read everything which was written (thereon) and **understood everything, and read the book of all the deeds of mankind, and of all the children of flesh that shall be upon the earth to the remotest generations.**

3 And forthwith I blessed the great Yahuah, the King

*Cf. Jub. 3:10, 4:3.*

*Enoch knew what would happen to the End Times from the Heavenly Tablets.*

of glory for ever, in that He has made all the works of the world, And I extolled Yahuah because of His patience. And blessed Him because of the children of men. 4 And after that I said: 'Blessed is the man who dies in righteousness and goodness, Concerning whom **there is no book of unrighteousness written**, And against whom no day of judgment shall be found.'

*Only the righteous are recorded in the Book of Life.*

5 And those **seven holy ones brought me and placed me on the earth before the door of my house**, and said to me: 'Declare everything to thy son Methuselah, and show to all thy children that **no flesh is righteous in the sight of Yahuah**, for He is their Creator. 6 **One year we will leave thee with thy son**, till thou givest thy (last) commands, that thou mayest **teach thy children and record (it) for them**, and testify to all thy children; and in the **second year** they shall **take thee** from their midst. 7 Let thy heart be strong. For the good shall announce righteousness to the good; The righteous with the righteous shall rejoice, And shall offer congratulation to one another. 8 But the sinners shall die with the sinners, And

*Cf. 76:14, 81:5; Jub. 7:38.*

*Enoch returned home and was taken yet.*

*He was taken 1 year later.*

the apostate go down with the apostate. 9 And **those who practice righteousness shall die on account of the deeds of men. And be taken away on account of the doings of the godless.'** 10 And in those days they ceased to speak to me, and I came to my people, blessing Yahuah of the world.

## CHAPTER 82:

1 And now, my son Methuselah, all these things I am recounting to thee and **writing down for thee**, and I have revealed to thee everything, and **given thee books concerning all these**: so **preserve, my son Methuselah, the books from thy father's hand, and (see) that thou deliver them to the generations of the world.** 2 I have given wisdom to thee and to thy children [And thy children that shall be to thee], That they may give it to their children for generations, This wisdom (namely) that passeth their thought. 3 And those who understand it **shall not sleep but shall listen with the ear that they may learn this wisdom. And**

*Methusaleh obeyed as Noah took these on the ark and Abraham read 1 Enoch in his day still. It remained inspired scripture thru the New Testament.*

*Cf. Job 23:12.* **it shall please those that eat thereof better than good food.** 4 Blessed are all the righteous, blessed are all those who walk in the way of righteousness and sin not as the sinners, in the reckoning of all their days in which the sun traverses the heaven, entering into and departing from the portals for **thirty days** with the heads of thousands of the order of the stars, together with the **four which are intercalated which divide the four portions of the** *Cf. Jub. 6:23, 29-32. 364-day year, 4 Intercalary days.* **year**, which lead them and enter with them **four days.** 5 Owing to them **men shall be at fault and not reckon them** in the whole reckoning of the year: yea, men shall be at fault, and not recognize *Cf. Jub. 6:32-38. Warning against use of any other calendar.* them accurately. 6 For they belong to the reckoning of the year and are truly recorded (thereon) for ever, one in the first portal and one in the third, and one in the fourth and one in the sixth, and **the year is completed in three** *Cf. Jub. 6:23, 29-32 364-day year, 4 intercalary days.* **hundred and sixty-four days.** 7 And the account thereof is **accurate and the recorded reckoning thereof exact;** for the luminaries, and months and **festivals**, and years and days, has Uriel shown and revealed

to me, to whom Yahuah of the *Enoch knew of Biblical Feasts such as Shavuot.* whole creation of the world hath subjected the host of heaven. 8 And he has power over night and day in the heaven to cause the light to give light to men—sun, moon, and stars, and all the powers of the heaven which revolve in their circular chariots.

9 And these are the orders of the stars, which set in their places and in their seasons and **festivals** and months. 10 And these are the names of those who lead them, who watch that they enter at their times, in their orders, in their seasons, in their months, in their periods of dominion, and in their positions.

11 Their **four leaders who divide the four parts of the year** enter first; and after them the **twelve leaders of the orders who divide the months**; and for the **three hundred and sixty (days) there are heads over** *Cf. Jub. 6:23, 29-32. 364-day year, 4 intercalary days.* **thousands who divide the days**; and for **the four intercalary days there are the leaders which sunder the four parts of the year.** 12 And these heads over thousands are *Seasons.* intercalated between leader and leader, each behind a station, but their leaders make

the division. **13** And these are the names of the leaders who divide the four parts of the year which are ordained: Milki'el, Hel'emmelek, and Mel'eyal, and Narel.

*Yahuah's ways are entrenched in His calendar even with full participation of the angels.*

**14** And the names of those who lead them: Adnar'el, and Iyasusa'el, and 'Elome'el— these three follow the leaders of the orders, and there is one that follows the three leaders of the orders which follow those leaders of stations that divide the four parts of the year. **15** In the beginning of the year Melkeyal rises first and rules, who is named Tam'aini, and **sun** and all the days of his dominion whilst he bears rule are **ninety-one days**. **16** And these are the signs of the days which are to be seen on earth in the days of his dominion: sweat, and heat, and calms; and all the trees bear fruit, and leaves are produced on all the trees, and the harvest of wheat, and

*Cf. Jub. 4:21. "rule of the sun."*

*Spring.* the rose-flowers, and all the flowers which come forth in the field, but the trees of the winter season become withered. **17** And these are the names of the leaders which are under them: Berka'el, Zelebs'el, and another who is added a head of a thousand, called Hiluyaseph: and the days of the dominion of this (leader) are at an end.

**18** The next leader after him is Hel'emmelek; whom one names the shining sun, and all the days of his light are **ninety-one days**. **19** And these are the signs of (his) days on the earth: glowing heat and

*Summer.* dryness, and the trees ripen their fruits and produce all their fruits ripe and ready, and the sheep pair and become pregnant, and all the fruits of the earth are gathered in, and everything that is in the fields, and the winepress: these things take place in the days of his dominion. **20** These are the names, and the orders, and the leaders of those heads of thousands: Gida'iyal, Ke'el, and He'el, and the name of the head of a thousand which is added to them, Asfa'el: and the days of his dominion are at an end.

# SECTION 4:

83-90

# THE BOOK OF DREAM VISIONS

## CHAPTER 83:

Cf. Jub. 4:19.
"vision of his sleep... until day of judgment."

Cf. Jub. 4:20.
Before 582 A.M. or before age of 60.

Cf. 85:3
Jub. 4:19.
Wife Edna.

Before age of 60.

**1** And now, my son Methuselah, I will show thee all my visions which I have seen, recounting them before thee. **2 Two visions I saw before I took a wife**, and the one was quite unlike the other: **the first when I was learning to write**: the **second before I took thy mother**, (when) I saw a terrible vision. And regarding them I prayed to Yahuah. **3** I had laid me down in the house of my grandfather Mahalalel, (when) I saw in a vision how the heaven collapsed and was borne off and fell to the earth. **4** And when it fell to the earth I saw how the earth was swallowed up in a great abyss, and mountains were suspended on mountains, and hills sank down on hills, and high trees were rent from their stems, and hurled down and sunk in the abyss. **5** And thereupon a word fell into my mouth, and I lifted up (my voice) to cry aloud and said: 'The earth is destroyed.' **6** And my grandfather **Mahalalel** waked me as I lay near him and said unto me: 'Why dost thou cry so, my son, and why dost thou make such lamentation? **7** And I recounted to him" the whole vision which I had seen, and he said unto me: 'A terrible thing hast thou seen, my son, and of grave moment is thy dream-vision as to the secrets of all the sin of the earth: **it must sink into the abyss and be destroyed with a great destruction**. **8** And now, my son, **arise and make petition to Yahuah of glory**, since thou art a believer, that **a remnant may remain on the earth**, and that He may not destroy the whole earth. **9** My son, from heaven all this will come upon the earth, and upon the earth there will be great destruction.' **10** After that I arose and prayed and implored and besought, and **wrote down my prayer for the generations of the world**, and I will show everything to thee, my son Methuselah. **11** And when I had **gone forth below and seen the**

Mahalalel, Enoch's Grand-father, father of Jared, was holy and understood the vision Enoch saw. This also proves Modern Jasher wrong that the patriarchs were holy during the days of Enos who was his grand-father.

Cf. 25.3, 27.3,5, 36:4, 40:3, 63:2, 75:3. "Yahuah of glory."

heaven, and the sun rising in the east, and the moon setting in the west, and a few stars, and the whole earth, and everything as He had known it in the beginning**, then I blessed Yahuah of Judgment and extolled Him because He had made the sun to go forth from the windows of the east, and he ascended and rose on the face of the heaven, and set out and kept traversing the path shown unto him.

# CHAPTER 84:

1 And I lifted up my hands in righteousness and blessed the Holy and Great One, and spake with the breath of my mouth, and with the tongue of flesh, which Elohim has made for the children of the flesh of men, that they should speak therewith, and He gave them breath and a tongue and a mouth that they should speak therewith: 2 'Blessed be Thou, Yahuah, King, Great and mighty in Thy greatness, Yahuah of the whole creation of the heaven. **King of kings** and Elohim of the whole world. And Thy power and kingship and greatness abide for ever and ever. And

*Cf. 9:4 "King of Kings." 1Tim. 6:15; Rev 17:14, 19:16.*

throughout all generations Thy dominion: And all **the heavens are Thy throne for ever, And the whole earth Thy footstool** for ever and ever. 3 For Thou hast made and Thou rulest all things, And **nothing is too hard for Thee**, Wisdom departs not from the place of Thy throne, Nor turns away from Thy presence. And Thou knowest and seest and hearest everything, And there is nothing hidden from Thee [for Thou seest everything]. 4 And now the angels of Thy heavens are guilty of trespass, And upon the flesh of men abideth Thy wrath until the great day of judgment. 5 And now, O Elohim and Yahuah and Great King, I implore and beseech Thee to fulfill my prayer. To leave me a posterity on earth. And not to destroy all the flesh of man. And make the earth without inhabitant, so that there should be an eternal destruction. 6 And now, my Yahuah, destroy from the earth the flesh which has aroused Thy wrath, but **the flesh of righteousness and uprightness establish as a plant of the eternal seed.** And hide not Thy face from the prayer of Thy servant, O Yahuah.'

*Cf. Isa. 66:1; Mat. 5:35; Act 7:49. Exact quote of 1 Enoch.*

*Cf. Luke 1:37. "For with God nothing shall be impossible."*

# 85-90
# THE SECOND DREAM VISION OF ENOCH:

## The History of the World to the Founding of the Messianic Kingdom a.k.a. the apocalypse of animals

## 86
### The Fall of the Angels and the Demoralization of Mankind

## 87
### The Advent of the Seven Archangels

## 88
### The Punishment of the Fallen Angels by the Archangels

# CHAPTER 85:

1 And after this I saw another dream, and I will show the whole dream to thee, my son. 2 And Enoch lifted up (his voice) and spake to his son Methuselah: 'To thee, my son, will I speak: hear my words— incline thine ear to the dream vision of thy father. 3 Before I took thy mother Edna, I saw in a vision on my bed, and behold a bull came forth from the earth, and that bull was white; and after it came forth a heifer, and along with this (latter) came forth two bulls, one of them black and the other red. 4 And that black bull gored the red one and pursued him over the earth, and thereupon I could no longer see that red bull.

5 But that black bull grew and that heifer went with him, and I saw that many oxen proceeded from him which resembled and followed him. 6 And that cow, that first one, went from the presence of that first bull in order to seek that red one but found him not, and lamented with a great lamentation over him and sought him. 7 And I looked till that first bull came to her and quieted her, and

from that time onward she cried no more. 8 And after that she bore another white bull, and after him she bore many bulls and black cows. 9 And I saw in my sleep that white bull likewise grow and become a great white bull, and from him proceeded many white bulls, and they resembled him.

10 And they began to beget many white bulls, which resembled them, one following the other, (even) many.

# CHAPTER 86:

1 And again I saw with mine eyes as I slept, and I saw the heaven above, and behold a star fell from heaven, and it arose and ate and pastured amongst those oxen. 2 And after that I saw the large and the black oxen, and behold they all changed their stalls and pastures and their cattle, and began to live with each other. 3 And again I saw in the vision, and looked towards the heaven, and behold I saw many stars descend and cast themselves down from heaven to that first star, and they became bulls amongst those cattle and pastured with

*Cf. Jub. 4:19. Wife Edna. Adam. Cf. Gen. 1:26-27. White in righteouness not skin color as Adamah, the soil means red. Eve/Havah. Cf. Gen. 2:22.*

*Cf. Gen. 4:1-2, 8; Jub. 4:2. Black, evil Cain killed Red, for blood, Abel. Not skin.*

*Cf. Jub. 4:1,9. Cain married Awan, the first daughter of Adam and Eve, his sister.*

*Cf. Gen. 4:17-26. Cain's lineage. Cain remained evil and left Adam to the East.*

*Cf. Jub. 4:7. Adam & Eve mourned over Abel 28 years.*

*Cf. Gen. 4:25; Jub. 4:7. Seth is born. Joy restored.*

*Cf. Gen. 5:4; Jub. 4:10. "...she bare yet nine sons." After Cain, Abel, Awan, Seth and Azura. 12 sons total plus daughters.*

*Cf. Gen. 4:26; Jub. 4:12. Seth was holy as were his generations. With Enos, his son, men began to call upon YHWH.*

*Cf. 6:6; Jub. 4:15; Gen. 6:1-2. In "Days of Jared" Watchers come to Earth to teach men initially.*

*Star = Angel, sons of Elohim or bene ha Elohim.*

*Cf. Gen. 6:1-4; Jub. 5:1-2; Jude 1:6; 2 Pet. 2:4. Angels mate with women. Offspring Nephilim giants = large black oxen. "all flesh corrupted.. their orders."*

*Cf. 6:6,8:1, 9:6, 10:4, 13:1. Angels fell by oath on Mt. Hermon, Israel.*

Cf. Gen. 6:4; Jub. 5:2. Nephilim corrupting orders procreating like horses with the daughters of men.

them [amongst them]. **4** And I looked at them and saw, and behold they all let out their privy members, like horses, and began to cover the cows of the oxen, and they all became pregnant and bare elephants, camels, and asses.

Cf. 7:2-4; Gen. 6:5; Jub. 5:2. Turned on mankind to devour them.

**5** And all the oxen feared them and were affrighted at them, and began to bite with their teeth and to devour, and to gore with their horns.

**6** And they began moreover to devour those oxen; and behold all the children of the earth began to tremble and quake before them and to flee from them.

# CHAPTER 87:

Cf. Jub. 5:7, 9, 7:22. "Each slay his neighbor."

**1** And again I saw how they began to gore each other and to devour each other, and the earth began to cry aloud.

**2** And I raised mine eyes again to heaven, and I saw in the vision, and behold there came

Cf. 85:3. White = holy not race.

forth from heaven beings who were like white men: and four

Cf. 20. The seven archangels. Cf. 81:5, 90:21-22, 90:31.

went forth from that place and three with them. **3** And those three that had last come forth grasped me by my hand and took me up, away from the generations of the earth, and

raised me up to a lofty place, and showed me a tower raised high above the earth, and all the hills were lower. **4** And one said unto me: "Remain here till thou seest everything that befalls those elephants, camels, and asses, and the stars and the oxen, and all of them."

Enoch is not in the Garden yet but views the sins of the Earth from a protected place above.

# CHAPTER 88:

Cf. 10:4; Jub. 5:10. Yahuah said to Raphael: 'Bind Azazel hand and foot, and cast him into the darkness...'

**1** And I saw one of those four who had come forth first, and he seized that first star which had fallen from the heaven, and bound it hand and foot and cast it into an abyss: now that abyss was narrow and deep, and horrible and dark. **2** And one of them drew a sword, and gave it to those elephants and camels and asses: then they began to smite each other, and the whole earth quaked because of them. **3** And as I was beholding in the vision, lo, one of those four who had come forth stoned (them) from heaven, and gathered and took all the great stars whose privy members were like those of horses, and bound them all hand and foot, and cast them in an abyss of the earth.

Cf. 10:4; Jub. 5:10; Matt. 8:12, 22:13, 25:30. Sinners will be "cast out into outer darkness: there shall be weeping and gnashing of teeth" on the Day of Judgment.

Cf. 14:6; Jub. 5:9.

Cf. 10:4, 54:4-5; Jub. 5:10; Jude 1:6, 2 Pet. 2:4.

## CHAPTER 89:

*Cf. 60. Michael instructed Noah of the coming Flood.*

**1** And one of those four went to that white bull and instructed him in a secret, without his being terrified: he was born a bull and became a man, and built for himself a great vessel and dwelt thereon; and three bulls dwelt with him in that vessel and they were covered in.

*Cf. Gen. 6:14, Jub. 5:21. "Make thee an ark."*

*Gen. 7:13, 16. Bulls = Shem, Ham, Japheth. Yahuah shut them in.*

**2** And again I raised mine eyes towards heaven and saw a lofty roof, with seven water torrents thereon, and those torrents flowed with much water into an enclosure.

*Cf. Gen. 1:8; Ps. 19:1, 150; Ez. 1:22-26, 10:1; Dan. 12:3. "Firmament."*

*Cf. Jub. 5:24. seven flood-gates of heaven.*

**3** And I saw again, and behold fountains were opened on the surface of that great enclosure, and that water began to swell and rise upon the surface, and I saw that enclosure till all its surface was covered with water.

*Cf. Jub. 5:25, 29, 6:2; Gen. 7:11. fountains opened on surface of firmament.*

**4** And the water, the darkness, and mist increased upon it; and as I looked at the height of that water, that water had risen above the height of that enclosure, and was streaming over that enclosure, and it

*Cf. Gen. 7:19-20. Fifteen cubits upward did the waters prevail, and the mountains were covered.*

stood upon the earth. **5** And all the cattle of that enclosure were gathered together until I saw how they sank and were swallowed up and perished in that water. **6** But that vessel floated on the water, while all the oxen and elephants and camels and asses sank to the bottom with all the animals, so that I could no longer see them, and they were not able to escape, (but) perished and sank into the depths. **7** And again I saw in the vision till those water torrents were removed from that high roof, and the chasms of the earth were leveled up and other abysses were opened. **8** Then the water began to run down into these, till the earth became visible; but that vessel settled on the earth, and the darkness retired and light appeared. **9** But that white bull which had become a man came out of that vessel, and the three bulls with him, and one of those three was white like that bull, and one of them was red as blood, and one black: and that white bull departed from them.

*Cf. Gen. 7:22. "All in whose nostrils was the breath of life, of all that was in the dry land, died."*

*Cf. Gen. 8:14, Jub. 5:29.*

*Cf. Jub. 5:29. Chasms of the Earth are the Great Deep Oceanic Ridges and Trenches known as the Rivers from Eden. Gen. 2 or Enoch's 7 Antediluvian Rivers, 77:5-7.*

*Noah = white righteous bull. Not race. Shem = righteous, Ham = red like Abel as his people will be martyred by Japheth who is evil black like Cain. These are not race but accurate to history.*

*After the Flood.*

**10** And they began to bring forth beasts of the field and birds, so that there arose different genera; lions, tigers, wolves, dogs, hyenas, wild boars, foxes, squirrels, swine, falcons, vultures, kites, eagles, and ravens; and among them was born a white bull.

*Abraham = white righteous bull.*

*Cf. Gen 16:12. Wild donkey/ass = Ishmael (some translations). White righteous bull = Isaac.*

**11** And they began to bite one another; but that white bull which was born amongst them begat a wild ass and a white bull with it, and the wild asses multiplied.

*Cf. Jub. 37:20, 24. Wild boar = Esau/Edom. Black = evil. Cf. Gen. 36:9-43. "Dukes of Edom."*

**12** But that bull which was born from him begat a black wild boar and a white sheep; and the former begat many boars, but that sheep begat twelve sheep.

*White righteous sheep = Jacob.*

*12 sheep = 12 tribes of Israel.*

**13** And when those twelve sheep had grown, they gave up one of them to the asses, and those asses again gave up that sheep to the wolves, and that sheep grew up among the wolves.

*Cf. Gen 37:28. Joseph was sold to the Ishmaelites (asses) who sold him to the wolves of Egypt.*

**14** And Yahuah brought the eleven sheep to live with it and to pasture with it among the wolves: and they multiplied and became many flocks of sheep.

*Cf. Gen. 47. Israel joins Joseph in Egypt.*

*Cf. Ex.1:8-10.*

**15** And the wolves began to fear them, and they oppressed them until they destroyed their little ones, and they cast their young into a river of much water: but those sheep began to cry aloud on account of their little ones, and to complain unto their Yahuah.

*Cf. Ex. 1:22.*

**16** And a sheep which had been saved from the wolves fled and escaped to the wild asses; and I saw the sheep how they lamented and cried, and besought their Yahuah with all their might, till that Yahuah of the sheep descended at the voice of the sheep from a lofty abode, and came to them and pastured them.

*Cf. Ex. 2. Moses born among the wolves.*

*Cf. Ex. 2:15. Moses fled to Midian with the Ishmaelites (wild asses).*

*Cf. Ex. 19. Yahuah descends on Mt. Sinai. Cf. Num. 10:33. Abides in the Ark of the Covenant among them.*

**17** And He called that sheep which had escaped the wolves, and spake with it concerning the wolves that it should admonish them not to touch the sheep.

*Cf. Ex. 2:15. Moses fled to Midian with the Ishmaelites (wild asses).*

*Cf. Ex. 3.*

**18** And the sheep went to the wolves according to the word of Yahuah, and another sheep met it and went with it, and the two went and entered together into the assembly of those wolves, and spake with them and admonished them not to touch the sheep from henceforth.

*Cf. Ex. 4:14. Aaron, brother of Moses.*

**19** And thereupon I saw the wolves, and how they oppressed the sheep exceedingly with all

*Cf. Ex. 5. "Let my people go."*

*Cf. Ex. 5:9.*

their power; and the sheep cried aloud. 20 And Yahuah came to the sheep and they began to smite those wolves: and the wolves began to make lamentation; but the sheep became quiet and forthwith ceased to cry out. 21 And I saw the sheep till they departed from amongst the wolves; but the eyes of the wolves were blinded, and those wolves departed in pursuit of the sheep with all their power. 22 And Yahuah of the sheep went with them, as their leader, and all His sheep followed Him: and His face was dazzling and glorious and terrible to behold. 23 But the wolves began to pursue those sheep till they reached a sea of water. 24 And that

*The plagues.*

*Cf. Ex. 13. The Exodus.*

*Cf. Ex. 14. Pharaoh pursued.*

sea was divided and the water stood on this side and on that before their face, and their Yahuah led them and placed Himself between them and the wolves. 25 And as those wolves did not yet see the sheep, they proceeded into the midst of that sea, and the wolves followed the sheep, and [those wolves] ran after them into that sea. 26 And when they saw Yahuah of the sheep, they turned to flee before His face, but that sea gathered itself together, and became as it had been created, and the water swelled and rose till it covered those wolves. 27 And I saw till all the wolves who pursued those sheep perished and were drowned.

*Ex. 14. Red Sea divided.*

*Ex. 14. Pillar of cloud and darkness separated them.*

*Ex. 14. Egyptians follow them into the sea to their doom.*

*Cf. Ex. 15. Yahuah provides water.*

28 But the sheep escaped from that water and went forth into a wilderness, where there was no water and no grass; and they began to open their eyes and to see; and I saw Yahuah of the sheep pasturing them and giving them water and grass, and that sheep going and leading them. 29 And that sheep ascended to the summit of that lofty rock, and

*Cf. Ex. 19. Moses goes up to Mt. Sinai.*

Yahuah of the sheep sent it to them. 30 And after that I saw Yahuah of the sheep who stood before them, and His appearance was great and terrible and majestic, and all those sheep saw Him and were afraid before His face. 31 And they all feared and trembled because of Him, and they cried to that sheep with them [which was amongst them]: "We are not able to stand before our Yahuah or to behold Him." 32 And that sheep which led them again ascended to the summit of that rock, but the sheep began to be blinded and to wander from the way which he had showed them, but that sheep wot not thereof. 33 And Yahuah of the sheep was wrathful exceedingly against them, and that sheep discovered it, and went down from the summit of the rock, and came to the sheep, and found the greatest part of them blinded and fallen away. 34 And when they saw it they feared and trembled at its presence, and desired to return to their folds. 35 And that sheep took other sheep with it, and came to those sheep which had fallen away, and began to slay them; and

*Cf. Ex. 19.Yahuah visits Sinai.*

*Cf. Ex. 20:19. "And they said unto Moses, Speak thou with us, and we will hear: but let not God speak with us, lest we die."*

*Cf. Ex. 32. The golden calf.*

*Cf. Ex. 32. The Levites killed the rebellious.*

the sheep feared its presence, and thus that sheep brought back those sheep that had fallen away, and they returned to their folds. 36 And I saw in this vision till that sheep became a man and built a house for Yahuah of the sheep, and placed all the sheep in that house. 37 And I saw till this sheep which had met that sheep which led them fell asleep: and I saw till all the great sheep perished and little ones arose in their place, and they came to a pasture, and approached a stream of water. 38 Then that sheep, their leader which had become a man, withdrew from them and fell asleep, and all the sheep sought it and cried over it with a great crying. 39 And I saw till they left off crying for that sheep and crossed that stream of water, and there arose the two sheep as leaders in the place of those which had led them and fallen asleep (lit. "had fallen asleep and led them"). 40 And I saw till the sheep came to a goodly place, and a pleasant and glorious land, and I saw till those sheep were satisfied; and that house stood amongst them in the pleasant land.

*Cf. Ex. 35. The Tabernacle is built.*

*Deut. 34:7. Moses died.*

*Num. 14:27. The adults of Israel 20 years old and above perished in the wilderness.*

*Deut. 34:7. Moses died.*

*Cf. Jos. 3. Israel crosses the Jordan River to enter the Promised Land.*

*Cf. Judges 2:18-19. The days of the Judges fit this exactly.*

41 And sometimes their eyes were opened, and sometimes blinded, till another sheep arose and led them and brought them all back, and their eyes were opened.

*Cf. 1 Sam. 17:43. Goliath claimed David saw him as a dog. Perhaps Philistines = dogs. Dogs and foxes are often seen as scavengers in the Bible.*

42 And the dogs and the foxes and the wild boars began to devour those sheep till Yahuah of the sheep raised up [another sheep] a ram from their midst, which led them.

*Cf. Jub. 37:20, 24. Wild boars = Edom/Esau.*

*Foxes = Ammonites/ Samaritans likely.*

43 And that ram began to butt on either side those dogs, foxes, and wild boars till he had destroyed them all.

*Ram = King Saul who died disgraced and unseemly.*

44 And that sheep whose eyes were opened saw that ram, which was amongst the sheep, till it forsook its glory and began to butt those sheep, and trampled upon them, and behaved itself unseemly.

*Samuel, lamb sent to David, another lamb to anoint him king. He grew into a ram and lead Israel after Saul.*

45 And Yahuah of the sheep sent the lamb to another lamb and raised it to being a ram and leader of the sheep instead of that ram which had forsaken its glory. 46 And it went to it and spake to it alone, and raised it to being a ram, and made it the prince and leader of the sheep; but during all these things those dogs oppressed the sheep.

47 And the first ram pursued that second ram, and that second ram arose and fled before it; and I saw till those dogs pulled down the first ram. 48 And that second ram arose and led the [little] sheep. 49 And those sheep grew and multiplied; but all the dogs, and foxes, and wild boars feared and fled before it, and that ram butted and killed the wild beasts, and those wild beasts had no longer any power among the sheep and robbed them no more of aught, And that ram begat many sheep and fell asleep; and a little sheep became ram in its stead, and became prince and leader of those sheep.

50 And that house became great and broad, and it was built for those sheep: (and) a tower lofty and great was built on the house for Yahuah of the sheep, and that house was low, but the tower was elevated and lofty, and Yahuah of the sheep stood on that tower and they offered a full table before Him.

*King Saul pursued David who fled and even when given the opportunity would not kill King Saul.*

*The Philistines (dogs) killed King Saul and his sons.*

*David eradicated much of the Nephilim giants from the land bringing peace.*

*David died.*

*Young Solomon rose to King, a ram.*

*King Solomon built the Temple.*

*Cf. John 2:16. "The temple is called 'God's house', but owing to sin of Israel 'your house.'*

*Cf. Matt. 23:37; Rom. 11:3. They killed the prophets.*

*Cf. 1Ki. 2:1, 11. Elijah lived after Solomon and was not killed but taken up. He, as Enoch, did not go to Heaven to reside but Enoch says Elijah joins him in the Garden of Eden. The Tree of Life is there to sustain them.*

**51** And again I saw those sheep that they again erred and went many ways, and forsook that their house, and Yahuah of the sheep called some from amongst the sheep and sent them to the sheep, but the sheep began to slay them. **52** And one of them was saved and was not slain, and it sped away and cried aloud over the sheep; and they sought to slay it, but Yahuah of the sheep saved it from the sheep, and brought it up to me and caused it to dwell there. **53** And many other sheep He sent to those sheep to testify unto them and lament over them. **54** And

*Cf. Mark 11:17.*

after that I saw that when they forsook the house of Yahuah and His tower they fell away entirely, and their eyes were blinded; and I saw Yahuah of the sheep how He wrought much slaughter amongst them in their herds until those sheep invited that slaughter and betrayed His place. **55** And He gave them over into the hands of the lions and tigers, and wolves and hyenas, and into the hand of the foxes, and to all the wild beasts, and those wild beasts began to tear in pieces those sheep. **56** And I saw that He forsook that their house and their tower and gave them all into the hand of the lions, to tear and devour them, into the hand of all the wild beasts, **57** And I began to cry aloud with all my power, and to appeal to Yahuah of the sheep, and to represent to Him in regard to the sheep that they were devoured by all the wild beasts, **58** But He remained unmoved, though He saw it, and rejoiced that they were devoured and swallowed and robbed, and left them to be devoured in the hand of all the beasts. **59** And He called **seventy shepherds**; and cast those sheep to them that they might pasture them, and He spake to the shepherds and their companions: "Let each individual of you pasture the sheep henceforward, and everything that I shall

*Lions and tigers = Babylon and Assyria who were joined by Samaria and the Edomites in destroying the 1st Temple. Wolves = Egyptians. Hyenas = Syria/ Samaria. Cf. Jer. 12:9; Is. 56:9; Ez. 34:5, 8.*

*Temple is destroyed.*

*Israel broke their covenant with Yahuah. He warned the consequence for such and he would not be righteous if he did not allow that.*

*See note next page.*

command you that do ye. 60 And I will deliver them over unto you duly numbered, and tell you which of them are to be destroyed—and them destroy ye." And He gave over unto them those sheep. 61 And He called another and spake unto him: "Observe and mark everything that the shepherds will do to those sheep; for they will destroy more of them than I have commanded them. 62 And every excess and the destruction which will be wrought through the shepherds, record (namely) how many they destroy according to my command, and how many according to their own caprice: record against every individual shepherd all the destruction he effects. 63 And read out before me by number how many they destroy, and how many they deliver over for destruction, that I may have this as a testimony against them, and know every deed of the shepherds, that I may comprehend and see what they do, whether or not they abide by my command which I have commanded them. 64 But they shall not know it, and thou shalt not declare it to them, nor admonish them, but only record against each individual all the destruction which the shepherds effect each in his time and lay it all before me." 65 And I saw till those shepherds pastured in their season, and they began to slay and to destroy more than they were bidden, and they delivered those sheep into the hand of the lions. 66 And the lions and tigers ate and devoured the greater part of those sheep, and the wild boars ate along with them; and they burnt that tower and demolished that house. 67 And I became exceedingly sorrowful over that tower because that house of the sheep was demolished, and afterwards I was unable to see if those sheep entered that house.

*This observer must be an angel as the time is too great for any man other than Enoch who is not this one.*

*The shepherds have seasons and each has a time.*

*Lions, Babylon sacked the Southern Kingdom and the Assyrians, tigers, took the Northern Tribes captive before.*

*Cf. Jub. 37:20. Wild boars = Edom. Cf. 1 Esd. 4:45. The Edomites burnt down the 1st Temple.*

*Enoch lamented over the loss of the 1st Temple. He will over the 2nd Temple defilement as well.*

**68** And the shepherds and their associates delivered over those sheep to all the wild beasts, to devour them, and each one of them received in his time a definite number: it was written by the other in a book how many each one of them destroyed of them. **69** And each one slew and destroyed many more than was prescribed; and I began to weep and lament on account of those sheep. **70** And thus in the vision I saw that one who wrote how he wrote down every one that was destroyed by those shepherds day by day, and carried up and laid down and showed actually the whole book to Yahuah of the sheep—(even) everything that they had done, and all that each one of them had made away with, and all that they had given over to destruction. **71** And the book was read before Yahuah of the sheep, and He took the book from his hand and read it and sealed it and laid it down.

*Only an angel would have such a view when Israel was in captivity.*

*Cf. 1 Esd. 5:56. Zerubbabel, Yahusha and brothers led the laying of the 2nd Temple foundation by order of Cyrus.*

*Cf. 1 Esd. 5:72-73. Edomites and the Samaritans/ Syrians opposed the Temple halting progress.*

*Cf. 1 Esd. 6. The Temple building is renewed and completed under King Darius.*

**72** And forthwith I saw how the shepherds pastured for twelve hours, and behold three of those sheep turned back and came and entered and began to build up all that had fallen down of that house; but the wild boars tried to hinder them, but they were not able. **73** And they began again to build as before, and they reared up that tower, and it was named the high tower; and they began again to place a table before the tower, but all the bread on it was polluted and not pure. **74** And as touching all this the eyes of those sheep were blinded so that they saw not, and (the eyes of) their shepherds likewise; and they delivered them in large numbers to their shepherds for destruction, and they trampled the sheep with their feet and devoured them.

**75** And Yahuah of the sheep remained unmoved till all the sheep were dispersed over the field and mingled with them (i. e. the beasts), and they (i. e. the shepherds) did not save them out of the hand of the beasts. **76** And this one who wrote the book carried it up, and showed it and read it before Yahuah of the sheep, and implored Him on their account, and besought Him on their account as he showed Him all the doings of the shepherds, and gave testimony before Him against all the shepherds. **77** And he took the actual book and laid it down beside Him and departed.

*Medo-Persia is conquered by the Greek Empire. Judaea is taken over peacefully. Greece never defiles the Temple. The Maccabees do.*

*Cf. Ps. 83:5-8; Dan. 8. Edom, Ishmael, Moab, Egyptian Essenes, Philistines, Assyrian replacements in Samaria, conquer the Temple and usurp the priesthood. The Temple is defiled and Judaea subdued. These are the birds and the leaders are known as eagles as they are Ezra's Eagle Empire to the end. This is not Rome but a confederation. Cf. 2nd Esd. 12-13.*

1 And I saw till that in this manner thirty-five shepherds undertook the pasturing (of the sheep), and they severally completed their periods as did the first; and others received them into their hands to pasture them for their period, each shepherd in his own period. 2 And after that I saw in my vision all the birds of heaven coming, the eagles, the vultures, the kites, the ravens; but the eagles led all the birds; and they began to devour those sheep, and to pick out their eyes and to devour their flesh. 3 And the sheep cried out because their flesh was being devoured by the birds, and as for me I looked and lamented in my sleep over that shepherd who pastured the sheep. 4 And I saw until those sheep were devoured by the dogs and eagles and kites, and they left neither flesh nor skin nor sinew remaining on them till only their bones stood there: and their bones too fell to the earth and the sheep became few. 5 And I saw until that twenty-three had undertaken the pasturing and completed in their several periods fifty-eight times.

*The confederation of birds of prey are joined by Philistines (dogs).*

*35 from 90:1 + 23 = 58.*

*Editors' Note: Enoch saw what he needed to see to expose the coming defiling of the Temple which ignited what will become Daniel's count for 2,300 years (see chart Ch. 93) as well as David's Psalm 83 War conquering the Temple and usurping the priesthood which happened in 165 B.C. What is clear is he did not possess copies of Daniel, 2nd Esdras, Isaiah, Ezekiel nor even Psalm as this is absent much detail a writer in the second century B.C. would have had access from the previous 600 years of the writings of the prophets. That serves as obvious evidence this was not written in the era of Hellenism but long before and instead, First Enoch is the origin of the thinking within those works. It is an illiterate assertion from those supposed scholars in the lead on the Dead Sea Scrolls, which is evidently this inept Pharisee paradigm of Charles continued, despite the mass archaeology explained away in the worst willing ignorance in our time. It is propaganda lined with scoffing not scholarship.*

*The Qumran local writings greatly condemn the Hasmoneans and Pharisees as the "sons of darkness," "wicked priests," "sons of Belial," etc. John the Baptist rose from among these sons of Zadok, exiled Temple Priests, who are the white righteous sheep. They were the voice crying out in the wilderness preparing the way as the forerunner to Messiah's coming in the Flesh.*

*Great Horn = Messiah is born as the Son of Man.*

6 But behold lambs were born by those white sheep and they began to open their eyes and to see, and to cry to the sheep, 7 Yea, they cried to them, but they did not hearken to what they said to them, but were exceedingly deaf, and their eyes were very exceedingly blinded.

8 And I saw in the vision how the ravens flew upon those lambs and took one of those lambs, and dashed the sheep in pieces and devoured them. 9 And I saw till horns grew upon those lambs, and the ravens cast down their horns; and I saw till there sprouted a great horn of one of those sheep, and their eyes were opened. 10 And it looked at them [and their eyes opened], and it cried to the sheep, and the rams saw it and all ran to it. 11 And notwithstanding all this those eagles and vultures and ravens and kites still kept tearing the sheep and swooping down upon them and devouring them: still the sheep remained silent, but the rams lamented and cried out. 12 And those ravens fought and battled with it and sought to lay low its horn, but they had no power over it. 13 And I saw till the shepherds and eagles and those vultures and kites came, and they cried to the ravens that they should break the horn of that ram and they battled and fought with it, and it battled with them and cried that its help might come.

*The Hasmoneans or Samaritans now mixed even in marriage with Herod, an Edomite given power by Rome.*

*Ravens = Pharisees/ Samaritan Priests who usurped the Temple sought to kill Messiah. Notice the ravens are the lead.*

*Yahusha would be crucified but He rose and conquered. Enoch skips to the end, however. The End Times are even more important.*

*Editors' Note: Charles separated verse 13 as if it was a different period grouping it within the Last Days which makes no sense whatsoever. He could not even see Messiah in this passage but inserted His enemies, the Maccabees (and their Pharisee priesthood they installed) as heroes in His stead. We find that extremely ignorant of the Bible and history — overt Pharisee propaganda. In all fairness, he did not have the Qumran scrolls. However, to miss Yahusha whom Enoch already knew and told of His coming and Second Coming seems more "willing ignorance" (2 Pet. 3).*

**14** And I saw till that man, who wrote down the names of the shepherds [and] carried up into the presence of Yahuah of the sheep [came and helped it and showed it everything: he had come down for the help of that ram]. **15** And I saw till Yahuah of the sheep came unto them in wrath, and all who saw Him fled, and they all fell into His shadow from before His face. **16** All the eagles and vultures and ravens and kites were gathered together, and there came with them all the sheep of the field, yea, they all came together, and helped each other to break that horn of the ram. **17** And I saw that man, who wrote the book according to the command of Yahuah, till he opened that book concerning the destruction which those twelve last shepherds had wrought, and showed that they had destroyed much more than their predecessors, before Yahuah of the sheep. **18** And I saw till Yahuah of the sheep came unto them and took in His hand the staff of His wrath, and smote the earth, and the earth clave asunder, and all the beasts and all the birds of the heaven fell from among those sheep, and were swallowed up in the earth and it covered them.

**19** And I saw till a great sword was given to the sheep, and the sheep proceeded against all the beasts of the field to slay them, and all the beasts and the birds of the heaven fled before their face.

*Cf. 2nd Esd. 13. The world unites to fight Yahusha in the end. They still want to break His horn but they have no power still.*

*All the powers, rulers and wicked against Yahusha, will be consumed in the Lake of Fire.*

*Editors' Note: We now see the continuation of Yahusha's story in the End Times. Notice, this is the same ram (v. 9-13) whose horn they are still trying to break thousands of years later. They failed in putting Him to death as He resurrected but Enoch skips right to the heart of the matter. Now, Yahusha returns in the Second Coming which Charles understood but failed to notice the same ram from the previous age, which is the first century. We find many such errors in thinking though his translations are very good passing the test of time. How can one calling themselves a Christian scholar overlook Messiah and the fact this same ram lived in the first century and the End Times yet is a ram of the Tribes of Israel? Then, to insert His enemies, the Maccabees/Pharisees who tried and still try to break His horn is illiterate. This is a paradigm of willing ignorance called scholarship, yet it is coated with Pharisee leaven which fails all of us. It penetrates the modern church who can't even see Qumran was a New Testament community.*

**20** And I saw till a throne was erected in the pleasant land, and Yahuah of the sheep sat Himself thereon, and the other took the sealed books and opened those books before Yahuah of the sheep.

*Cf. 14:18-23, 60:2; Dan. 7; 1 Ki. 22:19; Is. 6; Ez. 1, 3:22-24, 10:1. Biblical throne visions that match.*

**21** And Yahuah called those men the **seven first white ones**, and commanded that they should bring before Him, beginning with the first star which led the way, all the stars whose privy members were like those of horses, and they brought them all before Him.

*Cf. Rev. 20:12. "And the books were opened."*

*Cf. Rev. 1:4, 4:5, 8:2. "Seven spirits before throne."*

**22** And He said to that man who wrote before Him, being one of those seven white ones, and said unto him; "Take those seventy shepherds to whom I delivered the sheep, and who taking them on their own authority slew more than I commanded them." **23** And behold they were all bound, I saw, and they all stood before Him. **24** And the judgment was held first over the stars, and they were judged and found guilty, and went to the place of condemnation, and they were cast into an abyss, full of fire and flaming, and full of pillars of fire. **25** And those seventy shepherds were judged and found guilty, and they were cast into that fiery abyss. **26** And I saw at that time how a like abyss was opened in the midst of the earth, full of fire, and they brought those blinded sheep, and they were all judged and found guilty and cast into this fiery abyss, and they burned; now this abyss was to the right of that house. **27** And I saw those sheep burning and their bones burning.

*Cf. Rev. 20:15. "Cast into the lake of fire."*

*Cf. 27:2; Matt. 5:22,29,30. "Where Gehenna is the place of final punishment."*

**28** And I stood up to see till they folded up that old house; and carried off all the pillars, and all the beams and ornaments of the house were at the same time folded up with it, and they carried it off and laid it in a place in the south of the land. **29** And I saw till Yahuah of the sheep brought a **new house** greater and loftier than that first, and set it up in the place of the first which had been folded up: all its pillars were new, and its ornaments were new and larger than those of the first, the old one which He had taken away, and all the sheep were within it. **30** And I saw all the sheep which had been left, and all the beasts on the earth, and all the birds of the heaven, falling down and doing homage to those sheep and making petition to and obeying them in every thing. **31** And thereafter those three who were clothed in white and had seized me by my hand [who had taken me up before], and the hand of that ram also seizing hold of me, they took me up and set me down in the midst of those sheep before the judgment took place. **32** And those sheep were all white, and their wool was abundant and clean. **33** And all that had been destroyed and dispersed, and all the beasts of the field, and all the birds of the heaven, assembled in that house, and Yahuah of the sheep rejoiced with great joy because they were all good and had returned to His house. **34** And I saw till they laid down that sword, which had been given to the sheep, and they brought it back into the house, and it was sealed before the presence of Yahuah, and all the sheep were invited into that house, but it held them not. **35** And the eyes of them all were opened, and they saw the good, and there was not one among them that did not see. **36** And I saw that that house was large and broad and very

*Cf. Rev. 3:12; Heb. 12:22. "New Jerusalem."*

*Cf. Heb. 11:10, 13:14. "The city which hath foundations whose builder and maker is God."*

*Cf. Rev. 3:5 "Clothed in white raiment."*

full.

**37** And I saw that a white bull was born, with large horns, and all the beasts of the field and all the birds of the air feared him and made petition to him all the time. **38** And I saw till all their generations

*Cf. 1 Jn. 3:2.*

were transformed, and they all became white bulls; and the first among them became a lamb, and that lamb became a great animal and had great black horns on its head; and Yahuah of the sheep rejoiced over it and over all the oxen.

**39** And I slept in their midst: and I awoke and saw everything. **40** This is the vision which I saw while I slept, and I awoke and blessed Yahuah of righteousness and gave Him glory, **41** Then I wept with a great weeping, and my tears stayed not till I could no longer endure it: when I saw, they flowed on account of what I had seen; for everything shall come and be fulfilled, and all the deeds of men in their order were shown to me. **42** On that night I remembered the first dream, and because of it I wept and was troubled—because I had seen that vision.'

# THE EPISTLE OF ENOCH

# SECTION 5:

1 'And now, my son Methuselah, call to me all thy brothers and gather together to me all the sons of thy mother. For the word calls me. And the spirit is poured out upon me, That I may show you everything that shall befall you for ever.' 2 And thereupon Methuselah went and summoned to him all his brothers and assembled his relatives. 3 And he spake unto all the children of righteousness and said: 'Hear, ye sons of Enoch, all the words of your father. And hearken aright to the voice of my mouth; For I exhort you and say unto you, beloved: Love uprightness and walk therein. 4 And draw not nigh to uprightness with a **double heart**. And **associate not with those of a double heart**, But walk in righteousness my sons. And it shall guide you on good paths, And righteousness shall be your companion. 5 For I know that violence must increase on the earth And a great chastisement be executed on the earth, And all unrighteousness come



to an end: Yea, it shall be cut off from its roots, And its whole structure be destroyed. 6 And unrighteousness shall again be consummated on the earth. And all the deeds of unrighteousness and of violence And transgression shall prevail in a twofold degree. 7 And when sin and unrighteousness and blasphemy and violence in all kinds of deeds increase. And apostasy and transgression and uncleanness increase, a great chastisement shall come from heaven upon all these. And the holy Yahuah will come forth with wrath and chastisement to execute judgment on earth. 8 In those days violence shall be cut off from its roots, And the roots of unrighteousness together with deceit. And they shall be destroyed from under heaven. 9 And all the idols of the heathen shall be abandoned. And the temples burned with fire, And they shall remove them from the whole earth, And they (i. e. the heathen) shall be cast into the judgment of fire, And shall perish in wrath and in grievous judgment for ever. 10 And the righteous shall arise from their sleep, And wisdom shall arise and be given unto them. [11 And after that the roots of unrighteousness shall be cut off, and the sinners shall be destroyed by the sword...

shall be cut off from the blasphemers in every place, and those who plan violence and those who commit blasphemy shall perish by the sword.]

*Cf. Rev. 1:16, 19:15, 21; 2 Esd. 13:4, 10-1.*

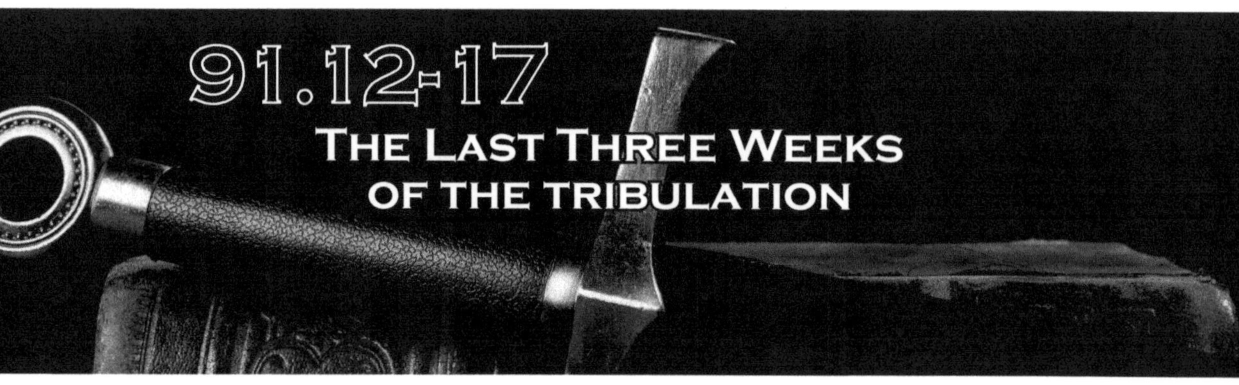


*The 10th week defines this is the last 7 parts or the 7 years of the Tribulation. This 8th, 9th and 10th week all occur at the end of the Great Tribulation. These are not the same periods nor a continuation of Ch. 93 in terms of time periods. These occur then not throughout history over millennia.*

*8th week: Day of Judgment.*

*Houses = New Jerusalem.*

*9th week: Day of Judgment.*

12 And after that there shall be another, the **eighth week**, that of righteousness. And a sword shall be given to it that a righteous judgment may be executed on the oppressors. And sinners shall be delivered into the hands of the righteous.

13 And at its close they shall acquire houses through their righteousness, And a house shall be built for the Great King in glory for evermore,

14 And after that, in the **ninth week** the righteous judgment shall be revealed to the whole world, And all the works of the godless shall vanish from all the earth, And the world shall be written

down for destruction. And all mankind shall look to the path of uprightness. 15 And after this, in the **tenth week in the seventh part**. There shall be the great eternal judgment, in which He will execute vengeance amongst the angels.

16 And the first heaven shall depart and pass away. And a new heaven shall appear. And all the powers of the heavens shall give sevenfold light.

17 **And after that there will be many weeks without number for ever**, And all shall be in goodness and righteousness, And sin shall no more be mentioned for ever.

*10th week: Day of Judgment at the end of the 7-year Tribulation. The 7th part.*

*Cf. Jub. 1:29.*

*Cf. 45:4-5, 72:1; 2 Pet. 3:13. "New Heavens, new Earth."*

*Cf. Is. 32:17; Rev. 21:4, Matt. 25:31-46; 2 Pet. 3:10-13; Rom. 6:23; Jn. 1:29.*

## CHAPTER 92:

*Enoch wrote this period. Otherwise, scholars have to assume the true Temple Priests were frauds which is ludicrous and illiterate. They did not use false names nor represent false doctrine.*

**1** **The book written by Enoch**—[Enoch indeed wrote this complete doctrine of wisdom (which is) praised of all men and a judge of all the earth] for all my children who shall dwell on the earth. And for the future generations who shall observe uprightness and peace. **2** **Let not your spirit be troubled on account of the times**; For the Holy and Great One has appointed days for all things. **3** And the righteous one shall arise from sleep, [Shall arise] and walk in the paths of righteousness, And all his path and conversation shall be in eternal goodness and grace. **4** He will be gracious to the righteous and give him eternal uprightness, And He will give him power so that he shall be (endowed) with goodness and righteousness, And he shall walk in eternal light, **5** And sin shall perish in darkness for ever. And shall no more be seen from that day for evermore.

*Cf. Jn. 14:1,27. "Let not your heart be troubled."*

*Cf. 2 Esd. 7:35.*

## CHAPTER 93:

**1** And after that Enoch both gave and began to recount **from the books. 2** And Enoch said 'Concerning the children of righteousness and concerning the elect of the world, And concerning **the plant of uprightness**, I will speak these things. Yea, I Enoch will declare (them) unto you, my sons: According to that which appeared to me in the heavenly vision. And which I have known through the word of the holy angels. And have learnt from the heavenly tablets.' **3** And Enoch began to recount **from the books** and said: 'I was born **the seventh in the first week**. While judgment and righteousness still endured. **4** And after me there shall arise in the **second week great wickedness**, And deceit shall have sprung up; And **in it there shall be the first end**. And in it **a man shall be saved** and after it is ended unrighteousness shall grow up, And **a law shall be made for the sinners.**

**5** And after that in **the third week** at its close **a man shall** be elected as the plant of righteous judgment and his posterity shall become the plant of righteousness for evermore. **6** And after that in **the fourth week**, at its close, Visions of the holy and righteous shall be seen, And **a law for all generations and an enclosure shall be made for them. 7** And after that in **the fifth week**, at its close. **The house of glory and dominion shall be built** for ever. **8** And after that in **the sixth week** all who live in it shall be blinded, And the hearts of all of them shall godlessly forsake wisdom. And in it **a man shall ascend**; And at its close **the house of dominion shall be burnt with fire**, And the **whole race of the chosen root shall be dispersed. 9** And after that in **the seventh week** shall an **apostate generation arise**, and many shall be its deeds, and all its deeds shall be apostate. **10** And at its close shall be elected **the elect righteous of the eternal plant of righteousness**. To receive sevenfold instruction concerning all His creation.

Cf. Jub. 7:39.

Messiah, not Israel. Cf. 10:16, 93:5, 10; Jub. 16:26, 21:24, 36:6.

Enoch quotes the Second Section: The Book of Parables again.

Cf. Jub. 3:10, 4:3. "heavenly tablets."

Enoch is 7th from Adam always and this is the 1st millennia.

Noah. First end = The Flood and nothing else.

Cf. 1 Tim. 1:9. "Law is not made for a righteous man but for the lawless."

Cf. Jub. 7:20. "Noah began to enjoin upon his sons' sons the ordinances and commandments."

Abraham.

Messiah, not Israel. Cf. 10:16, 93:2, 10; Jub. 16:26, 21:24, 36:6.

Cf. Ex.19. Mt. Sinai. Law given and Tabernacle built.

Cf. 1 Ki. 6; 2 Chr. 3:1–14. The 1st Temple is built.

Cf. Matt. 15:14. Pharisees are the blind leading the blind who usurped the Temple.

Cf. Matt. 15:14. Pharisees are the blind leading the blind who usurped the Temple.

Cf. Acts 1:9-11; Mark 16:19, 20; Luke 24:50–53. Yahusha is the only man who ascended.

70 A.D. 2nd Temple destroyed. Israel scattered.

Messiah, not Israel. Cf 10:16, 93:2, 5; Jub. 16:26, 21:24, 36:6.

Final era and 2nd Coming.

[11 For who is there of all the children of men that is able to hear the voice of the Holy One without being troubled? And who can think His thoughts? And who is there that can behold all the works of heaven? 12 And how should there be one who could behold the heaven, and who is there that could understand the things of heaven and see a soul or a spirit and could tell thereof, or ascend and see all their ends and think them or do like them? 13 And who is there of all men that could know what is the breadth and the length of the earth, and to whom has been shown the measure of all of them? 14 Or is there any one who could discern the length of the heaven and how great is its height, and upon what it is founded, and how great is the number of the stars, and where all the luminaries rest?]

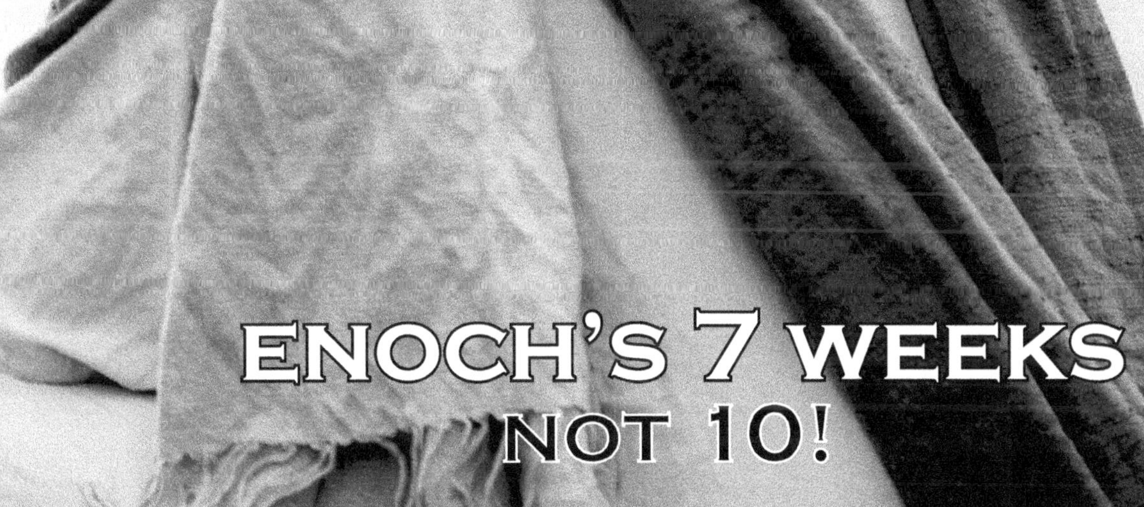

# ENOCH'S 7 WEEKS

Enoch defines the time of man from Creation to the Final Age as seven weeks *(not 10)*. He defines historical markers that clarify these periods of weeks or Sabbaths in Hebrew, are set on 1,000-year compartments. This cannot be confused with Chapter 91 which we will explain is all on the Day of Judgment at the end of the Great Tribulation *(7th part)* and this is Chapter 93, two chapters later. Essentially, Enoch defines a period of 7,000 years, a millennial Sabbath period which completes and then, still enters the next millennium. This is consistent with all such prophetic timelines in 1 Enoch, 2nd Esdras and Daniel 8 *(see chart next spread)*.

**Week 1** — 93:3 — **5000-4,001 B.C**
Enoch is apparent when he tells us he was born the seventh which we know he is seventh from Adam and in the First Week. This is the first 1,000 years. There is no other sensible time period and no other seventh to consider. Jubilees 4:16 says he was born: 11th Jubilee, 5th Week, 4th Year. 522 Years From Creation.

**Week 2** — 93:4 — **4000-3001 B.C.**
After a kiloyear, the entire Earth was becoming increasingly corrupt – Man, plants and animals. This brings "the first end" which is the Flood about 1,308 A.M. The man being saved is Noah and Noah taught Law and sacrificed on Sabbaths and early Feasts such as Shavuot just as Moses detailed in Jubilees 6-10. There are only two ends in all of scripture. Approx. 3,500 B.C.

**Week 3** — 93:5 — **3000-2001 B.C.**
This third week identifies righteous Abraham whose seed will be the Messiah – "the eternal plant of righteousness forever." Abraham was tested in 2003 A.M laying down law in 2052 A.M. the year he died. This occurred at the close of the 3rd week, Estimated 2100 B.C.

**Week 4** — 93:6 — **2000-1001 B.C.**
In the fourth week, Yahuah's presence is seen on Mt. Sinai. Covenant is renewed for the first nation to do so, the law is given to Israel and the Tabernacle is built. Estimated 1700 B.C.

**Week 5** — 93:7 — **1000-1 B.C.**
The fifth week has only one anchor and it is undeniable. *"The house of glory and dominion shall be built..."* The Temple is built estimated 970 B.C. within this millennium.



**Week 6** — 93:8 — **1 A.D.-1000 A.D.**
The temple is usurped and controlled by the blind – Pharisees. A man ascends. That is Yahusha. The Temple is burned with fire which is the final destruction of the 2nd Temple *(70 A.D.)*. Israel is scattered. This era can be no other than specifically the First Century which is the sixth millennium in Enoch's timeline.

**Week 7** — 93:9 — **1001-2,000 A.D**
The final apostate generation arises in the seventh week. *"And at its close shall be elected the elect righteous of the eternal plant of righteousness."* Once this 7,000 years closes, the end comes in its time and the Day of Final Judgment is near. The Day of Judgment is defined in Chapter 91.



*Based on our modern Roman calendar.*

Just as with the Jubilee which is 49 years but we celebrate the 50th year, it appears the millennium operates on that rule. We complete 7,000 years and then, there is but a short time remaining. Two chapters prior, Enoch mentioned an 8th week where the righteous are given a sword and the wicked are judged. This is the Day of Judgment not a similar period to this 7 weeks. In the 9th week of Chapter 91, the wicked are judged for the world to see which is still the Day of Judgment not another 1,000 years. Enoch did not have Daniel and Revelation yet he was accurate here and serves as their origins. In the 10th week of Chapter 91, the "great eternal judgment" is executed by Yahusha. This remains the same day as the other two weeks. The reason for this is made clear when in the 10th week, it is defined as the "tenth week in the seventh part." These are not millennia as the 7 Weeks of Enoch. These are the Tribulation of 7 years in which Judgment is executed on the seventh part of 7 years or at the end of the Great Tribulation.

Before the Flood, Enoch was precise yet misunderstood by many scholars as they attempt to take his 7 weeks or 7,000 years and turn it into 10,000 or similar by adding a passage from two chapters earlier which is a distinctly different period of measure. Understand the word week in Ancient Hebrew is Sabbath. These are Sabbath ages of 1,000 years according to Enoch's timing in history. We are reminded in Jubilees 4:30, Psalm 90:4, and 2 Peter 3:8, a day in Yahuah's time is as 1,000 years. Essentially just as with the Jubilee, we complete one full Sabbath of millennia or 7,000 years and the next age is the final age of this era. Of course, then all begins anew without the wicked.

**A CONSISTENT TIMELINE:**

**1 ENOCH 10.12:
70 GENERATIONS: WATCHERS BOUND
1 ENOCH 10.14: WATCHERS BOUND UNTIL
THE END OF ALL GENERATIONS
ENOCH'S 70 GENERATIONS = 7,000 YEARS**

**2ND ESDRAS 7:31:
AFTER 7 DAYS, DEAD RAISED/JUDGMENT
7 DAYS = 7,000 YEARS**

**7 WEEKS = 7,000 YEARS
WE COMPLETE THAT MILLENNIAL SABBATH CYCLE
WHICH THEN COMES THE END OF THE ERA IN THE
BEGINNING OF THE NEXT WEEK.
CHAPTER 91 IS ALL WITHIN THE 7 YEARS
OF THE GREAT TRIBULATION, A DIFFERENT
SABBATH CYCLE MISAPPLIED BY MANY
SCHOLARS WHO ADD TO THIS 7 WEEKS
WITH A PASSAGE WELL DEFINED AS DIFFERENT
FROM TWO CHAPTERS EARLIER.**

## THE VISION OF DANIEL 8: OUR INTERPRETATION

Just as Enoch, Daniel was steeped in the same mindset as he read and used First Enoch as inspired scripture. He saw a vision which Gabriel assisted in understanding that Medo-Persia*(20: ram)* would be conquered by Alexander the Great*(21: goat with 1 Great Horn)* as happened in 331 B.C. well after Daniel. Alexander's power was split into four kings/generals*(22: horns, 323 B.C.)*. Daniel is building to a trigger point for a very specific event to come. At the end of Greece's reign, a smaller power within the Greek Empire defined as located in the territory of Ptolemy I in the North of Israel*(9)* and South of Turkey*(not Ptolemy's)*, attacks Judaea and defiles the Temple in Jerusalem including usurping the priesthood. This is not Rome which is not a little horn of Ptolemy I who is a horn of Greece. It cannot be Greece either but a smaller power within.

## DANIEL'S TIME PERIOD TO BEGIN THE COUNT:

In the vision, time progresses beyond Medo-Persia to the very end of Greece's reign about 168 B.C. Then, the Temple is defiled*(11)*. The daily sacrifice was taken away*(11)* in the worst of ways as this leads to the replacement of the Temple Priests with a new unlawful breed of Samarian priests called Pharisees, Sadducees and Scribes who elevate themselves above Yahuah*(11)*. They took away the Temple Priest's sacrifice by usurping the priesthood as they *"practiced and prospered"(12)* thus voiding all sacrifices made there and defiling the Temple. This lasted until after Messiah when the Temple was destroyed again. Daniel defines the daily sacrifice stolen away by reason of transgression*(12)*. This is not a one-time event. It is a conquest of the Temple, a trespassing and theft. The Greeks never did such *[Comm. on Nahum, p.505, 22]*. The exiled Temple Priests write of this event in their Qumran local documents*[Comm. on Hab., p. 515, Comm. on Isaiah, p. 499, 22]*.

# THE IGNITION POINT: "TRANSGRESSION OF DESOLATION"

At the end of Greece's reign and during the vacuum of power shifting to Rome, this event occurred in 165 B.C. when the Hasmonean foreigners came from the Northwest of Judaea *(9)* in the former territory of Dan which was part of Samaria not Judaea. They took ownership of the Temple and that is undeniable as they were still there in the New Testament. There are no Pharisees in the Old Testament and their party did not exist in Judaea until 165 B.C. They conquered the Temple just as Psalm 83 and Daniel 8 predicted representing the same mix of powers which list does not include Greece nor Rome. In the very end, this is the same order from which "the Assyrian" *(23: beast, Isa. 10:24, 31:8)* will rise as they are the initial replacements of the Northern Lost Tribes from Assyria *(2 Ki. 17)* which will bring us to the end of the 2,300 days or years really.

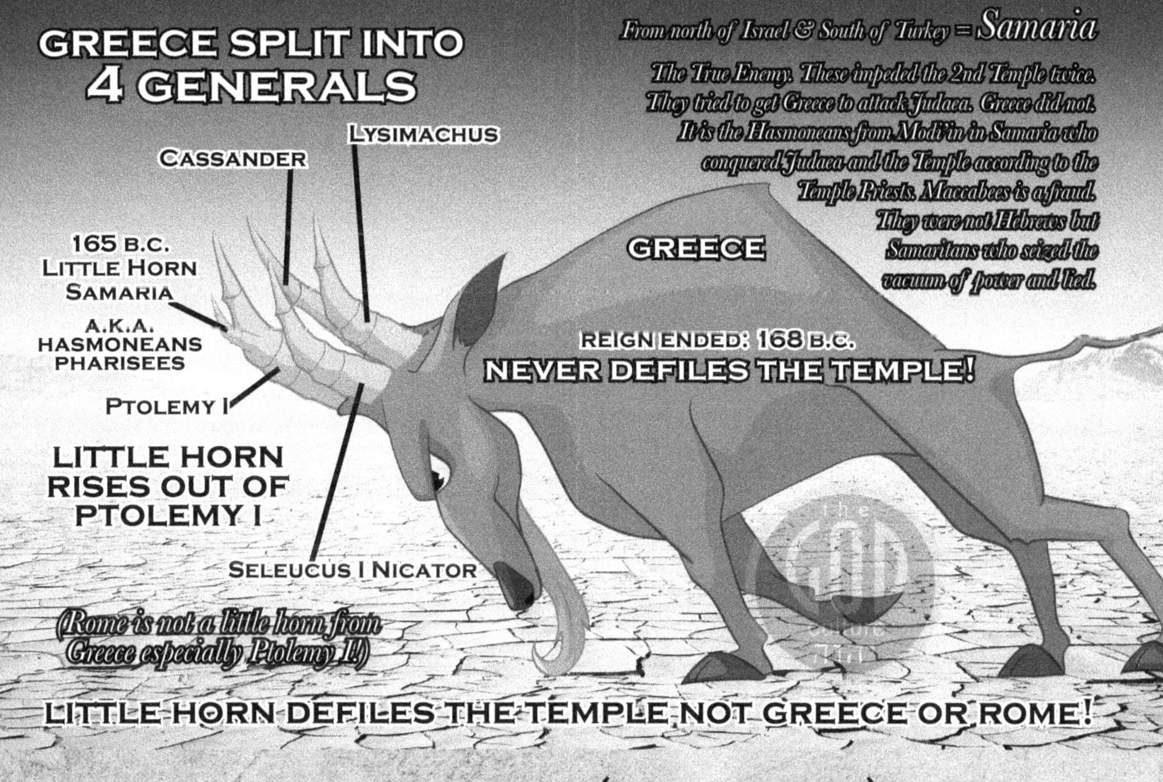



## THE CALCULATION (APPROXIMATE):

165 B.C. *(approx.)* is the ignition point to begin the count of 2,300 years until the Day of Judgment. No man knows the day or hour but Yahusha is unambiguous we will know the season as He admonished us to be ready *(Matt. 24:42-44)*. Are you?

**165 B.C. TO YEAR 2021 = 2,186 YEARS PASSED
*RECONCILED TO ROMAN CALENDAR + 8 YEARS
2,194 YEARS PASSED SINCE 165 B.C.
2,300 YEARS TOTAL - 2,194 PASSED = 106 YEARS LEFT

YEAR 2021 + 106 YEARS LEFT = YEAR 2127

APPROXIMATELY 100 YEARS UNTIL TRIBULATION**
Daniel, Enoch, and Ezra all agree. We are very close.

## CHAPTER 94:

*Cf. 1Tim. 1:15, 4:9. "Worthy of all acceptation."*

1 And now I say unto you, my sons, love righteousness and walk therein; For the paths of righteousness are worthy of acceptation, But the paths of unrighteousness shall suddenly be destroyed and vanish. 2 And to certain men of a generation shall the paths of violence and of death be revealed, And they shall hold themselves afar from them, And shall not follow them. 3 And now I say unto you the righteous: Walk not in the paths of wickedness, nor on the paths of death, And draw not nigh to them, lest ye be destroyed. 4 But seek and choose for yourselves righteousness and an elect life, And walk in the paths of peace. And ye shall live and prosper. 5 And hold fast my words in the thoughts of your hearts, And suffer them not to be effaced from your hearts; For know that sinners will tempt men to evilly-entreat wisdom, So that no place may be found for her, And no manner of temptation may minish.

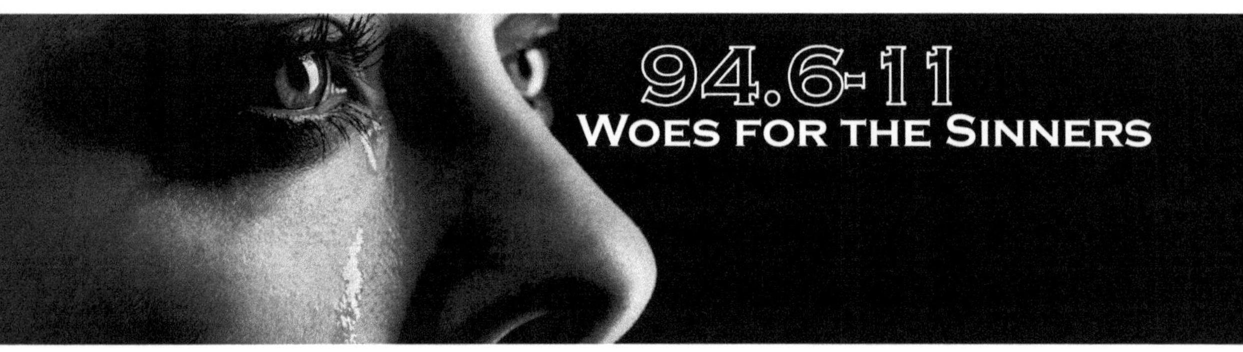


6 Woe to those who build unrighteousness and oppression And lay deceit as a foundation; For they shall be suddenly overthrown, And they shall have no peace. 7 Woe to those who build their houses with sin; For from all their foundations shall they be overthrown; And by the sword shall they fall. [And those who acquire gold and silver in judgment suddenly shall perish.] 8 Woe to you,

ye rich, for ye have trusted in your riches, And from your riches shall ye depart. Because ye have not remembered the Most High in the days of your riches. 9 Ye have committed blasphemy and unrighteousness. And have become ready for the day of slaughter, And the day of darkness and the day of the great judgment. 10 Thus I speak and declare unto you: He who hath created you will overthrow you, And for your fall there shall be no compassion, And your Creator will rejoice at your destruction. 11 And your righteous ones in those days shall be a reproach to the sinners and the godless.

# 95

# ENOCH'S GRIEF: FRESH WOES AGAINST THE SINNERS

## CHAPTER 95:

1 Oh that mine eyes were [a cloud of] waters that I might weep over you. And pour down my tears as a cloud of waters: That so I might rest from my trouble of heart! 2 "Who has permitted you to practice reproaches and wickedness? And so judgment shall overtake you, sinners. 3 Fear not the sinners, ye righteous; For again will Yahuah deliver them into your hands, That ye may execute judgment upon them according to your desires.

*Cf. Jub. 32:18-19. The righteous rule and judge.*

4 Woe to you who fulminate anathemas which cannot be reversed: Healing shall therefore be far from you because of your sins. 5 Woe to you who requite your neighbor with evil; For ye shall be requited according to your works, 6 Woe to you, lying witnesses, And to those who weigh out injustice, For suddenly shall ye perish. 7 Woe to you, sinners, for ye persecute the righteous; For ye shall be delivered up and persecuted because of injustice, And heavy shall its yoke be upon you.

## CHAPTER 96:

**1** Be hopeful, ye righteous; for suddenly shall the sinners perish before you, And ye shall have lordship over them according to your desires. [**2** And in the day of the tribulation of the sinners, Your children shall mount and rise as eagles, And higher than the vultures will be your nest, And ye shall ascend and enter the crevices of the earth. And the clefts of the rock for ever as coneys before the unrighteous. And the sirens shall sigh because of you and weep.] **3** Wherefore fear not, ye that have suffered; For healing shall be your portion, And a bright light shall enlighten you, And the voice of rest ye shall hear from heaven. **4** Woe unto you, ye sinners, for your riches make you appear like the righteous, But your hearts convict you of being sinners, And this fact shall be a testimony against you for a memorial of (your) evil deeds. **5** Woe to you who devour the finest of the wheat. And drink wine in large bowls. And tread under foot the lowly with your might. **6** Woe to you who drink water from every fountain, For suddenly shall ye be consumed and wither away, Because ye have forsaken the fountain of life. **7** Woe to you who work unrighteousness And deceit and blasphemy: It shall be a memorial against you for evil. **8** Woe to you, ye mighty, Who with might oppress the righteous; For the day of your destruction is coming. In those days many and good days shall come to the righteous—in the day of your judgment.

*Cf. Jub. 32:18-19. The righteous rule and judge.*

*Cf. Is. 40:31. "But they that wait upon the LORD shall renew their strength; they shall mount up with wings as eagles."*

*Coneys = rabbits.*

*Cf. Matt. 23:5, 6:1. As the Pharisee do falsely even today.*

# 97
# THE EVILS IN STORE FOR SINNERS AND THE POSSESSORS OF UNRIGHTEOUS WEALTH

## CHAPTER 97:

1 Believe, ye righteous, that the sinners will become a shame And perish in the day of unrighteousness. 2 Be it known unto you (ye sinners) that the Most High is mindful of your destruction. And the angels of heaven rejoice over your destruction. 3 What will ye do, ye sinners, And whither will ye flee on that day of judgment, When ye hear the voice of the prayer of the righteous? 4 Yea, ye shall fare like unto them. Against whom this word shall be a testimony: "Ye have been companions of sinners." 5 And in those days the prayer of the righteous shall reach unto Yahuah, And for you the days of your judgment shall come. 6 And all the words of your unrighteousness shall be read out before the Great Holy One, And your faces shall be covered with shame. And He will reject every work which is grounded on unrighteousness. 7 Woe to you, ye sinners, who live on the mid ocean and on the dry land. Whose remembrance is evil against you. 8 Woe to you who acquire silver and gold in unrighteousness and say: "We have become rich with riches and have possessions; And have acquired everything we have desired. 9 And now let us do what we purposed: For we have gathered silver, And many are the husbandmen in our houses, And our granaries are (brim) full as with water." 10 Yea and like water your lies shall flow away; For your riches shall not abide But speedily ascend from you; For ye have acquired it all in unrighteousness, And ye shall be given over to a great curse.

*Cf. 47:2, 99:3, 16, 104:3, 22:5-7; Rev. 6:10 "Righteous souls cry out for vengeance."*

*Beach houses.*

*Cf. Rev. 3:17.*

## CHAPTER 98:

1 And now I swear unto you, to the wise and to the foolish, For ye shall have manifold experiences on the earth.

2 For ye men shall put on more adornments than a woman, And colored garments more than a virgin: In royalty and in grandeur and in power, And in silver and in gold and in purple. And in splendor and in food they shall be poured out as water. 3 Therefore they shall be wanting in doctrine and wisdom, And they shall perish thereby together with their possessions; And with all their glory and their splendor, And in shame and in slaughter and in great destitution, Their spirits shall be cast into the furnace of fire. 4 I have sworn unto you, ye sinners, as a mountain has not become a slave, And a hill does not

*Cf. Matt. 13:42.*

252

Cf. Gen. 3; 2 Esd. 7:48; Rom 5:12. "Wherefore, as by one man sin entered into the world."

become the handmaid of a woman. **Even so sin has not been sent upon the earth. But man of himself has created it**, And under a great curse shall they fall who commit it.

Cf. Pro. 28:13; Ps. 69:5, 90:8, 44:20-21; Jer. 16:17-18; Luke 12:1-2; Heb. 4:12-13. No hidden sins.

5 And barrenness has not been given to the woman. But on account of the deeds of her own hands she dies without children. 6 I have sworn unto you, ye sinners, by the Holy Great One, That all your evil deeds are revealed in the heavens. And that none of your deeds of oppression are covered and hidden.

Cf. Jer. 31:34. "...for I will forgive their iniquity, and I will remember their sin no more." For Him to forget, there most certainly was a record. How else could he be a righteous judge?

7 And do not think in your spirit nor say in your heart that ye do not know and that ye do not see that every sin is every day recorded in heaven in the presence of the Most High. 8 From henceforth ye know that all your oppression wherewith ye oppress is written down every day till the day of your judgment.

9 Woe to you, ye fools, for through your folly shall ye perish: and ye transgress against the wise, and so good hap shall not be your portion. 10 And now, know ye that ye are prepared for the day of destruction: wherefore do not hope to live, ye sinners, but ye shall depart and die; for ye know no ransom; for ye are prepared for the day of the great judgment, for the day of tribulation and great shame for your spirits. 11 Woe to you, ye obstinate of heart, who work wickedness and eat blood: Whence have ye good things to eat and to drink and to be filled? From all the good things which Yahuah the Most High has placed in abundance on the earth; therefore ye shall have no peace. 12 Woe to you who love the deeds of unrighteousness:    wherefore do ye hope for good hap unto yourselves? Know that ye shall be delivered into the hands of the righteous, and they shall cut off your necks and slay you, and have no mercy upon you. 13 Woe to you who rejoice in the tribulation of the righteous; for no grave shall be dug for you. 14 Woe to you who set at naught the words of the righteous; for ye shall have no hope of life.

Cf. Jub. 7:29, 22:22.

Enoch knew not to eat blood! He knew the Law! Noah did as well and he knew what was a clean and unclean animal as he took extra sets of the clean on the ark.

15 Woe to you who write down lying and godless words; for they write down their lies that men may hear them and act godlessly towards (their) neighbor. 16 Therefore they shall have no peace but die a sudden death.

## CHAPTER 99:

1 Woe to you who work godlessness, And glory in lying, and extol them: Ye shall perish, and no happy life shall be yours. 2 Woe to them who pervert the words of uprightness. And transgress the eternal law. And transform themselves into what they were not [into sinners]: They shall be trodden under foot upon the earth. 3 In those days make ready, ye righteous, to raise your prayers as a memorial, And place them as a testimony before the angels, That they may place the sin of the sinners for a memorial before the Most High. 4 In those days the nations shall be stirred up, And the families of the nations shall arise on the day of destruction. 5 And in those days the destitute shall go forth and carry off their children, And they shall abandon them, so that their children shall perish through them: Yea, they shall abandon their children (that are still) sucklings, and not return to them. And shall have no pity on their beloved ones. 6 And again I swear to you, ye sinners, that sin is prepared for a day of unceasing bloodshed. 7 And they who worship stones, and grave images of gold and silver and wood (and stone) and clay, and those who worship impure spirits and demons, and all kinds of idols not according to knowledge, shall get no manner of help from them. 8 And they shall become godless by reason of the folly of their hearts, And their eyes shall be blinded through the fear of their hearts And through visions in their dreams. 9 Through these they shall become godless and fearful; For they shall have wrought all their work in a lie. And shall have worshipped a stone: Therefore in an instant shall they perish. 10 But in those days blessed are all they who accept the words of wisdom, and understand

*Cf. 47:2, 97:3-5, 99:16, 104:3, 22:5-7; Rev. 6:10 "Righteous souls cry out for vengeance."*

*Cf. 9:1-3,11,15:2, 40:7, 47:2; Rev. 8:3-4 "Angel with golden censer of incense."*

*Cf. Acts 10:4. "Thy prayers... are gone up for a memorial before God."*

*Cf. Jub. 22:17; Rev. 9:20.*

them, And observe the paths of the Most High, and walk in the path of His righteousness. And become not godless with the godless; For they shall be saved. 11 Woe to you who spread evil to your neighbors; For you shall be slain in Sheol. 12 Woe to you who make deceitful and false measures, And (to them) who cause bitterness on the earth; For they shall thereby be utterly consumed. 13 Woe to you who build your houses through the grievous toil of others, And all their building materials are the bricks and stones of sin; I tell you ye shall have no peace. 14 Woe to them who reject the measure and eternal heritage of their fathers and whose souls follow after idols; For they shall have no rest, 15 Woe to them who work unrighteousness and help oppression. And slay their neighbors until the day of the great judgment. 16 For He shall cast down your glory, And bring affliction on your hearts. And shall arouse His fierce indignation, And destroy you all with the sword; And all the holy and righteous shall remember your sins.

*Cf. 47:2, 97:3-5, 99:3, 104:3, 22:5-7; Rev. 6:10 "Righteous souls cry out for vengeance."*

# 100
# THE SINNERS DESTROY EACH OTHER: JUDGMENT OF THE FALLEN ANGELS: THE SAFETY OF THE RIGHTEOUS: FURTHER WOES FOR THE SINNERS

## CHAPTER 100:

1 And in those days in one place the fathers together with their sons shall be smitten. And brothers one with another shall fall in death till the streams flow with their blood. 2 For a man shall not withhold his hand from slaying his sons and his sons' sons, And the sinner shall not withhold his hand from his honored brother: From dawn till sunset they shall slay one another

3 And the **horse shall walk up to the breast in the**

*Cf. Rev. 14:20. "Blood came out of the winepress even unto the horses' bridles."*

**blood of sinners**, And the chariot shall be submerged to its height. 4 In those days the angels shall descend into the secret places and gather together into one place all those who brought down sin, And the Most High will arise on that day of judgment To execute great judgment amongst sinners. 5 And over all the righteous and holy He will appoint guardians from amongst the holy angels to guard them as the **apple of an eye**, until He makes an end of all wickedness and all sin, and though the righteous sleep a long sleep, they have naught to fear. 6 And (then) the children of the earth shall see the wise in security. **And shall understand all the words of this book**, And recognize that their riches shall not be able to save them in the overthrow of their sins. 7 Woe to you, sinners, on the day of strong anguish, Ye who afflict the righteous and burn them with fire: Ye shall be requited according to your works. 8 Woe to you, ye obstinate of heart. Who watch in order to devise wickedness: Therefore shall

*Cf. Deut. 32:10 Ps. 17:8; Lam. 2:18; Zec. 2:8. "...the apple of his eye." Origin: 1 Enoch.*

*Enoch says his book will be read in the Last Days and bring repentance.*

fear come upon you and there shall be none to help you.

9 Woe to you, ye sinners, on account of the words of your mouth. And on account of the deeds of your hands which your godlessness has wrought. In blazing flames burning worse than fire shall ye burn. 10 And now, know ye that from the angels He will inquire as to your deeds in heaven, from the sun and from the moon and from the stars in reference to your sins because upon the earth ye execute judgment on the righteous. 11 And He will summon to testify against you every cloud and mist and dew and rain; for they shall all be withheld because of you from descending upon you, and they shall be mindful of your sins. 12 And now give presents to the rain that it be not withheld from descending upon you, nor yet the dew, when it has received gold and silver from you that it may descend. 13 When the hoar-frost and snow with their chilliness, and all the snow-storms with all their plagues fall upon you, in those days ye shall not be able to stand before them.

## CHAPTER 101:

1 Observe the heaven, ye children of heaven, and every work of the Most High, and fear ye Him and work no evil in His presence. 2 If He closes the windows of heaven, and withholds the rain and the dew from descending on the earth on your account, what will ye do then?

*Cf. Jub. 12:4.*

3 And if He sends His anger upon you because of your deeds, ye cannot petition Him; for ye spake proud and insolent words against His righteousness: therefore ye shall have no peace. 4 And see ye not the sailors of the ships, how their ships are tossed to and fro by the waves, and are shaken by the winds, and are in sore trouble? 5 And therefore do they fear because all their goodly possessions go upon the sea with them, and they have evil forebodings of heart that the sea will swallow them and they will perish therein. 6 Are not the entire sea and all its waters, and all its movements, the work of the Most High, and has He not set limits to its doings, and confined it throughout by the sand? 7 And at His reproof it is afraid and dries up, and all its fish die and all that is in it; but ye sinners that are on the earth fear Him not. 8 Has He not made the heaven and the earth, and all that is therein? Who has given understanding and wisdom to every thing that moves on the earth and in the sea? 9 Do not the sailors of the ships fear the sea? Yet sinners fear not the Most High.

## CHAPTER 102:

1 In those days when He hath brought a grievous fire upon you, Whither will ye flee, and where will ye find deliverance? And when He launches forth His word against you, will you not be affrighted and fear? 2 And all the luminaries shall be affrighted with great fear, And all the earth shall be affrighted and tremble and be alarmed. 3 And all the angels shall execute their commands and shall seek to hide themselves from the presence of the Great Glory, And the children of earth shall tremble and quake; And ye sinners shall be accursed for ever, And ye shall have no peace. 4 Fear ye not, ye souls of the righteous. And be hopeful ye that have died in righteousness. 5 And grieve not if your soul into Sheol has descended in grief, And that in your life your body fared not according to your goodness, But wait for the day of the judgment of sinners And for the day of cursing and chastisement, 6 And yet when ye die the sinners speak over you: "As we die, so die the righteous. And what benefit do they reap for their deeds? 7 Behold, even as we, so do they die in grief and darkness. And what have they more than we? From henceforth we are equal. 8 And what will they receive and what will they see for ever? **Behold, they too have died, And henceforth for ever shall they see no light**." 9 I tell you, ye sinners, ye are content to eat and drink, and rob and sin, and strip men naked, and acquire wealth and see good days.

10 Have ye seen the righteous how their end falls out, that no manner of violence is found in them till their death?

11 "Nevertheless they perished and became as though they had not been, and their spirits descended into Sheol in tribulation."

*Cf. 22. The chambers where souls sleep in Sheol not a burning Hell.*

*Origin of Isaiah's words: Cf. Is. 14:9-11. Chiefs and kings will ridicule the righteous that we suffer the same fate. Yet, they only understand the physical death for their spirits will be consumed and believers will live eternally.*

*Righteous do not go to a burning Hell. Sheol is a general term including the chambers where souls sleep. Cf. 22.*

## CHAPTER 103:

1 Now, therefore, I swear to you, the righteous, by the glory of the Great and Honored and Mighty One in dominion, and by His greatness I swear to you, 2 I know a mystery and have **read the heavenly tablets**. And have **seen the holy books**, And have found written therein and inscribed regarding them:

*Cf. Jub. 3:10, 4:3. "heavenly tablets."*

3 That all goodness and joy and glory are prepared for them, and written down for the spirits of those who have died in righteousness. And that manifold good shall be given to you in recompense for your labors, And that your lot is abundantly beyond the lot of the living. 4 And the spirits of you who have died in righteousness shall live and rejoice. And their spirits shall not perish, nor their memorial from before the face of the Great One unto all the generations of the world: wherefore no longer fear their contumely.

*Insulting language.*

5 Woe to you, ye sinners, when ye have died, If ye die in the wealth of your sins, And those who are like you say regarding you: "Blessed are the sinners: they have seen all their days. 6 And now they have died in prosperity and in wealth. And have not seen tribulation or murder in their life; And they have died in honor. And judgment has not been executed on them during their life." 7 Know ye, that their souls will be made to descend into Sheol and they shall be wretched in their great tribulation.

*Cf. Jub. 7:29, 22:22.*

8 And into darkness and chains and a burning flame where there is grievous judgment shall your spirits enter; And the great judgment shall be for all the generations of the world. Woe to you, for ye shall have no peace. 9 Say not in regard to the righteous and good who are in life: "In our troubled days we have toiled laboriously and experienced every trouble. And met with much evil and been consumed, And have become few and our spirit small. 10 And we have been destroyed and have not found any to help us even with a word: We have been tortured [and destroyed], and not hoped to see life from day to day.

11 We hoped to be the head and have become the tail: We have toiled laboriously and

had no satisfaction in our toil; And we have become the food of the sinners and the unrighteous, And they have laid their yoke heavily upon us. 12 They have had dominion over us that hated us and smote us; And to those that hated us we have bowed our necks But they pitied us not. 13 We desired to get away from them that we might escape and be at rest, But found no place whereunto we should flee and be safe from them. 14 And we complained to the rulers in our tribulation, And cried out against those who devoured us. But they did not attend to our cries and would not hearken to our voice. 15 And they helped those who robbed us and devoured us and those who made us few; and they concealed their oppression, and they did not remove from us the yoke of those that devoured us and dispersed us and murdered us, and they concealed their murder, and remembered not that they had lifted up their hands against us."

# 104

## ASSURANCES GIVEN TO THE RIGHTEOUS: ADMONITIONS TO SINNERS AND THE FALSIFIERS OF THE WORDS OF UPRIGHTNESS

## CHAPTER 104:

1 I swear unto you, that in heaven the angels remember you for good before the glory of the Great One: and your names are written before the glory of the Great One.

*In the Book of Life.*

2 Be hopeful; for aforetime ye were put to shame through ill and affliction; but now ye shall shine as the lights of heaven, ye shall shine and ye shall be seen, and the portals of heaven shall be opened to you. 3 And in your cry, cry for judgment, and it shall appear to you; for all your tribulation shall be visited on the rulers, and on all who helped those who plundered you. 4 Be hopeful, and cast not away your hope; for ye shall have great joy as the angels of heaven. 5 What shall ye be obliged to do? Ye shall not have to hide on the day of the great judgment and ye shall not be found as sinners, and the eternal judgment shall be far from you for all the generations of the world. 6 And now fear not,

*The innumerable multitude of martyrs in Rev. 7:9-17 which is separate from the 144,000 born in Heaven, get to Heaven somehow. Men do not until then. These portals explain how.*

*Cf. 47:2, 97:3-5, 99:3, 16, 22:5-7; Rev. 6:10 "Righteous souls cry out for vengeance."*

Cf. 2 Cor. 6:14.

ye righteous, when ye see the sinners growing strong and prospering in their ways: be not companions with them, but keep afar from their violence; for ye shall become companions of the hosts of heaven. 7 And, although ye sinners say: "All our sins shall not be searched out and written down" nevertheless they shall write down all your sins every day. 8 And now I show unto you that light and darkness, day and night, see all your sins. 9 Be not godless in your hearts, and lie not and alter not the words of uprightness, nor charge with lying the words of the Holy Great One, nor take account of your idols; for all your lying and all your godlessness issue not in righteousness but in great sin. 10 And now I know this mystery, that sinners will alter and pervert the words of righteousness in many ways, and will speak wicked words, and lie, and practice great deceits, and write books concerning their words.

*This can fully witnessed today.*

11 But when they write down truthfully all my words in their languages, and do not change or minish ought from my words but write them all down truthfully—all that I first testified concerning them, 12 Then, I know another mystery, that books shall be given to the righteous and the wise to become a cause of joy and uprightness and much wisdom. 13 And to them shall the books be given, and they shall believe in them and rejoice over them, and then shall all the righteous who have learnt therefrom all the paths of uprightness be recompensed.'

*Now that is awesome!!!*

# 105
## ELOHIM AND THE MESSIAH TO DWELL WITH MAN

## CHAPTER 105:

1 In those days Yahuah bade (them) to summon and testify to the children of earth concerning their wisdom: Show (it) unto them; for ye are their guides, and a recompense over the whole earth. 2 For **I and My Son will be united with them for ever** in the paths of uprightness in their lives; and ye shall have peace: rejoice, ye children of uprightness. Amen.

*Note: Before there was an Aman-ra, Enoch used Amen. That is because the Hebrew word Amen never derives from ra. That is illiterate.*

Cf. Gen. Ap.

Noah was not what we call white in race. He was white as snow as an albino. Thru his lineage all races would be continued and he was likely a mixture or sort. He was born with white, long hair. This is not characteristic of any race ven that of white. Many would characterize albinos as having glowing eyes. Noah spoke as a newborn. This was not normal.

Lamech feared Noah was the product of Angels mating with women which defined his age. Noah was fully human, however, with a special purpose.

**1**. And after some days my son Methuselah took a wife for his son Lamech, and she became pregnant by him and bore a son. **2**. And his body was white as snow and red as the blooming of a rose, and the hair of his head and his long locks were white as wool, and his eyes beautiful. And when he opened his eyes, he lighted up the whole house like the sun, and the whole house was very bright. **3**. And thereupon he arose in the hands of the midwife, opened his mouth, and conversed with Yahuah of righteousness. **4**. And his father Lamech was afraid of him and fled, and came to his father Methuselah. **5**. And he said unto him: 'I have begotten a strange son, diverse from and unlike man, and resembling the sons of the Elohim of heaven; and his nature is different and he is not like us, and his eyes are as the rays of the sun, and his countenance is glorious.

**6**. And it seems to me that he is not sprung from me but from the angels, and I fear that in his days a wonder may be wrought on the earth.

**7**. And now, my father, I am here to petition thee and implore thee that thou mayest go to Enoch, our father, and learn from him the truth, for **his dwelling-place is amongst the angels**."

**8**. And when Methuselah heard the words of his son, he came to me to the **ends of the earth**; for he had heard that I was there, and he cried aloud, and I heard his voice and **I came to him**. And I said unto him: 'Behold, here am I, my son, wherefore hast thou come to me? **9**. And he answered and said: 'Because of a great cause of anxiety have I come to thee, and because of a disturbing vision have I approached. **10**. And now, my father, hear me: unto Lamech my son there hath been born a son, the like of whom there is none, and his nature is not like man's nature, and the color of his body is whiter than snow and redder than the bloom of a rose, and the hair of his head is whiter than white wool, and his eyes are like the rays of the sun, and he opened his eyes and thereupon lighted up the whole house. **11** And he arose

This is long after Enoch is taken.

Garden of Eden. Holy of Holies.

Cf. Gen. Ap. "He went at once to Parwain and he found him there." Parwaim is Sepharwaim where Ophir migrated to the land of the Garden. Enoch exits the Garden. No one goes in. Cf. 65:1. Noah also visits Enoch at the Garden of Eden entrance later.

# NOAH'S BIRTH

in the hands of the midwife, and opened his mouth and blessed Yahuah of heaven. **12**. And his father Lamech became afraid and fled to me, and did not believe that he was sprung from him, but that he was in the likeness of the angels of heaven; and behold I have come to thee that thou mayest make known to me the truth.' **13**. And I, Enoch, answered and said unto him: 'Yahuah will do a new thing on the earth, and this I have already seen in a vision, and make known to thee that in the generation of my father Jared some of the angels of heaven transgressed the word of Yahuah.

**14**. And behold they commit sin and transgress the law, and have united themselves with women and commit sin with them, and have married some of them, and have begot children by them.

**17**. And they shall produce on the earth **giants** not according to the spirit, but according to the flesh, and there shall be a great punishment on the earth, and the earth shall be cleansed from all impurity. **15**. Yea, there shall come a great destruction over the whole earth, and there shall be a deluge and a great destruction for one year. **16**. And this son who has been born unto you shall be left on the earth, and his three children shall be saved with him: when all mankind that are on the earth shall die [he and his sons shall be saved]. **18**. And now make known to thy son Lamech that he who has been born is in truth his son, and call his name Noah; for he shall be left to you, and he and his sons shall be saved from the destruction, which shall come upon the earth on account of all the sin and all the unrighteousness, which shall be consummated on the earth in his days.

**19**. And after that there shall be still more unrighteousness than that which was first consummated on the earth; for I know the mysteries of the holy ones; for He, Yahuah, has showed me and informed me, and **I have read (them) in the heavenly tablets**.

## CHAPTER 107:

1 And I saw written on them that generation upon generation shall transgress, till a generation of righteousness arises, and transgression is destroyed and sin passes away from the earth, and all manner of good comes upon it. 2 And now, my son, go and make known to thy son Lamech that this son, which has been born, is in truth his son, and that (this) is no lie." 3 And when Methuselah had heard the words of his father Enoch—for he had shown to him everything in secret—he returned and showed (them) to him and called the name of that son Noah; for he will comfort the earth after all the destruction.

*Everything in scripture points to the remnant keeping His Law in the Last Days. Cf. Rev 12:17, 14:12, 22:14; 2 Jn. 1:6; 1 Jn. 2:3-4, 3:22, 24, 5:2-2; Jn.14:15, 21, 15:10. 2 Esd. 13:38: "he shall destroy them without labor, by the law which is like unto fire." The same "Law of Life." 2 Esd. 14:30 (Old Test.) and Rom. 8:2 (New). His law does not change.*

## CHAPTER 108:

1 Another book which Enoch wrote for his son Methuselah and for those who will come after him, and **keep the law in the last days**. 2 Ye who have done good shall wait for those days till an end is made of those who work evil, and an end of the might of the transgressors. 3 And wait ye indeed till sin has passed away, for **their names shall be blotted out of the book of life and out of the holy books**, and their seed shall be destroyed for ever, and their spirits shall be slain, and they shall cry and make lamentation in a place that is a chaotic wilderness, and in the fire shall they burn; for there is no earth there. 4 And I saw there something like an invisible cloud; for by reason of its depth I could not look over, and I saw a flame of fire blazing brightly, and things like shining mountains circling and sweeping to and fro.

*Cf. Rev. 20:12, 2nd Esd. 14:30; Psa 69:28, 109:13-14. "...blotted out of the book of the living."*

5 And I asked one of the holy angels who was with me and said unto him: 'What is this shining thing? For it is not a heaven but only the flame of a blazing fire, and the voice of weeping and crying and lamentation and strong pain.' 6 And he said unto me: 'This place which thou seest—here are cast the spirits of sinners and blasphemers, and of those who work wickedness, and of those who pervert every thing that Yahuah hath spoken through the mouth of the prophets—(even) the

*Lake of Fire, Gehenna, Tartarus. The burning Hell is opened in the end and not before.*

things that shall be. 7 For some of them are written and inscribed above in the heaven, in order that the angels may read them and know that which shall befall the sinners, and the spirits of the humble, and of those who have afflicted their bodies, and been recompensed by Elohim; and of those who have been put to shame by wicked men: 8 Who love Elohim and loved neither gold nor silver nor any of the good things which are in the world, but gave over their bodies to torture. 9 Who, since they came into being, longed not after earthly food, but regarded everything as a passing breath, and lived accordingly, and Yahuah tried them much, and their spirits were found pure so that they should bless His name. 10 And all the blessings destined for them **I have recounted in the books**. And He hath assigned them their recompense, because they have been found to be such as **loved heaven more than their life in** **the world**, and though they were trodden under foot of wicked men, and experienced abuse and reviling from them and were put to shame, yet they blessed Me. 11 And now I will summon the spirits of the good who belong to the generation of light, and I will transform those who were born in darkness, who in the flesh were not recompensed with such honor as their faithfulness deserved. 12 And I will bring forth in shining light **those who have loved My holy name**, and I will seat each on the throne of his honor. 13 And they shall be resplendent for times without number; for righteousness is the judgment of Elohim; for to the faithful He will give faithfulness in the habitation of upright paths. 14 And they shall see those who were born in darkness led into darkness, while the righteous shall be resplendent. 15 And the sinners shall cry aloud and see them resplendent, and they indeed shall go where days and seasons are prescribed for them.'

Cf. 48:7; 1 Jn. 2:15.

Cf. Rev 12:11. "...they loved not their lives unto the death." John Quoted Enoch Again.

Cf. Eph. 5:8; 1 Th. 5:5; John 12:36; Luke 16:8. "Children/sons of light."

Cf. Rev. 3:21, 20:4; Matt. 19:28. "Sit with me on my throne."

# BIBLIOGRAPHY:


### Translation Originally From:

The Book of Enoch or 1 Enoch, Translated from the Editor's Ethiopic Text. By R.H. Charles, D.Litt., D.D. Oxford at the Clarendon Press. 1912.

### Other General Sources of Note:

The Complete Dead Sea Scrolls in English. Revised Edition. By Geza Vermes. Penguin Books. London, NY. Revised 2004. Originally Published 1962. Page number in reference. [22]

The Book of Jubilees: The Torah Calendar. By Timothy Schwab and Anna Zamoranos. 2021. Based on the Original Translation by R.H. Charles, 1903. Free eBook at www.bookofjubilees. org

2nd Esdras: The Hidden Book of Prophecy. By Timothy Schwab and Anna Zamoranos. 2021. Based on the Original 1611 King James Version. Free eBook at www.2esdras.org

### Cited, Numbered Sources:

1. "The Canon of Scripture." Blue Letter Bible citing "What Everyone Needs To Know About The Bible." By Don Stewart. The Basic Bible Study Series. Publisher Dart Press, Orange, California. https://www.blueletterbible.org/faq/canon.cfm

2. Clark Pinnock, Biblical Revelation, Grand Rapids: Baker Book House, 1973, p. 104. Quoted by Blue Letter Bible.

3. 2014 Lecture at University of Chicago Divinity School sponsored by Jewish Federation of Chicago. Rachel Elior. Professor, Hebrew University of Jerusalem. https://www.youtube.com/watch?v=wLit979B60Y&t=3621s

4. Strong's Concordance "Awan" #H5770. Blue Letter Bible. (Note Ancient Hebrew never had a "V" so the word is Awan not Avan).

5. 1. "Where to See Some of the World's Oldest and Most Interesting Maps." By Jennifer Billock. Smithsonian Magazine. July 18, 2017.

2. "Geography and Ethnography: Perceptions of the World in Pre-Modern Societies." By Kurt A. Raaflaub & Richard J. A. Talbert. 2009. John Wiley & Sons. p. 147. 3. Map from: Wikimedia Commons. Map of the World from Sippar (Tell Abu Habba), Iraq, 6th century BCE. On display at the British Museum in London. By Osama Shukir Muhammed Amin.

6. "Books of Enoch Collection." By Scriptural Research Institute. 2020. p. 106.

7. "Rapha." Abarim Publications.

8. "The Dead Sea Scrolls and the Christian Myth." By John M. Allegro. 1992.

9. "The Mystery of the Essenes." By H. Spencer Lewis, F.R.C. From "The Mystical Life of Jesus." Rosicrucian Digest No. 2. 2007. p. 3.

10. "Natural History." Pliny the Elder. Book V. p. 277.

11. "The Life of Flavius Josephus." 1:2. The Genuine Works of Flavius Josephus the Jewish Historian. Translated from the Original Greek, according to Havercamp's accurate Edition.

12. 1770, Bonne Map of Israel. Rigobert Bonne 1727 – 1794. AdobeStock.

13. Madaba Mosaic Map(left), c. 6th century A.D. St. George's Church. Jordan. AdobeStock.

14. 1836, Tanner Map of Palestine, Israel, Holy Land. AdobeStock.

15. NASA/Goddard Space Flight Center Scientific Visualization Studio U.S. Department of Commerce, National Oceanic and Atmospheric Administration, National Geophysical Data Center, 2006, 2-minute Gridded Global Relief Data (ETOPO2v2). Horace Mitchell (NASA/GSFC): Lead Animator.

16. 1845, Chambers Map of Palestine, Israel, Holy Land. AdobeStock.

17. 1852, Philip Map of Palestine, Israel, Holy Land. AdobeStock.

18. Ein Gedi Photos: Chalcolithic Temple, Essene Synagogue, Tile mosaic Peacock symbols. AdobeStock.

19. *Antiquities of the Jews* — Book VIII, Chapter 6:4 and 7:1. Flavius Josephus.

20. "Enoch and Qumran Origins: New Light on a Forgotten Connection." Gabriele Boccaccini, Editor. William B. Erdemans Publishing Co. Grand Rapids, MI and Cambridge, UK. 2005. p. 137.

21. "The Complete Dead Sea Scrolls In English Revised Edition." "The Damascus Document." Translated By Geza Vermes, 2004, Penguin Classics Books. London, England. First Published 1962. Revised Edition 2004. p. 139.3. Flavius Josephus, Antiquities of the Jews, 18:16.

22. The Complete Dead Sea Scrolls in English. Revised Edition. By Geza Vermes. Penguin Books. London, NY. Revised 2004. Originally Published 1962. Page number in reference.

23. "The World's Largest Caldera Discovered In The Philippine Sea." By David Bressan. Forbes Magazine. Oct. 21, 2019.

24. "Dudael." Wikipedia. Feb. 24, 2022.

25. Strong's Concordance. Blue Letter Bible.

26. Ancient Hebrew Research Center. By Jeff A. Benner. Ancient-Hebrew.org. 2019.

27. Philippines #1 in Gold in History. The Search for King Solomon's Treasure. The Lost Isles of Gold and the Garden of Eden. By Timothy Schwab and Anna Zamoranos. 2020. 1. "Ancient Mining: Classical Philippine Civilization." Wikipedia. Extracted August 9, 2019. and "Cultural Achievements of Pre-Colonial Philippines." Wikipedia. Extracted August 9, 2019. 2. "The Edge of Terror: The Heroic Story of American Families Trapped in the Japanese-occupied Philippines." By Scott Walker. Thomas Dunne Books. St. Martin's Press. New York. Chap. 3 - The Gold Miners, 1901-1937. p. 44. 3. "Philippine Civilization and Technology." By Paul Kekai Manansala. Asia Pacific University. 4. "Encyclopedic Dictionary of Archaeology — Philippines, the." Compiled by Barbara Ann Kipfer, Ph.D. Kluwer Academic/ Plenum Publishers. New York, London, Moscow. 2000. p. 436. 5. "Miners Shun Mineral Wealth of the Philippines." By Donald Greenlees. NY Times. May 14, 2008. Citing The Fraser Institute. 6. "Trillion — Dollar Philippine Economic Goldmine Emerging From Murky Pit." By Ralph Jennings. Forbes Magazine. Apr. 5, 2015. 7. "Mining for Gold in the Philippines." By Nicole Rashotte. Gold Investing News. Sept. 10th, 2019.

28. Philippines #1 in Pearl. The Search for King Solomon's Treasure. The Lost Isles of Gold and the Garden of Eden. By Timothy Schwab and Anna Zamoranos. 2020. 1. "This $100 Million Pearl Is The Largest and Most Expensive in the World." By Roberta Naas. Forbes Magazine. Aug 23, 2016. 2. "Pinoy in Canada Discovers Strange Family Heirloom is Actually a Giant Pearl Worth $90 Million." Buzzooks.com. May 23, 2019.

29. Romblon Philippines Strongest Onyx. The Search for King Solomon's Treasure. The Lost Isles of Gold and the Garden of Eden. By Timothy Schwab and Anna Zamoranos. 2020. 1. "ROMBLON: 8 Awesome Places You Should Visit in Romblon!" Our Awesome Planet. Sept. 7, 2016. 2. "The Romblon Marble." Ellaneto Tiger Marble Trader, Romblon. 2010. 3. "Marvelous Marble" By Robert A. Evora. Manila Standard. Jan. 16, 2014.

30. "The Center of the Center of Marine Biodiversity on Earth." 1. "Environmental Biology of Fishes." K.E. Carpenter and V.G. Springer. 2005. 72: 467-480. 2. "Center of the Center of Marine Diversity." CNN. Apr. 30, 2012. 3. "100 Scientists Declare RP as World's 'Center of Marine Biodiversity." By Katherine Adraneda. June 8, 2006. The Philippine Star reporting on "Philippines Environmental Monitor, 2005" by the World Bank.

31. "Havilah." Hitchcock's Dictionary of Bible Names from BibleHub.org and KingJamesBibleDictionary.com, Strong's Concordance #H2341. Blue Letter Bible.

32. "Eve - Havah." Strong's Concordance #H2332. Blue Letter Bible.

33. "Alabaster, Mineral." and "Marble, Rock." By Editors of Encyclopaedia Britannica. Encyclopaedia Britannica. Updated Jan. 24, 2018 and Jan. 24, 2020.

34. "Indonesia's Mountains of Fire." By Daniel Quinn. Indonesia Expat. June 30, 2014. Indonesia's Volcanological Survey. Laporan Kebencanaan Geologi. Apr. 2, 2019.

35. "Book of Enoch." Wikipedia. Feb. 28, 2022.

36. "A modern facsimile of Martin Behaim's 1492 Erdapfel map. Behaim Globe (1492–1493) Ernst Ravenstein: Martin Behaim. His Life and his Globe." London 1908. Public Domain.

41. "The giant undersea rivers we know very little about" By Richard Gray. BBC News. July 6, 2017. Citing Dan Parsons, PhD, Sedimentologist, University of Hull, UK.

42. "The Thanksgiving Hymns (iQH, 1Q36, 4Q427-32). Hymn 14." The Complete Dead Sea Scrolls. By Geza Vermes. Penguin Classics. P. 278.

43. "Chapter Eight. Traditions Common To 4 Ezra And The Dead Sea Scrolls." By E.J.C. Tigchelaar and F. García Martínez. Qumranica Minora I. Qumran Origins and Apocalypticism. Series: Studies on the Texts of the Desert of Judah, Volume: 63. Publisher: Brill. 01 Jan 2007. 153–168.

44. F. García Martínez, "Qumran Origins and Early History: A Groningen Hypothesis," Folia Orientalia 25 (1989): 113–36.

53. "Commentary on Habakkuk." The Complete Dead Sea Scrolls in English. Revised Edition. By Geza Vermes. Penguin Books. London, NY. Revised 2004. Originally Published 1962. p. 510-511.

54. Commentary on Nahum, P. 505. The Complete Dead Sea Scrolls in English. Geza Vermes. Penguin Classics. Revised Edition. Published 1962. Revised 2004.

55. Commentary on Habukkuk, P. 515. The Complete Dead Sea Scrolls in English. Geza Vermes. Penguin Classics. Revised Edition. Published 1962. Revised 2004.

56. "Blessings (iQSb=iQ28b), The Blessing of the Prince of the Congregation." The Complete Dead Sea Scrolls in English. Geza Vermes. Penguin Classics. Revised Edition. Published 1962. Revised 2004. p. 389. 100 B.C. dating: J. T. Milik (DJD, I, 118-29).

60. "Antiquities of the Jews — Book XI." Josephus. Chapter 3.1. Chapter 11.133.

61. "Evergreen." Wikipedia. Jan. 19, 2022.